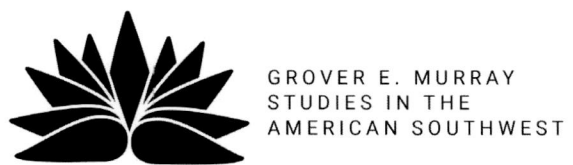

GROVER E. MURRAY
STUDIES IN THE
AMERICAN SOUTHWEST

ARTISTS OF THE HORSE

CAPTURING THE SPIRIT OF AMERICA'S WEST

HEIDI BRADY AND SCOTT WHITE

TEXAS TECH UNIVERSITY PRESS

This book is typeset in Adobe Caslon Pro. The paper used in this book meets the minimum requirements of ANSI/NISO Z39.48-1992 (R1997). ♾

Designed by Hannah Gaskamp
Cover design by Hannah Gaskamp

On the cover: *Big Sky Buckskin* (James Cole "Buckeye" Blake).
On the back, clockwise from top left: *Partners* (Emily McCartney), *High Clouds and Shadows* (Tim Solliday), *An American Icon* (Martin Grelle), *To the Fire* (Con Williams).

Library of Congress Cataloging-in-Publication Data

Names: Brady, Heidi, author. | White, Scott, 1953– author. Title: Artists of the Horse: Capturing the Spirit of America's West / Heidi Brady and Scott White. Description: Lubbock, Texas: Texas Tech University Press, [2025] | Series: Grover E. Murray Studies in the American Southwest | Summary: "Profiles of contemporary photographers, painters, and sculptors whose work portrays horses of the American West."—Provided by publisher.
Identifiers: LCCN 2024039515 | ISBN 978-1-68283-237-0 (cloth)
Subjects: LCSH: Artists—United States—Biography. | Artists—West (U.S.)—Biography. | Horses in art. | West (U.S.)—In art.
Classification: LCC N6536.B73 2024 | DDC 700/.46361—dc23/eng/20240918
LC record available at https://lccn.loc.gov/2024039515

Printed in Korea

25 26 27 28 29 30 31 32 33 / 9 8 7 6 5 4 3 2 1

Texas Tech University Press
Box 41037
Lubbock, Texas 79409-1037 USA
800.832.4042
ttup@ttu.edu
www.ttupress.org

This book is dedicated first and foremost to my parents Adelaide and Fred Brady, who fostered my love of God, Who is the reason for everything. I also dedicate this book to my family: my husband Wade Nichols, sons Mark and Ty, daughters-in-law Ashleigh and Marissa, and our dear grandchildren Mason, Angelina, Matthew, and Rylee.

DR. HEIDI BRADY

I dedicate this book to our families who supported us during all the interviews, revisions, and edits. I thank my partner in this project, Dr. Heidi Brady, whose opinions and viewpoints I value greatly. Thanks also to my friend Rhonda Hole for the technical assist.

DR. SCOTT WHITE

Contents

Foreword

I've been a huge fan of Western art and Western artists since I was very young, so I was thrilled when Scott White and Heidi Brady asked me to be a small part of this book. *Artists of the Horse: Capturing the Spirit of America's West* is a comprehensive look at twenty amazing Western artists from around the world. It includes their most important works and influences.

My name is Barry Corbin, and I'm often recognized for the Westerns I've been in. I'm proud of that because I love that genre, and horses have always been a huge part of my life. In my mind there is not a more beautiful animal on the face of this earth than the horse.

These artists in various mediums illustrate the interdependence and companionship of horses in the ranching culture. Probably the only thing harder than capturing a horse's essence in sculpting, painting, and photography is actually being a day-to-day hardworking cowboy. These talents have captured not only the essence of the horse but in some cases the soul of the cowboy too.

Thanks to Heidi's and Scott's hard work in putting this project together, I feel certain that the art and artists in this book will influence future generations of Western artists for years to come. This book is not just for the Western art fan's library but for art lovers and horse lovers everywhere.

BARRY CORBIN

Introduction

Recorded history may prove that no animal has had such a profound impact on man and civilization as the horse. *Equus caballus* has significantly helped man and his endeavors over time by playing major roles in survival, transportation, warfare, expansion, farming, ranching, and sport. Because of this, the importance of the horse to man and the significance of their relationships are reflected in the art of every culture since the dawn of prehistoric caves to the present times. This is certainly true in the American West, where cowboys, Native Americans, and settlers all depended on the horse. We find depictions of these beautiful animals on the American frontier from the earliest times when such art began to appear. Today, the horse remains a persistent subject and iconic image for contemporary Western painting, sculpture, photography, and drawing.

The horse, just as it was in an earlier work by these authors (*Horses in the American West*), remains the principal focus of this book. The twenty contemporary Western artists featured here fully integrate the horse into the stories of their art in their own individual creative styles. This book is not meant to be a comprehensive history of Western art but is a study of a select few. The chapters, or profiles, are taken from hours of interviews with the artists so that the point of view for each can be presented in their own voices. The artists come from a wide variety of backgrounds and display a common humility, which comes from a deep appreciation of the way of life of the West depicted on their canvases and in sketches, photography, or sculpture. Throughout all these works and across their stylistic choices, the horse, as a partner in work and as a companion, remains a strong, integral aspect of the way of the West.

In the process of creating this work, Dr. Brady and Dr. White interviewed each artist, sometimes more than once, and then transcribed each interview before shaping the information into a biographical chapter. Each artist was asked to select six images they thought best represented their work and achievements. Although these artists share common themes, their styles and interpretations of the horse are varied due to their personal backgrounds, experience with horses, and preferred artistic expressions. In discussing their approach to portraying the horse, most of the artists emphasize the importance of anatomical correctness in the horses they portray. Most agree that without the correct conformation and proportions of the horse in the art, other elements such as color, lighting, and the flow of the mane and tail become inconsequential. Some of the artists achieved their knowledge of horses through studying the formulas used by earlier painters of horses, and some gained an intimacy of horses by working with them each day. Just as each person carries unique features, the same can be said for each horse and each breed. Many of the horses shown within this book depict actual horses with unique attributes and personalities.

Motion, emotion, action, and the energy of the horse are both challenges and opportunities for each featured artist. Some of the individuals profiled are drawn to the challenge of portraying difficult action scenes, such as capturing a bucking horse or the lightning-fast reactions of the cowboy and horses in the roping pen. Emotion and tension are created, and the athleticism of the horse is shown as dynamic and powerful. With masterful manipulations within each medium, the artists try to seize moments or freeze time for an instant.

One aspect of the iconic horse of the West represents wildness and freedom. Some photographers in this book beautifully capture these characteristics in their work with feral horses. Others illustrate the versatility of the horses of the large ranches and highlight the partnership of man and horse as they work together to get tough jobs done. This unique partnership is on display throughout the book. Long days, hard terrain, stubborn cattle, or just the loneliness of working out in the pastures creates a need for a partner that can endure and respond. This relationship is seen over and over again in the artworks featured in this book.

Another theme of these artists is to show and preserve Western heritage, either as it was or as it exists now. Each artist must pay attention not only to the gear and tack appearing in the images but also to the type of horse, and details have to correctly fit the time period depicted. These artists have relied on their own knowledge of equine anatomy, mannerisms, energies, and intelligence. In addition, they exhibit the strengths of managing color, light, action, and conformity to proportion needed to portray these magnificent animals in the vignettes of art.

We hope that as readers peruse this book, they are able to reflect on the beautiful and powerful images of the horse and take a moment to ponder the remarkable lives and stories of the artists who created them. The personal expression and artistic approaches of these artists are reflective of the ideas, culture, and codes of the American West. This book will preserve these important contributions of capturing the horse in the art of the American West for future generations.

ARTISTS OF THE HORSE

PART 1

Painting and Drawing

Martin Grelle

CHAPTER 1

Martin Grelle

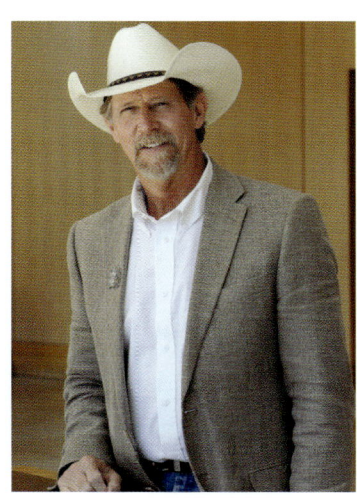

Martin Grelle is from the small town of Clifton, Texas, which lies at the top of the scenic rolling Hill Country. He has spent seventy years in this beautiful area with his wife Joyce because, as he says, "It's a great place to live, and we never found a good reason to leave." His family lived on a small farm and ranch about 15 miles west of Clifton. A short time later, his father purchased a small country store, which they renamed Crossroads Grocery, at the intersection of two rural roads, where they sold groceries and fuel. The store became a landmark in the community, and although Crossroads Grocery is no longer there, the area is still known as Crossroads. Grelle's father had an opportunity a few years later to become the local distributor for Mobil Oil Company, and the family moved into Clifton. Grelle remembers that he was fascinated with the old Mobil Oil calendars that his dad gave away each year, especially the photos, and he tried doing paintings of them, learning as he went.

When we were living in a little house across from the Crossroads Grocery, some of my first artwork was just crayons on mom's wall. For whatever reason, I guess God just put that bug in me, but I've always been really interested and fascinated with drawing and painting. Some of the first paintings that I did were with paint by number sets that my mom gave me. When I finished doing the paint by number images, I kept the paint and tried to do some of my own work.

In fifth grade, Grelle's teacher gave him his first book on art techniques and instruction. In high school, although he spent much of his time playing sports, especially football, he still found time to draw small portraits of classmates and horses. A significant event for Grelle came after a National Honor Society meeting, when he was able to visit with professional artist James Boren. Boren and artist Melvin Warren had just moved to Clifton, which Grelle considers to be fortuitous and a blessing. Prior to meeting these professionals, Grelle had no idea that he could possibly make a living as an artist.

During his school years, Grelle received some scholarship offers to play football and run track at several colleges; however, just a few weeks after graduation, these plans abruptly ended when his father became ill. Grelle had to remain home and help run the family oil distributorship business. With most of his friends off to college, Grelle began to paint on a regular basis. In 1974, Joanne Spieler, a friend who owned a small art gallery, arranged a one-man show of Grelle's work in Clifton. These works included drawings and paintings of horses set in the rural area of Clifton.

In 1975, Grelle was able to enroll for a semester at McLennan Community College in Waco to take art classes. The classes were beneficial for his career, especially the life drawing courses. However, from that experience he came to the conclusion that realism in art was not stressed in the setting of college academia, so he decided that he was better served using the art classroom in his own backyard at Clifton with Jim Boren. Grelle would often ride horses at Boren's property. Over time Boren became his mentor, and Grelle would take his works to the artist's studio to get critiqued, which immensely helped Grelle's artistic growth.

When Boren passed away, his wife Mary Ellen gave Grelle one of his geldings, which meant a great deal to Grelle.

Grelle became aware that being with horses and riding them makes all the difference in understanding how the muscles work and how the horse moves.

I've got books on anatomy on horses that I've used . . . and I have lots of photographs of horses that I've taken over the years. Studying those photos is how I first learned how to draw them. The best thing is to just get out, have horses out there and just try to do quick sketches, or quick little paintings. There's a lot to learn about how horses move . . . what happens when they move and how they are built, and observing them from life, is still the best way to learn it.

Grelle does not feel that a person can portray the horse just by looking at photographs, no matter how many photographs they study.

In the late 1970s and early 1980s, Grelle began to explore painting American Indian scenes. He has Choctaw heritage in his family on his father's side, and it became a big part to of expanding his storytelling in his artwork. He says, "As I had the ability to travel more and could afford it financially, I was able to broaden my scope. I've always been interested in history and am proud of my heritage. I wanted to learn more and further myself."

As for the artwork depicting American Indian subjects, Grelle has attended many reenactments through the years. Accuracy is foremost to him in capturing and preserving the lifeways of the various tribes of the American Indian. At times, he has to make modifications on the horses he's painting to better reflect the type of horses present in the 1800s. Grelle says, "I'll try to get that as accurate as I can. I also try to show the difference in their body language when they're bareback rather than saddled up." Grelle conducts a great deal of research on the artifacts used by the American Indian tribes and details in their equipment. He has an extensive library of reference books and materials for that purpose.

Because of his attention to detail in each of his paintings, Grelle's schedule is rigorous in the studio, especially when preparing for a show. He can work up to sixteen hours a day, seven days a week, for months at a time.

The preeminence of the horse remains central to Grelle's work. He feels strongly that it is vital to individualize the horses in his paintings. He tries to capture the character and individual nature of horses, including their different builds and the varied expressions they each have around their eyes. He also wants to portray the horse's role in the West.

The horse was so important in Western United States culture, not only with the American Indian . . . but all the other people that went out West to try to find a new way of life—the cavalry soldiers, farmers, ranchers. The horse remains important even today.

Grelle was invited to become a member of the Cowboy Artists of America in 1995 and has won several awards at their Annual Exhibition since that time. He has received numerous other awards, including the Prix de West Purchase Award (twice), the Briscoe Legacy Award, the Booth Museum's Artist of Excellence Award, and many others. For thirty years, he and his friend Bruce Greene, also from Clifton, have taught a weekend workshop for other artists to give back to Western art by mentoring others as they both were mentored as young artists.

Grelle paints and stores his artifacts in a studio near his home outside of Clifton. He keeps three Quarter Horses and two ponies for the grandchildren. He states that he received a great deal of support for his artistic endeavors through the years from his parents and from his two brothers and a sister, who are all creative in their own right. "I had a lot of support from the community growing up, which was really nice, and I still have that support today actually. There's just a good group of people here . . . and people get excited about the successes that [we] have been blessed to have."

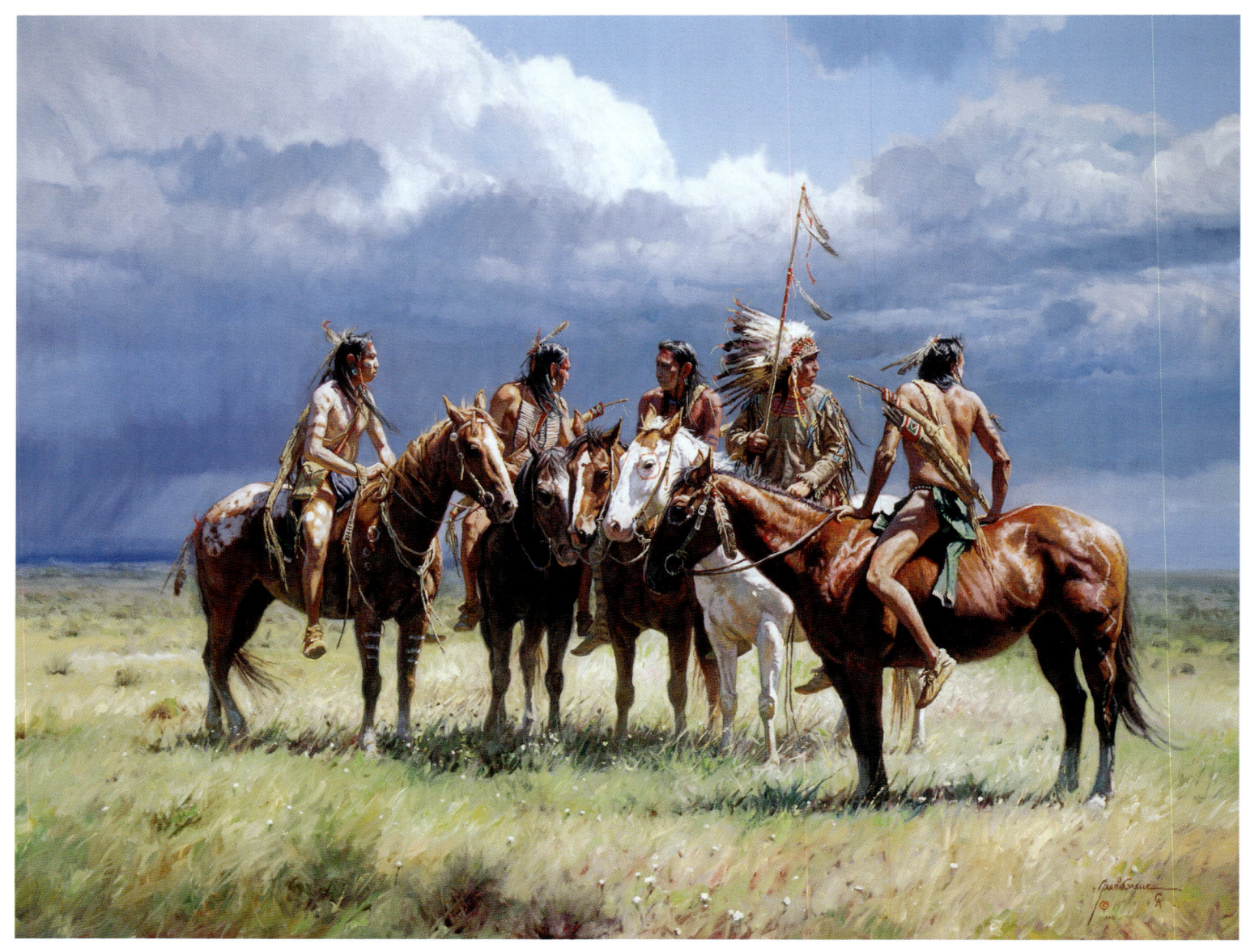

Waiting on the Wolves

(Oil on linen, 40" × 54", 2011)

"This painting depicts a small Apsáalooke war party as they wait for their scouts, or 'wolves' as they were called, to return with their report. Wolves were sent out, usually in pairs, to do reconnaissance for the pipe carrier, or leader, of the party. The information gathered by these wolves was critical to the success of the party."

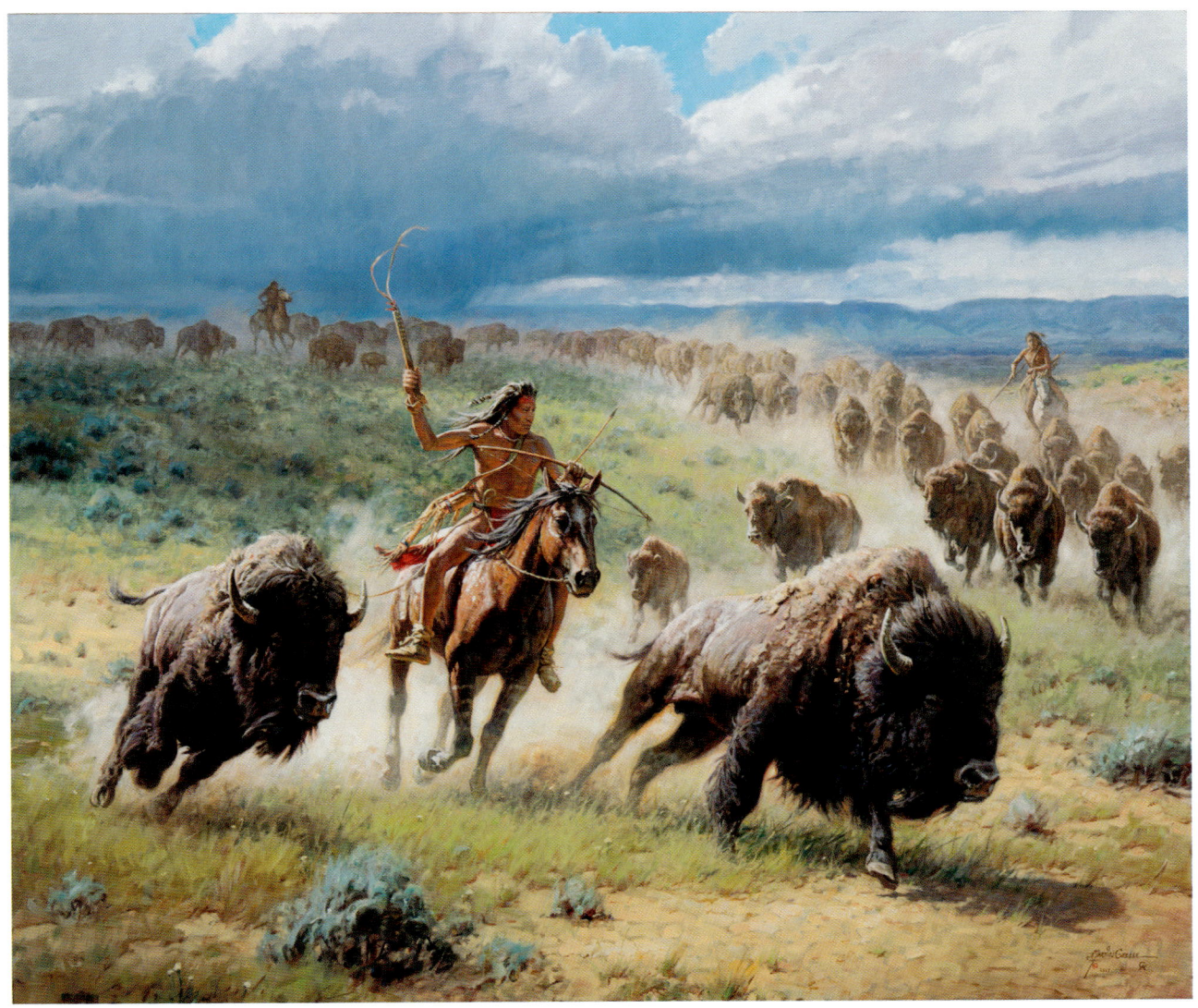

Chasing Thunder

(Oil on linen, 46" × 54", 2017)

"There are many firsthand descriptions of American Indian buffalo hunts available for reading, and this painting is based on those descriptions. The hunters would carry only what they needed and usually rode bareback. My goal was to capture the excitement of the chase and have the viewer imagine the sights and sounds of it. What an incredible experience it would have been—and the sound made by hundreds, even thousands, of running buffalo surely must have sounded like rolling thunder."

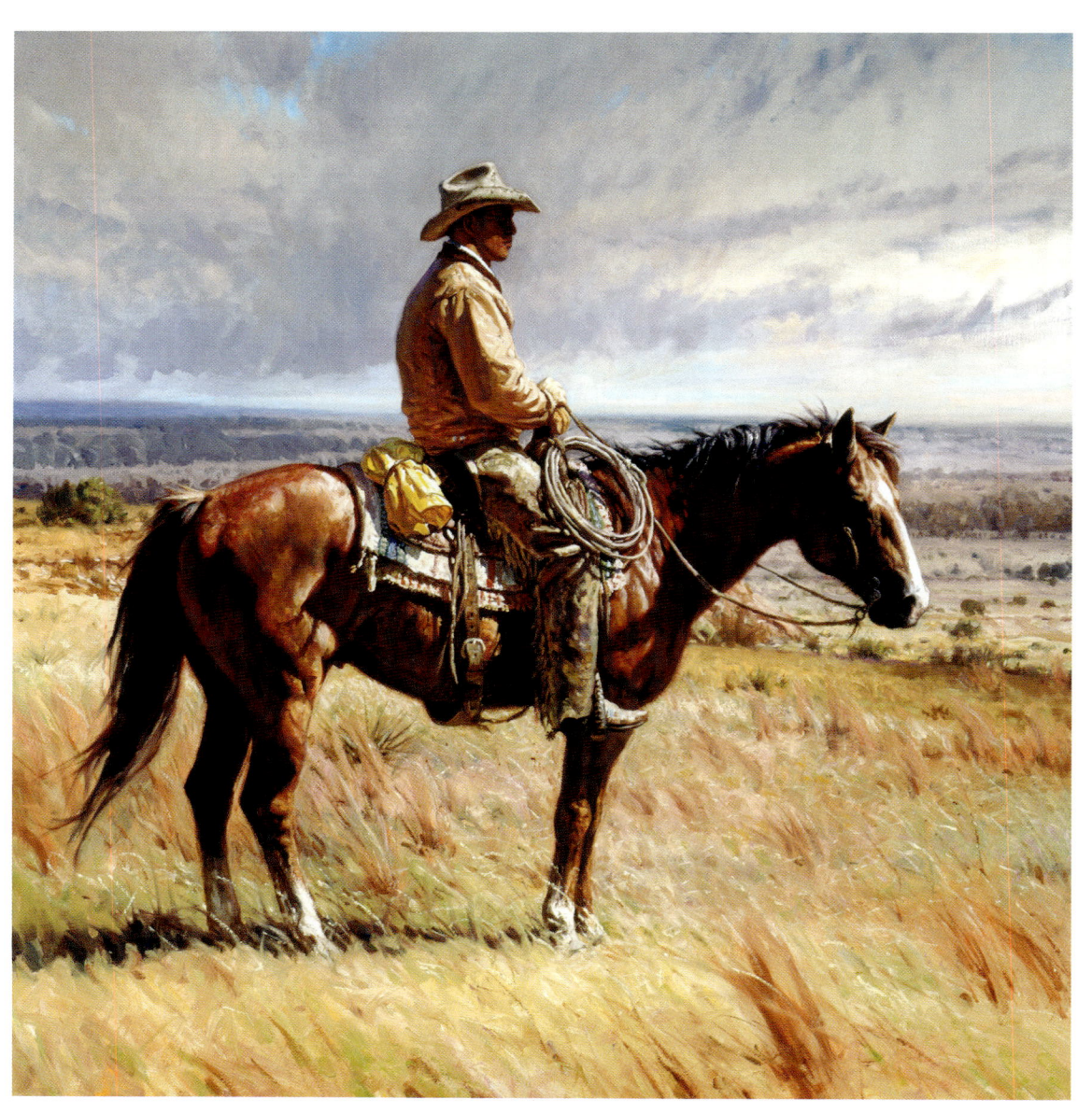

An American Icon

(Oil on linen, 36" × 36", 2003)

"The image of the American cowboy is an image that is recognized in almost all, if not all, the countries of the world. I have been fortunate to share time with cowboys on many ranches in this country, mostly in Texas, and they are some of the best people I've ever been around. This painting is a tribute to the American Cowboy and all they represent."

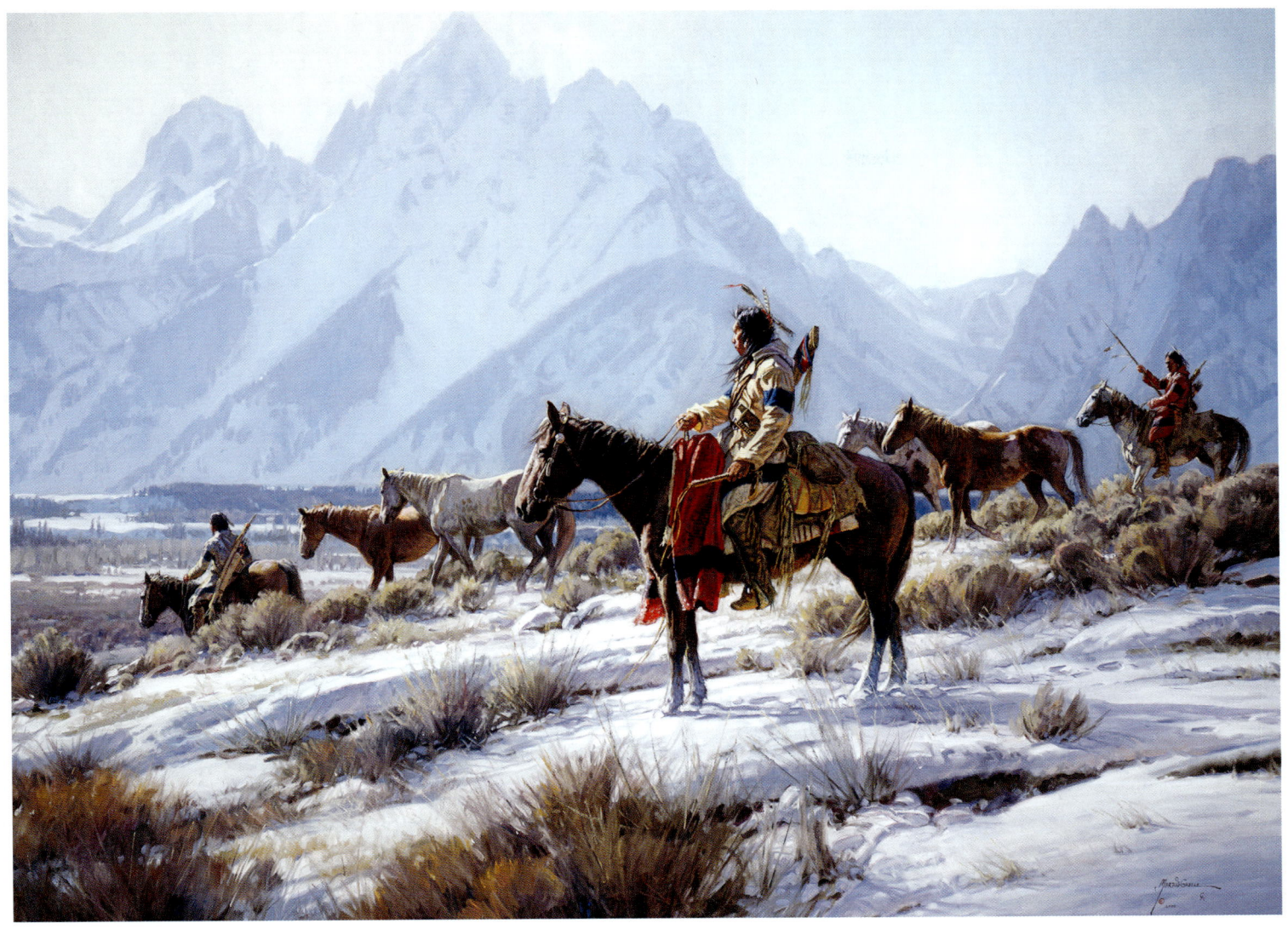

Apsáalooke Horse Hunters

(Oil on linen, 48" × 66", 2008)

"In reading a book on the Apsáalooke, or Crow, I was struck by a passage which said their people were happy in all seasons of the year, and that even in the sometimes brutally cold winter months they went about their lives as usual. The hunting of game in winter, to supplement the stores of food which were taken in the late summer and fall, was important, but they also continued with the taking of horses from enemy tribes. It was an important part of a warrior's existence—bringing wealth and coups that brought honor and respect."

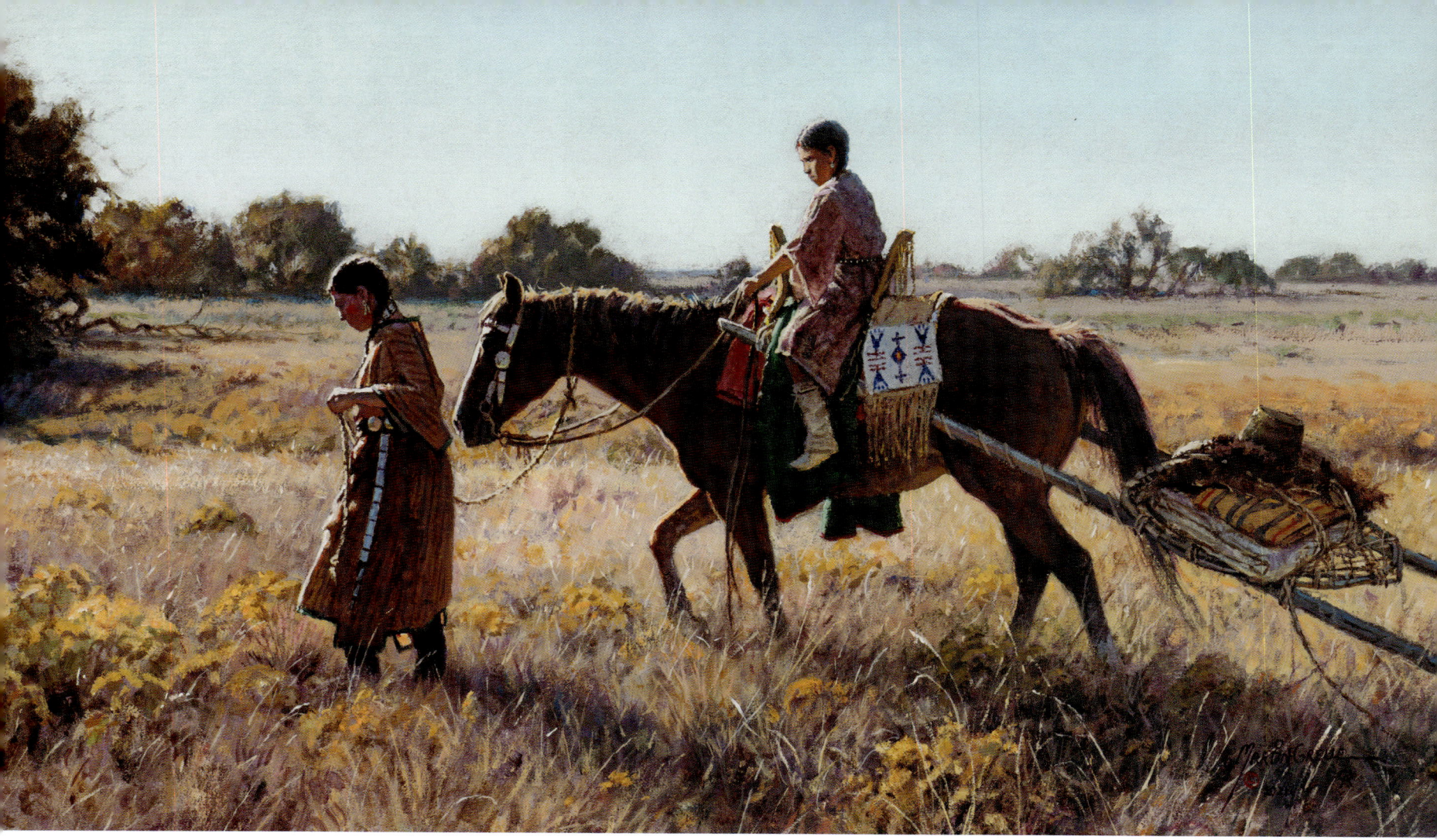

Morning Move

(Acrylic on linen, 14" × 24", 2021)

"This painting shows a Cheyenne mother with her young daughter as they move to a new campsite. The horse is pulling a travois with some of their possessions loaded onto it. The young girl rides while holding the reins, but the mother holds a lead rope as well, indicating that the horse is probably a risk for pulling the travois. These moves were a frequent event in the lives of the various tribes, and the women could tear down, load, and get moving to their new location in an amazingly short amount of time."

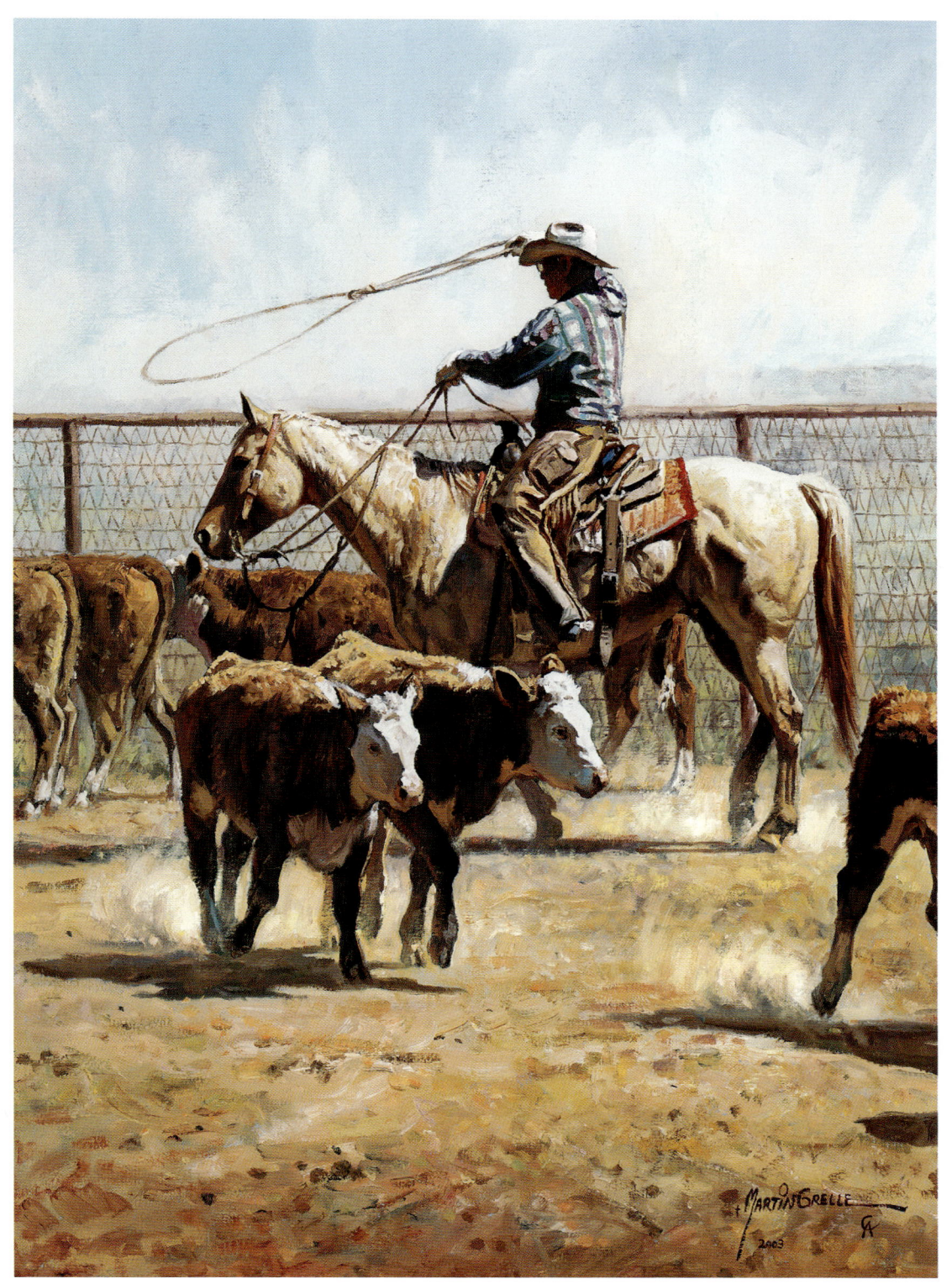

In the Texas Dust

(Oil on linen, 24" × 18", 2003)

"As a member of the Cowboy Artists of America, I have had the opportunity through our Annual Trail Ride to go out with working cowboys on many top ranches. My first ride was on the well-known 6666 Ranch at Guthrie, Texas, in the spring of 1996, and the CAA has returned to that ranch several times over the years. This painting was taken from references I got on that first ride. There was a severe drought during this time, and the dust was ever-present during our time there."

Teal
Blake

CHAPTER 2

Teal Blake

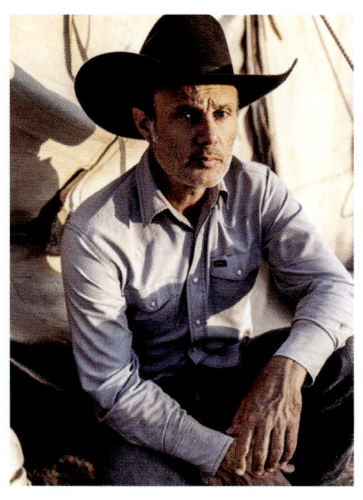

Teal Blake was raised in "Charlie Russell country" in Augusta, Montana, a town on the eastern front of the Rocky Mountains eighty miles north of Helena. When he wasn't off exploring and hunting with his .22 or riding horses, he loved to spend his time in his father's studio. Young Blake was constantly in trouble at school for drawing on every piece of paper in every class. His father, famed Western artist Buckeye Blake, would give his son scraps of matte board on which to draw and paint watercolors, but he never forced his son to draw or practice.

He never pushed it on me—he'd say, "Hey, if you want to watch this is what I'm doing now." And so it kept me from . . . getting run off or burnt out. I learned so much better by watching and seeing than reading anything. . . . And so I was able to watch him be a professional artist for forty years. . . . Seeing and watching him getting to put his head down and work and actually make a living at it, I knew I could make a living out of being an artist."

Blake began to show cutting horses at the age of seven. The family moved to Sun Valley, Idaho, and there, he "fell into rodeo" and participated in rodeo through high school riding bulls and team roping. He later enrolled in Montana State University on a rodeo scholarship, majoring in art. He was disillusioned by the structured art courses and assignments that he felt were not relevant. Blake shared that he "right there . . . checked out—at that time I was young and rodeoing and working on ranches and chasing the West. I did not want to be in a classroom learning about art history."

Blake thought at this time that he was going to rodeo professionally the rest of his life while working on several ranches at the same time. According to Blake, "The last thing I thought I was going to do was to set up an easel in the corner of the room and be stationary from then on."

One winter in Texas, however, he took a break from chasing the rodeo and set up his easel and paints, which refocused his direction back to art. He said, "I sat down in front of it and that was it—I quit entering rodeos then and it [the art] started taking shape then—I took the bull by the horns." His first show was in 2007 at the Phippen Western Art show in Prescott, Arizona. He won Best of Watercolor and Best of Show for his work, which was a candid painting of a bay horse in a red half-top trailer (see *Texas Half-Top*). This image was inspired while Blake was working at Buster Welch's in Snyder, Texas. He has returned to this scene several times throughout his career.

Blake's inspiration comes from his constant observations and sketches as he travels to different ranches. He does quick drawings in Moleskine sketchbooks that are always with him. He jots down notes about the day, encapsulating things that photographs cannot capture. These sketches spark his memory when he begins a painting and can be added to pieces already progressing. Blake also uses pictures for reference for his works; however, he tries to rely more on his memories of senses, smells, and light from the day than on the photographs. He says that he takes his sketchbooks with him when he is out on the wagon, in his truck, or in his tent to "sketch what [he] saw that day and write down notes . . . there's these little things that you're never gonna see again with the camera."

Blake's connection to horses is very strong, being raised in a family with strong traditions for raising premium Quarter Horses. His father, Buckeye, is in the Cowboy Hall of Fame for breeding the foundation lines of horses that have had such a strong influence on the breed. The family was known for raising high-quality cutting horses. Being around these horses provided the anatomy classroom for Blake, although his interest was also drawn to the wild horses of the West. He says, "I grew up seeing wild horses all the time. The second I was old enough to have my own place, I immediately had a Mustang, and I've got two now. I think there's something to holding on to that history of the West. . . . It's kind of a neat medicine to me." He tries to be very respectful of the major role the horse has had in the settling of the West when he is working on a painting and adds, "The horse is the iconic image of the West."

In painting his horses, capturing the character of the horse is very important to Blake. In his portrait of horses, each horse is represented as an individual, something to distinguish him from the others. He particularly likes the looks of the rangy horses of the past. He says, "I'm drawn to the skinny raw-boned Charlie Russell horses. . . . You look at the older horses and Remington's horses—cavalry horses and cow horses were tough with Roman noses—big feathered-footed things and had these great looks about them to paint."

Other artists besides his father have influenced the art of Teal Blake. The books and art of Will James were a strong inspiration, but he also likes the simplicity and strength of Maynard Dixon. Blake believes that artists can at times be like sponges in soaking up their surroundings and experiences. Watercolors are Blake's preferred and most comfortable medium, although for the past several years, he has been working in oils.

Blake's favorite personal horse is a cutting horse he raised and trained name Modelo Blue, or "Mo" for short. The horse has done it all, from showing to roping and ranching. Blake's son Luca has been learning to ride on this horse. Says Blake, "He is the best horse I have ever owned, and if I could ever get another horse half as good as him, I will be lucky."

Blake's son Luca is also artistic and loves to draw and paint. He has a little easel and works alongside his father, just as Blake did with his father. Blake's grandmother and grandfather on his dad's side were also both artistic, "so it's kind of neat . . . that he has that as well . . . it really traveled down the bloodline."

Blake published a children's book based on stories he told his son over the years of the adventures on a jackalope ranch. This book, *J is for Jackalope*, was the winner of the Western Heritage Award for Children's Literature.

In 2014, Blake was selected to be in the Cowboy Artists of America (CAA), which he considers a very humbling experience. At the time, he was the youngest artist to enter that prestigious group of artists. He is a winner of many awards including the Joe Beeler CAA Foundation Award, the Academy of Western Artists Artist of the year (2017), Silver Medal CAA watercolors (2015), and Gold Medal CAA watercolor award (2016 and 2017).

Blake currently lives in Fort Worth, Texas, with his son Luca.

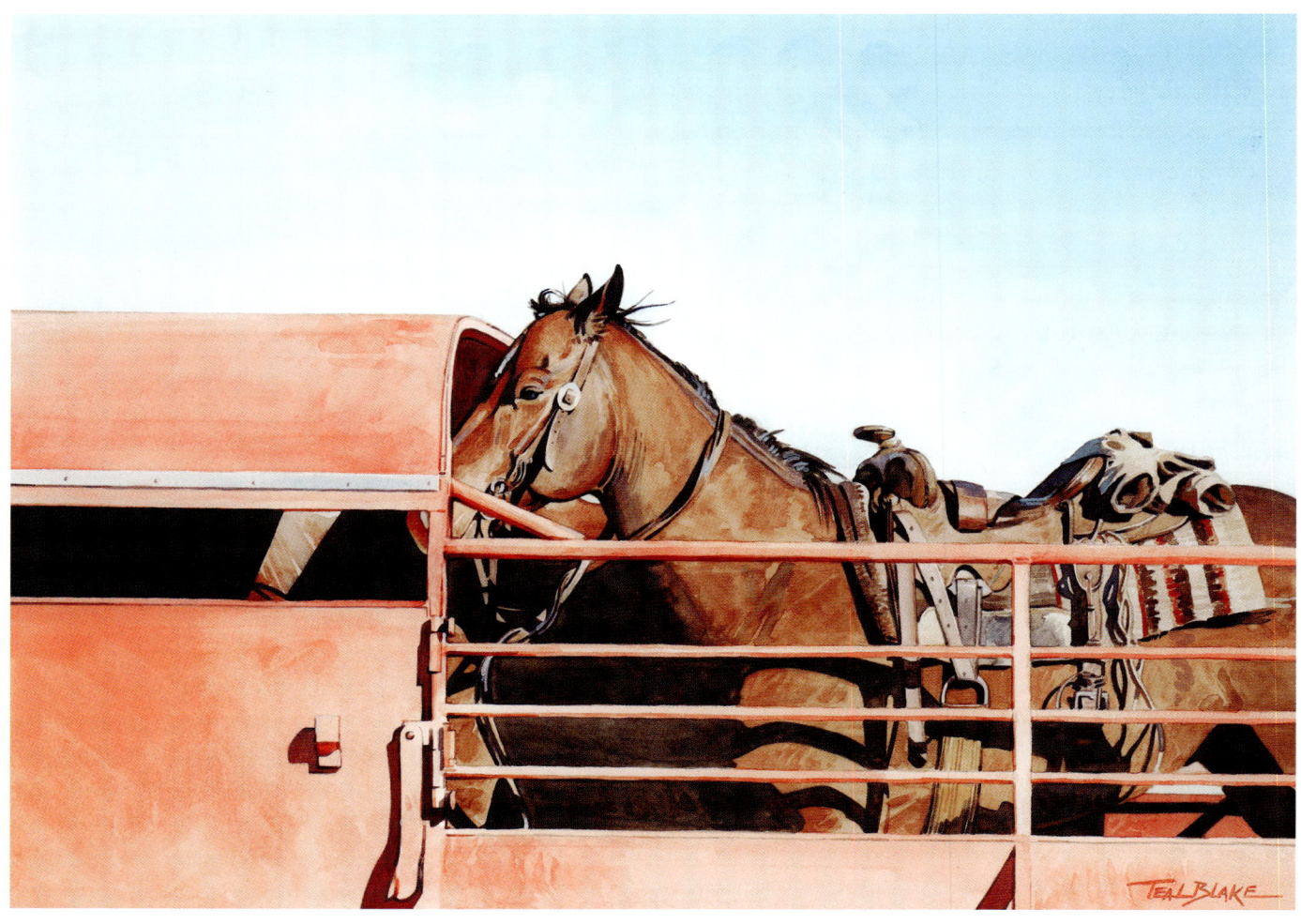

Texas Half-Top

(Watercolor, 16" × 24", 2008)

"I did a little piece of a bay horse in a red trailer—it was just a low half-top piece and it was from when I was working at Buster Welch's out of Snyder. And I wasn't sure what anybody was going to think of it, because I guess it wasn't the normal Western thing . . . but it did really well."

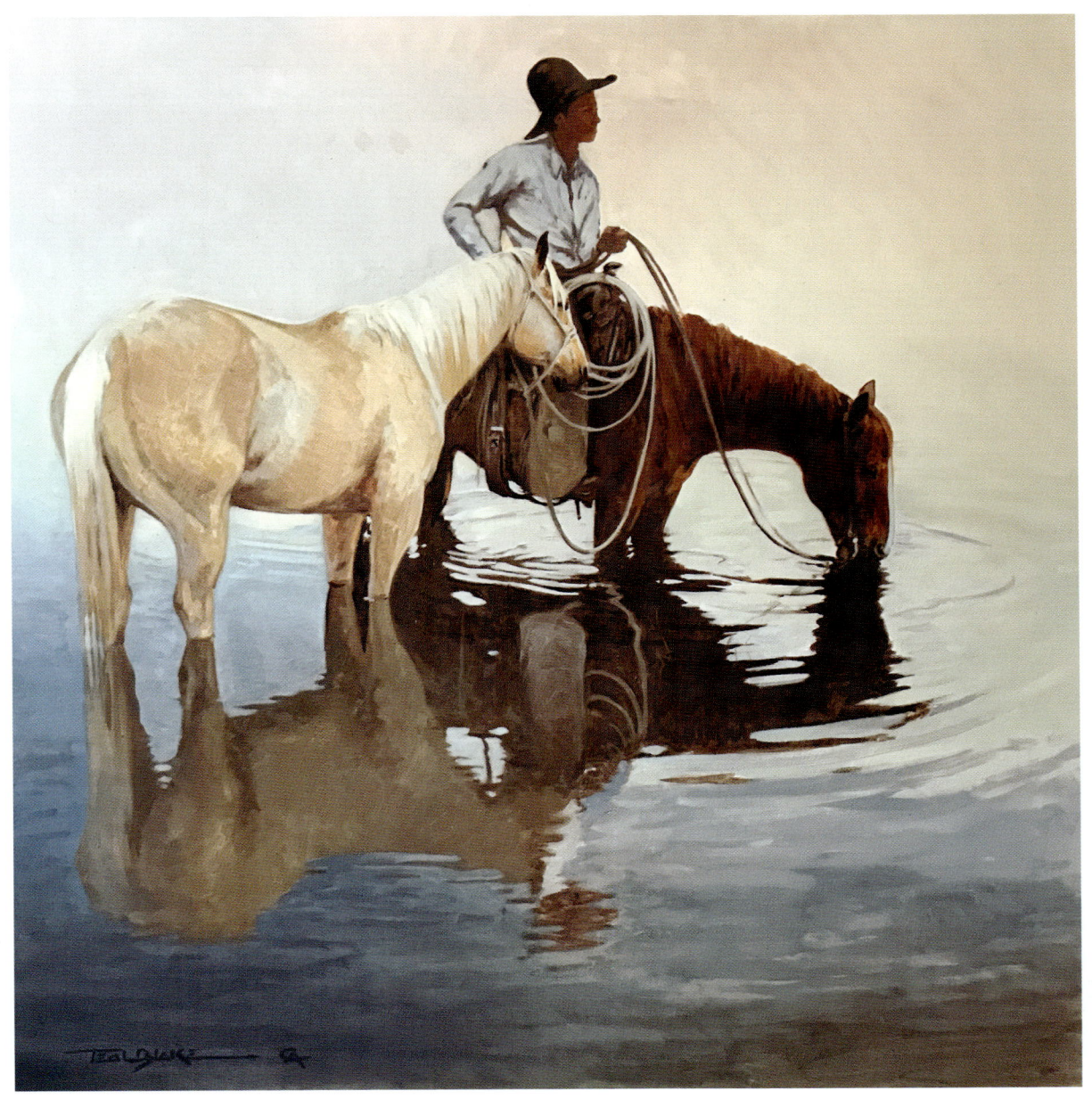

Ranch Water

(Oil, 40" × 40", n.d.)

"*Ranch Water* is a focus on the candid moment with horse and rider, serenity, and small ripples."

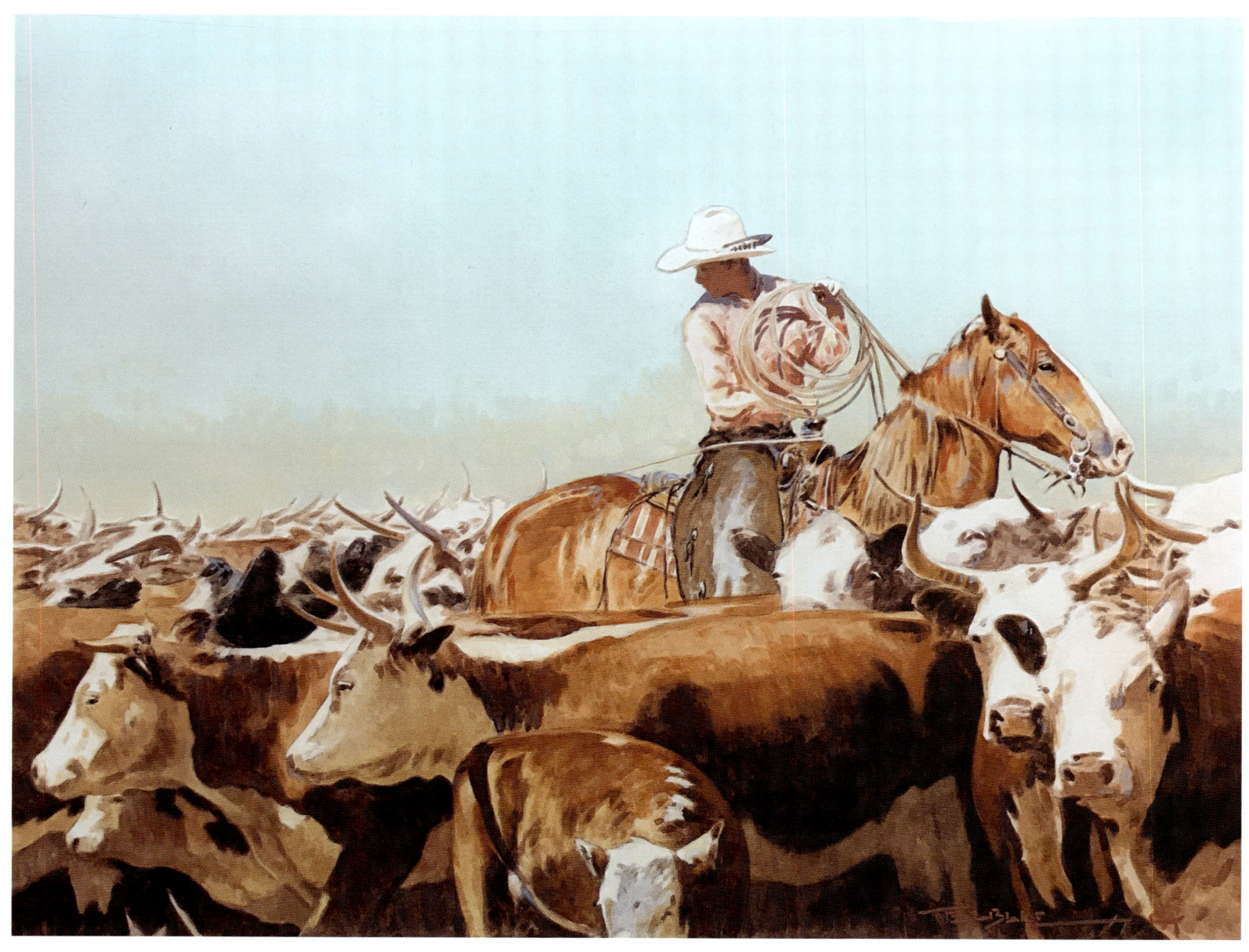

Lookin' for the Little Ones

(Watercolor, 24" × 30", 2019)

"Lookin' for the Little Ones is an ode to the ranches I grew up on in Montana—
everything was Herefords for the longest time."

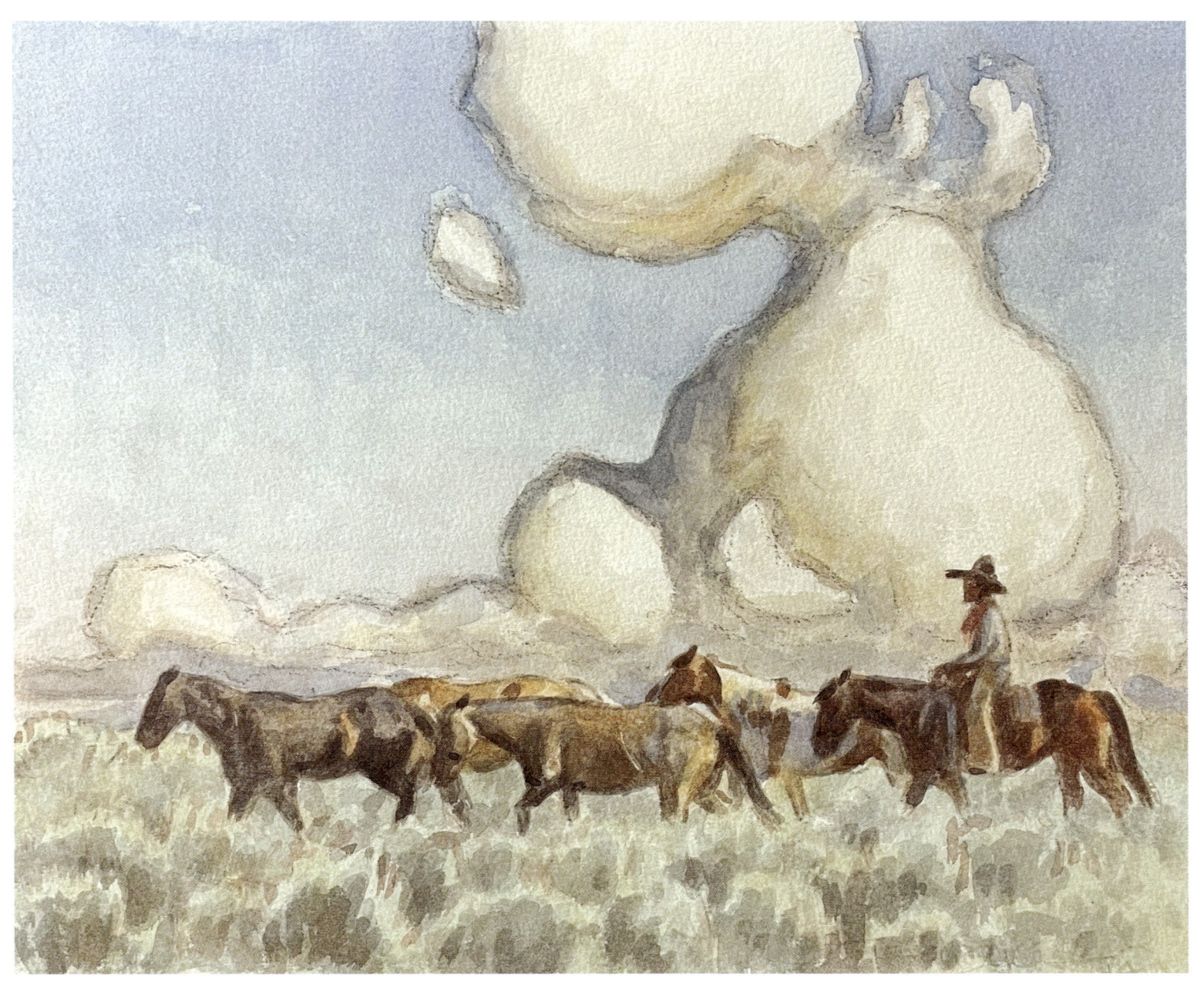

West

(Watercolor, 8″ × 10″, 2018)

Big sky. Sage. And horses.

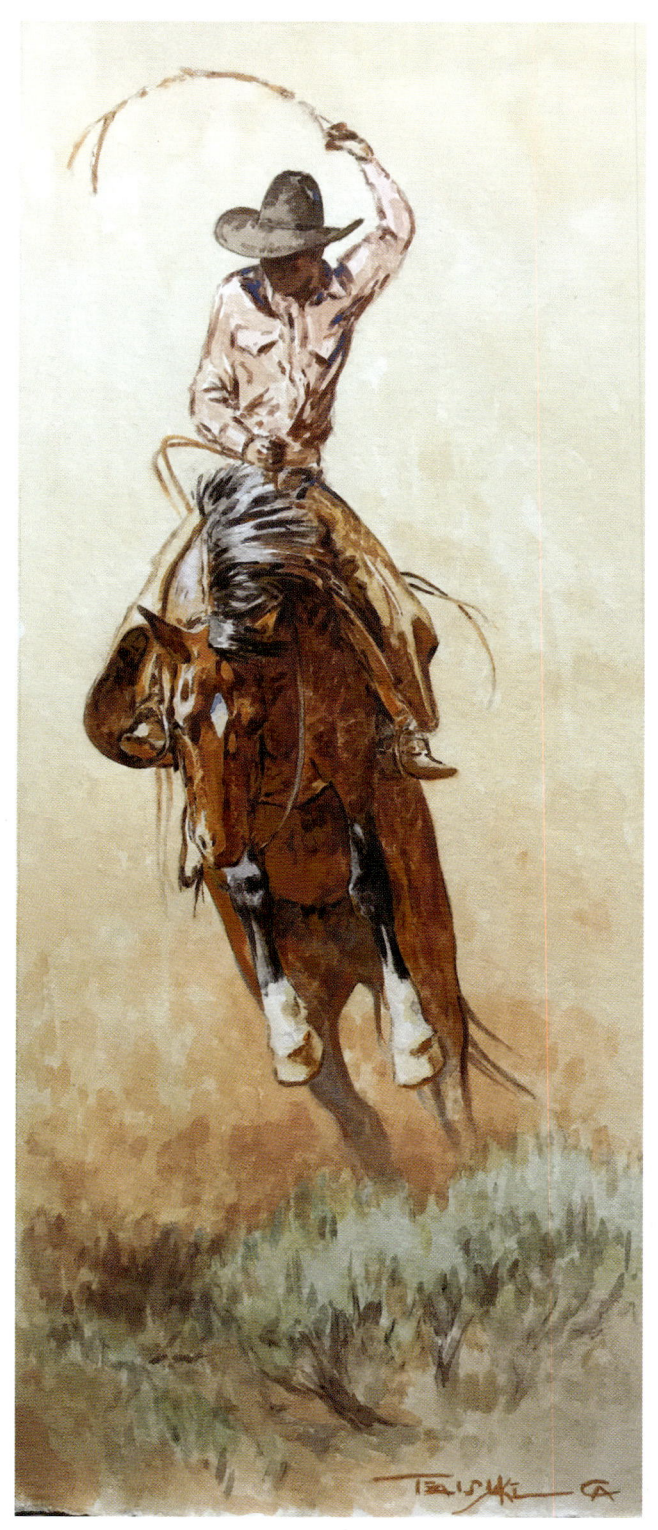

Into the Sage

(Watercolor, 16″ × 28″, 2018)

"This was me trying to fit a bucking horse into a vertical piece of paper. I wanted it to show the height and drop of a bronc."

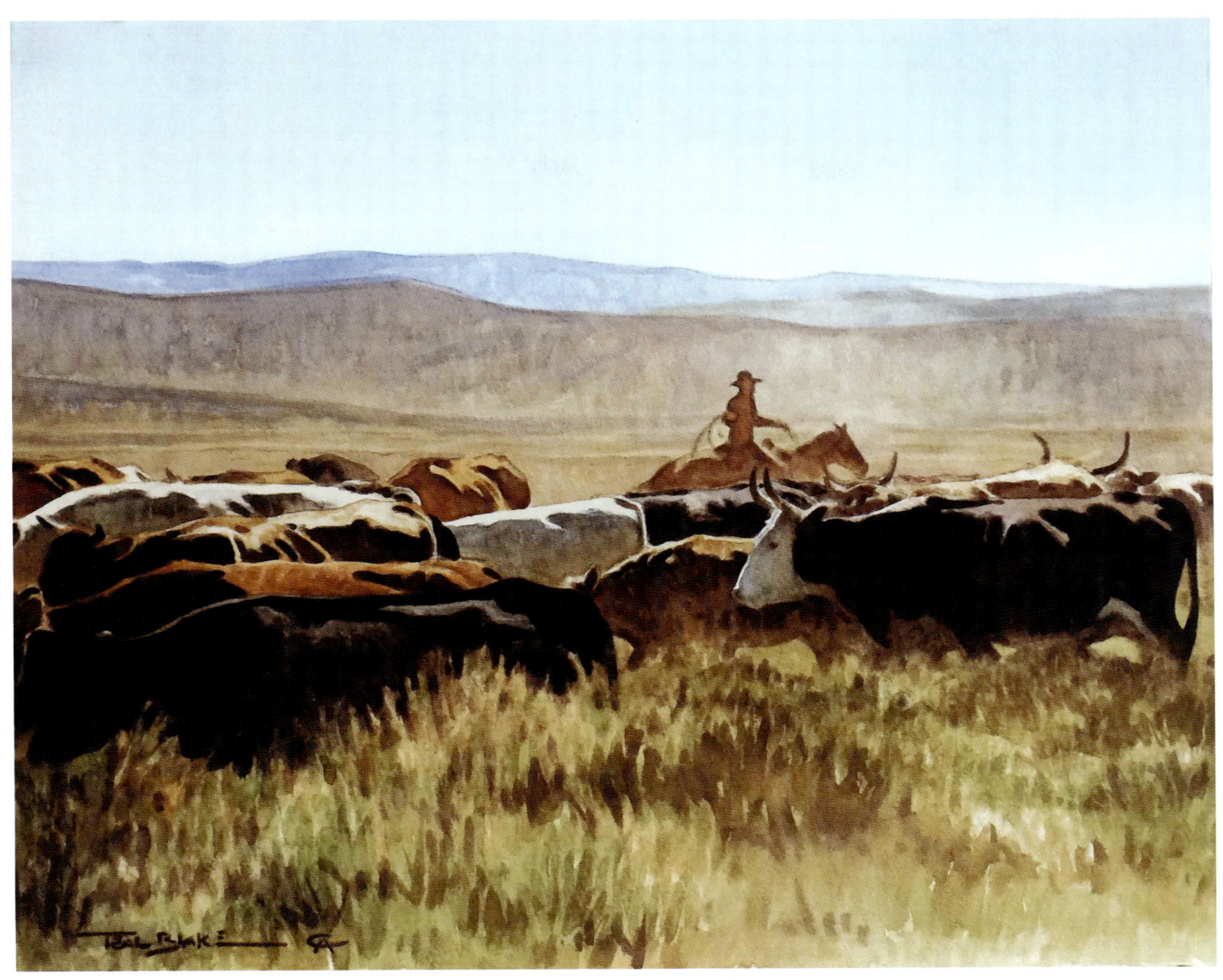

Headed for the Oxbow

(Watercolor, 16" × 20", 2018)

"Headed for the Oxbow was from a ranch I worked on near Tularosa, New Mexico.
The distance made for great atmosphere."

Mary Ross Buchholz

CHAPTER 3

Mary Ross Buchholz

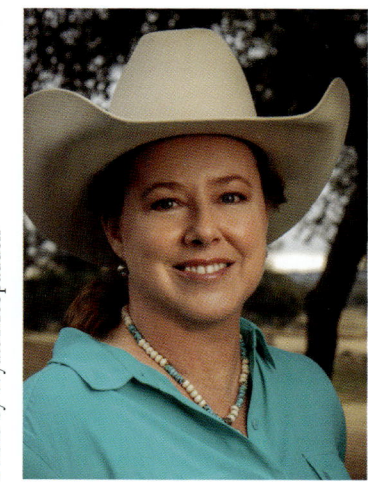

Photo by Wyatt McSpadden

Mary Ross Buchholz grew up on a ranch in Sonora, Texas, as a sixth-generation rancher. Both her mother and father came from pioneer ranching families from Sutton, Crockett, and Schleicher Counties. She married Bob Buchholz, also a rancher, from Dripping Springs, Texas. The family now lives east of Eldorado and operates the same place that the artist's great-grandfather once ranched. This area sits on the western edge of the Edwards Plateau and lends itself to diverse ranching enterprises.

Buchholz attended Texas A&M University, where she majored in animal science with a science option. When she married, she gave up the pursuit of going to veterinary school to return to the ranch and start a family. The couple now have three grown boys and together they raise cattle, sheep, goats, border collies, and Quarter Horses. When the children were young, it was important for Buchholz to stay at home rather than get a job in town. She states, "Raising the boys with our own values and beliefs was paramount." Since childhood, Buchholz has had a strong passion for drawing. With a twist of fate, a career in art ultimately was developed—and it fit the goal of staying home with the children wonderfully.

Buchholz is largely a self-taught artist, although she has taken many art classes and workshops over the span of her career. She credits her mother with pointing her in the direction of becoming an artist. The two took art lessons together, visited many museums, and traveled to Europe to see the great masters of art.

I love drawing. Actually, I started out more classically in the beginning. I loved to do paintings or drawings from life, whether it was during a workshop or just on my own. I'm drawn to portraits and interested in capturing the life within a person or an animal.

Buchholz is best known for her images in charcoal and graphite, although she is accomplished in sculpting and painting as well. Her motivation to create art is her love of horses and ranching. She feels lucky that her subjects are right outside her back door. She knows her subject well, and there are many things on the ranch that keep her motivated to continue to create her drawings. She says, "I see possibilities around every corner and every bush." If a model is needed for a certain angle or detail, her husband or another family member is happy to pose while she tweaks her drawing.

The main focus of Buchholz's art is to depict the working stock horse and the daily lives of genuine working cowboys and ranchers. In breaking into the art world, she set goals for herself and one by one met those goals. Her journey involved working hard, not giving up, and always striving to improve and continue learning. She says, "And the rest is history, I guess. Who would have thought a small-town girl would wind up being a Western artist?"

Buchholz uses her own reference photos and may use several photographs to design one piece. She makes sure not to copy photos to the last detail but uses them only as helpful references. Even though her artwork may seem highly detailed, her drawing skills impart the illusion of detail without all the information really being there. Buchholz is also known for her close-ups, such as on a horse's eye. She feels these close-up drawings can help bring the viewer into the work and the details that are often missed. She wants her art to not only look real but feel real—both at a distance and up close.

When using charcoal and graphite, I enjoy subtly rendering the details, the different textures and the individual characteristics of my

subjects. I marvel at how black and white images seem timeless and impart a simplicity without other distractions. I feel this is one reason why I choose to use charcoal and graphite as my primary medium.

Buchholz credits her father for teaching her about the conformation of the horse and learning to evaluate livestock in general. Her 4-H experiences and her studies in animal science and anatomy also have furthered her art career and helped her to develop her style.

At times, Buchholz has been invited to visit and gather reference photos at other ranches such as the 6666 Ranch in Guthrie, Texas. Being able to see the cowboys in a different region with their unique or varying styles of clothing or tack is exciting to Buchholz, knowing that it will provide new content and variety in her artwork. Ultimately, Buchholz feels honored to create portraits of these cowboys and their horses.

Buchholz teaches workshops annually for students in drawing. When teaching, she emphasizes to her students the importance of the value scale and the transitions from shadows into light. She feels the mid-tones are the most difficult for young artists, and she helps them better understand these tones. She often uses charcoal in her works to achieve the darkest values, although this approach can be challenging.

I can spend quite a bit of time on the transitions and getting it to read properly. There is a time that you need to let your intuition take over. You need to step back and squint at the work, which helps get the details out of the way. I draw in layers just like a painter. It's a time-consuming process using charcoal and graphite. Sometimes people don't realize the amount of hours that go into a piece.

In her drawings, one of Buchholz's primary goals is to capture the viewer's attention, both up close and from a distance. She intentionally moves the viewer's eye around her artwork by using more detail or contrast in the focal areas. She says, "It's kind of like a dance. Little hints and sparkles across the painting is what I like to achieve." She accomplishes this by composition, overall balance, and other techniques such as dramatic lighting. More difficult than dramatic lighting is subtle lighting. She will also include negative space and areas of rest in her works.

Buchholz is known to focus on the eye of the horse in her work. She states that the eye is her favorite part of the horse: "I truly enjoy making the eye feel liquid and fluid—the luminosity of the eye puts a smile on my face. I enjoy trying to capture the eye, reflecting the personality of the horse. You can tell a lot about a horse through its eyes."

Buchholz's biggest influences in art include French artist Rosa Bonheur, whose large-scale paintings from the 1800s captured the magnificence of animals, including horses. Bonheur's painting *The Horse Fair* is Buchholz's favorite. She was able to see many of Bonheur's works in the museums she visited with her mother. The late Bill Owen has also had an impact on her as an artist. Among the influential workshops that Buchholz participated in are those of Huihan Liu and Tony Ryder.

Buchholz has participated in many prominent art shows including *Night of the Artists* at the Briscoe Western Art Museum; *Great Wonders* at the National Cowboy & Western Heritage Museum; *The Coors Western Art Show* in Denver, Colorado; *The Russell* at the C. M. Russel Museum; *Summer Stampede* at the National Ranching Heritage Center; and *Cowgirl Up!*. She has received numerous prestigious awards. Her most recent honors include the *Small Works, Great Wonders* art show 2024 "Cynthia Post Memorial Directors' Choice Award" at the National Cowboy & Western Heritage Museum, the Briscoe Western Art Museum 2023 Night of Artists "William B. Travis Patrons' Choice Award" and the 2023 Academy of Western Artists "Artist of the Year Award." She has been the subject of many featured articles in magazines such as *Western Horseman*, *Western Art Collector*, *Art of the West*, and *Western Art & Architecture*.

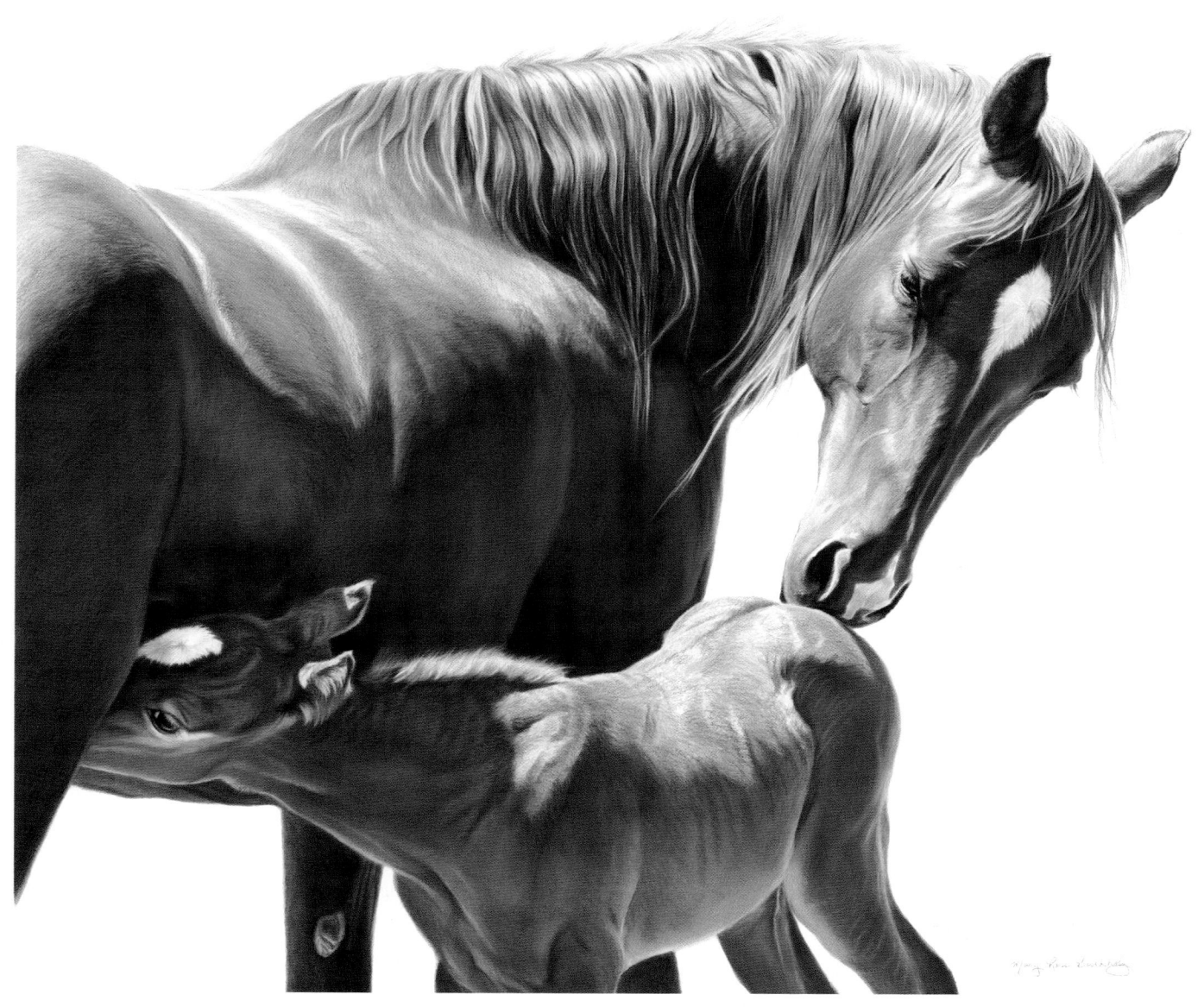

Mother's Day

(Graphite and charcoal, 22" × 27", 2020)

"There's an overall feeling that I want to end up with—I'm trying to convey that emotion or that sensitivity of this mare and her nursing colt. The mare arches her neck and sniffs the tail of the little foal. This to me is a sensitive moment. This sensation or emotion goes through me when I see that; being a mother I never tire of seeing mares and foals interact. I could sit and watch them all day long."

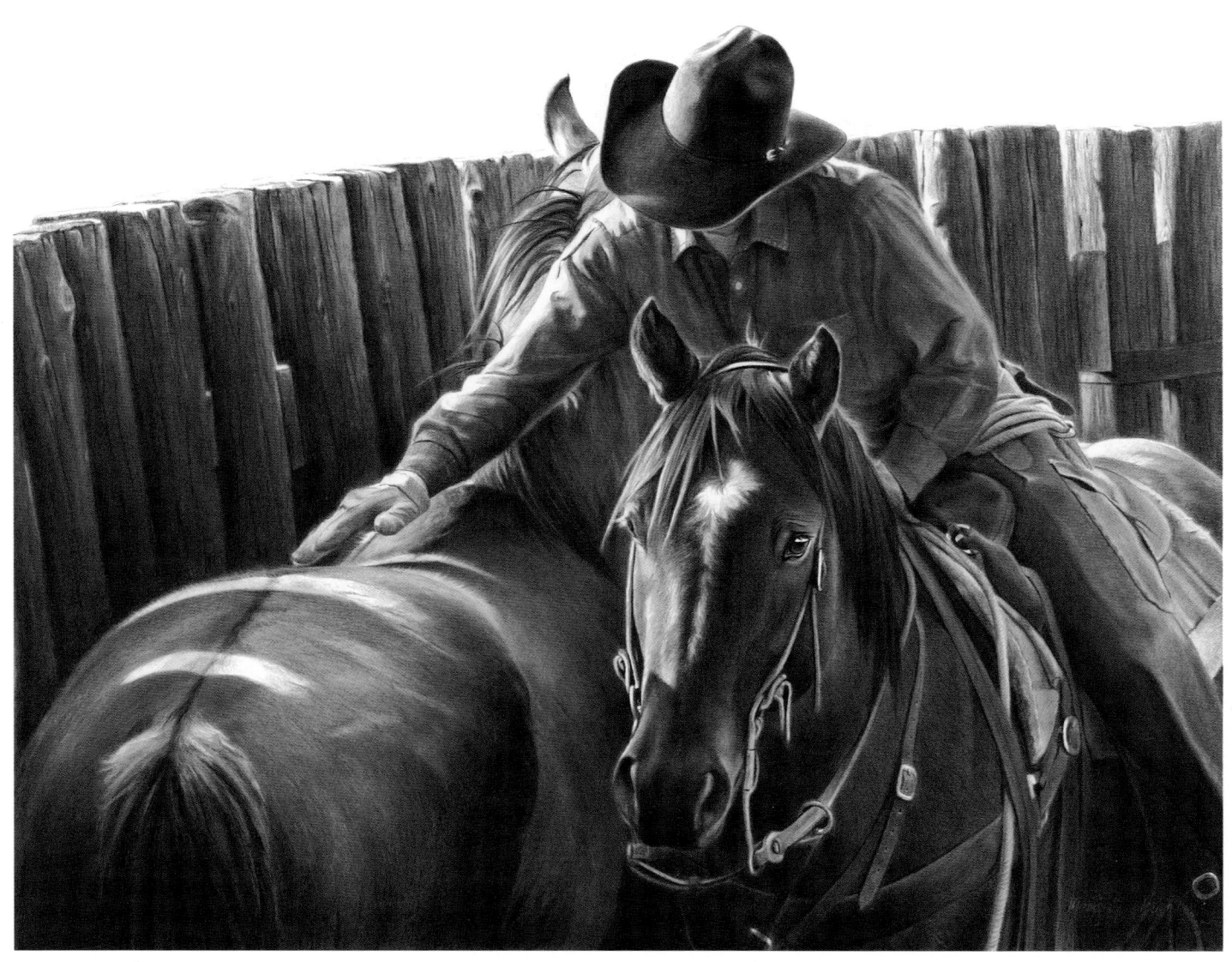

Gentlin' Touch

(Graphite and charcoal, 21.5" × 27.25", 2015)

"This young cowboy starts a colt by crowding him in the round pen and giving him a gentle touch. It's an important part of his training. The cowboy's mount, who is calm, helps the colt become more receptive to the cowboy's presence. This drawing has a unique composition, and I enjoyed drawing the shadows and highlights shining through the round pen posts."

Takin' Hold

(Graphite and charcoal,
19″ × 16″, 2017)

"The raw power of a tripping horse in action is something to behold. The rider has set the trip and the steer is about to hit the ground. This is the setup for a winning run. I enjoyed capturing this moment at the annual Roping Fiesta in San Angelo, Texas. Many things contribute to this being a powerful piece. It's the lighting, the shadows, the composition, the action of the horse and rider and the detail in the tack."

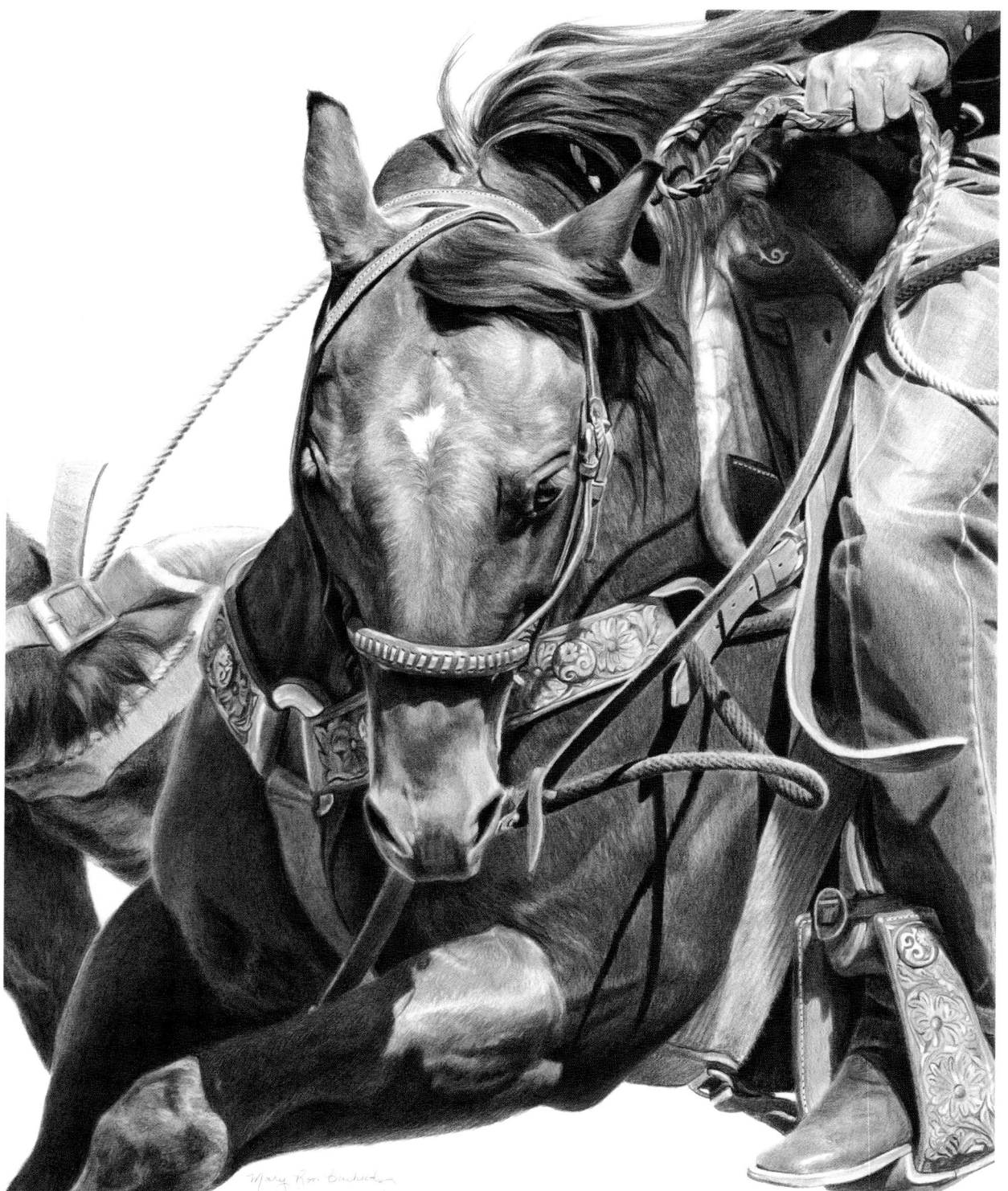

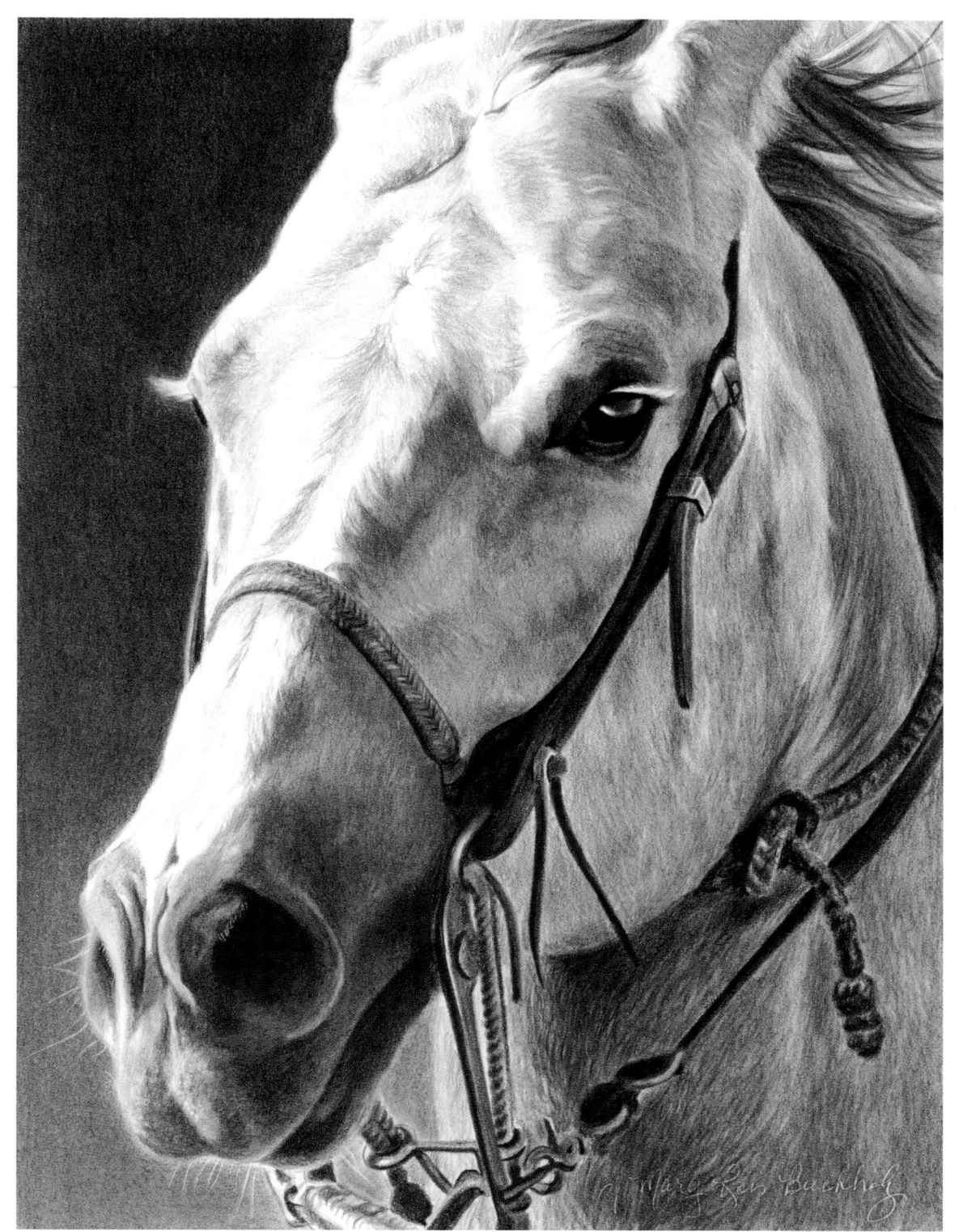

Going for It

(Graphite and charcoal,
11" × 8.5", 2017)

"I enjoying creating artworks that get up close and personal. This drawing is a complete package full of action along with dramatic lighting and subtly rendered details and tack. The eyes are my favorite part of an animal. I feel like that's where you're able to see the life; as people say, the eye captures the soul of the horse. I want my pieces to not only look real but feel real. I'm always mindful of the subject's personality and hope each piece is portrayed with honesty and simplicity."

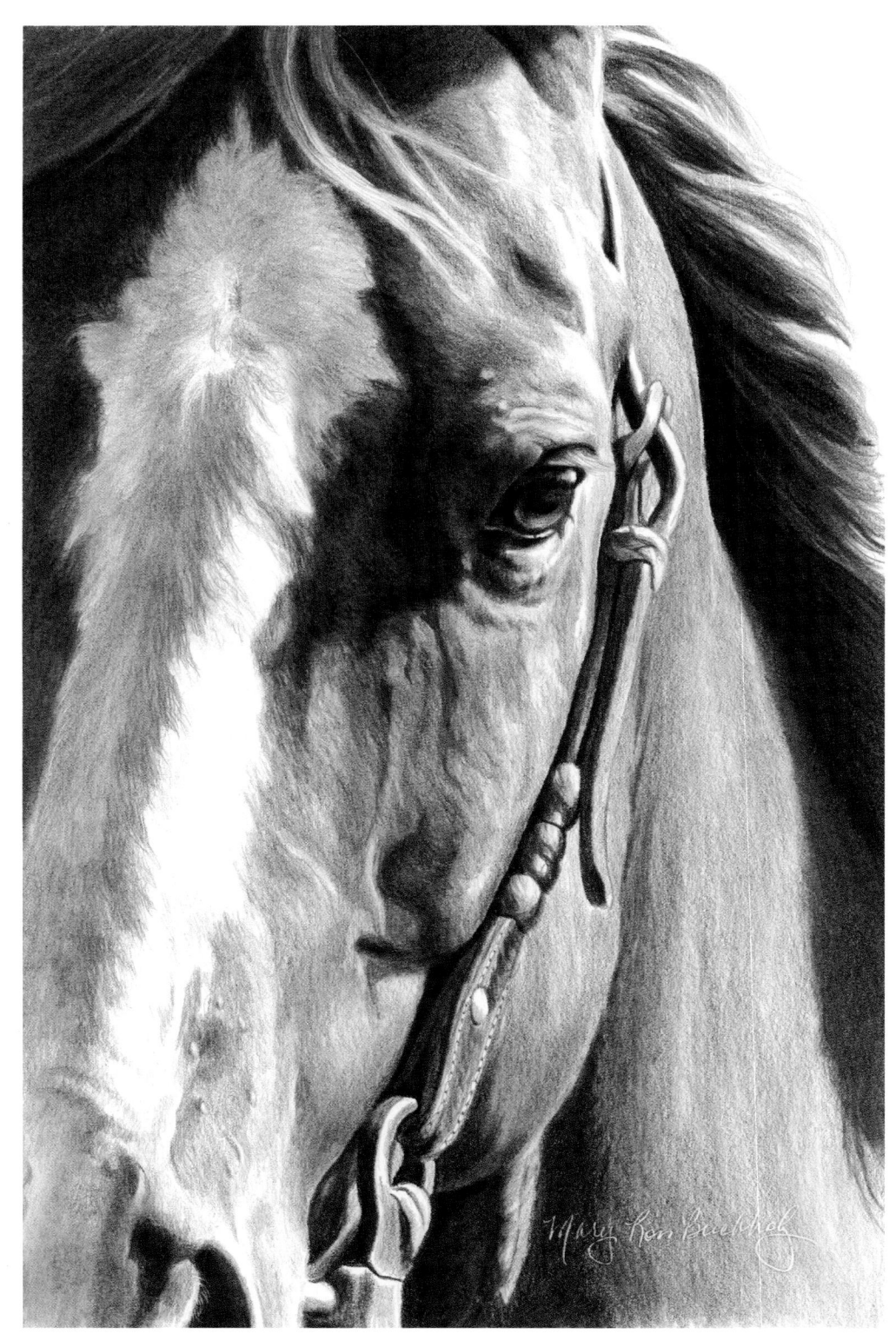

He's Focused

(Graphite and charcoal, 11.5" × 8", 2018)

"This is my husband's roping horse, Don. He is a tried-and-true roping horse that gives consistent runs every time. He stays focused, has speed and heart: all qualities anyone would love to have in a horse."

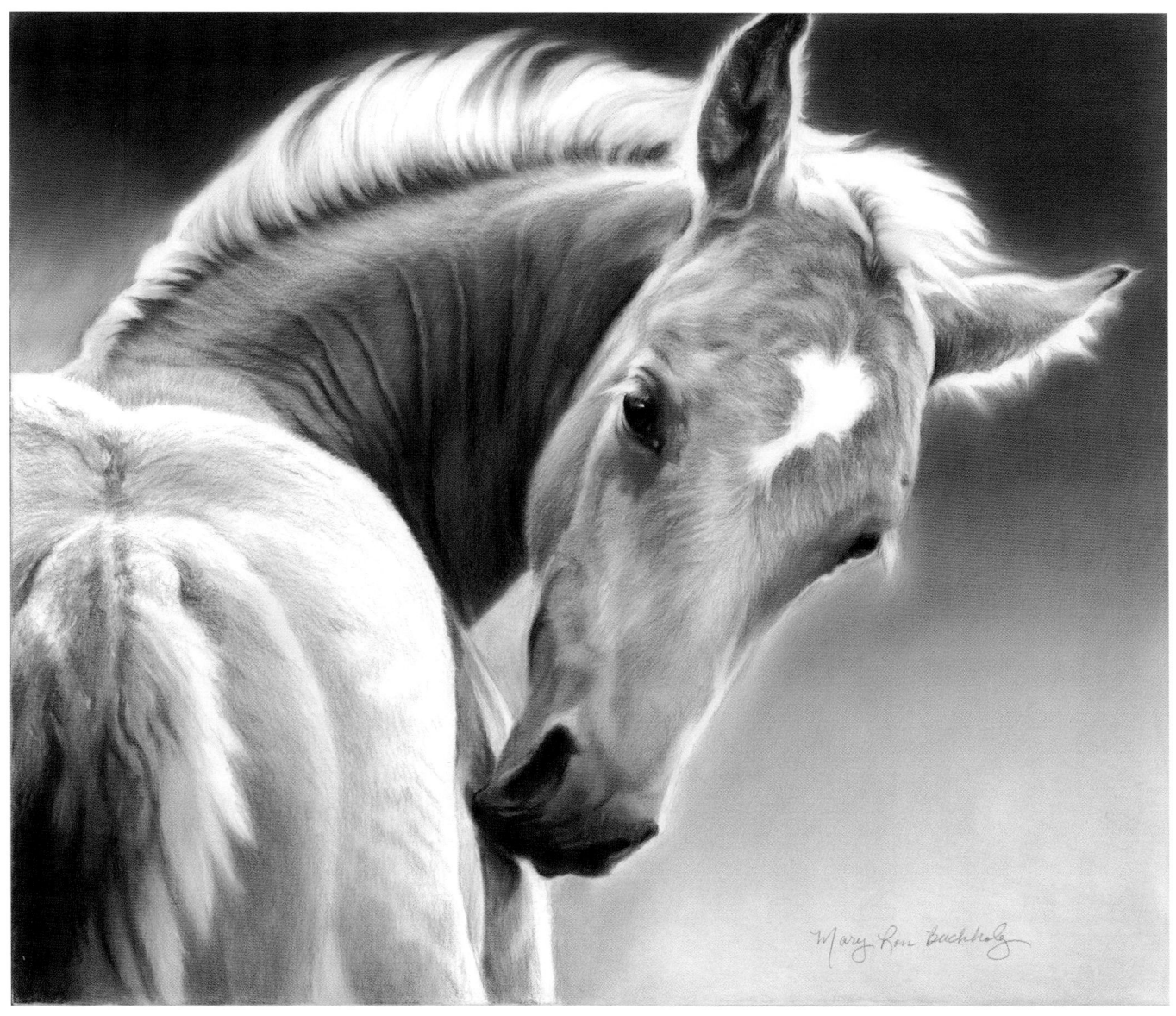

Nibble Nibble

(Graphite and charcoal, 12″ × 14″, 2020)

"Our buckskin filly is a looker. The light passes through her mane as she arches to scratch her ribs. One can't help but notice the soft downy coat and muzzle of this filly. The dramatic lighting, subtle details and the pleasing composition all pull the viewer into this piece."

Xiang Zhang

CHAPTER 4

Xiang Zhang

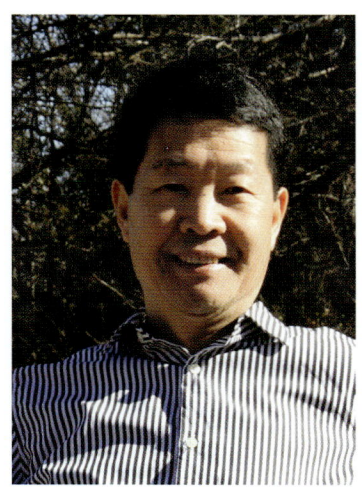

Xiang Zhang (pronounced Shang Zang) was born in the Year of the Horse on the Chinese calendar in Chengdu, a city in the province of Sichuan, China. His parents were professors at Sichuan University. Zhang began painting when he was a young boy, learning the traditional Chinese methods beginning at age four. Early on, he was interested in drawing art featuring horses. He would walk to school, passing farmers and their horses in the fields, and would stop to sketch the horses, beginning his life-long connection with the animals through art. Zhang's mother had some training in art and learned watercolor painting from her Christian high school teacher who had come to China from England. Zhang's parents both encouraged his passion for art and introduced him to some artists to learn drawing and oil painting when he was ten years old.

Zhang's formal schooling came to a sudden halt in 1966 because of the Cultural Revolution in China. All schools (elementary, middle, and high schools) were closed until the revolution ended, ten years later. This did not stop Zhang from studying art and painting. He continued to go to the countryside, often with his painting friends, where he would paint portraits of the farmers for practice.

When some of the schools reopened in 1977, Zhang was accepted by two fine art institutes. For four years, he attended the Central Academy of Drama in Beijing and completed a degree in set design. His work was heavily influenced by the Russian masters. Every morning he would spend four hours drawing, painting, and learning art theory, followed in the afternoon by studies of costume design, architecture, theater history, and set design. After graduation, the government sent him to teach in the TV Department at Beijing Broadcast Institute for three and a half years. However, Zhang had aspirations to leave China and go to America to continue his training in art. After the Cultural Revolution came to an end, he was able to read and discover what was going on in the rest of the world. He set his goals on getting an American education in fine art.

To accomplish this aim, Zhang moved to New Orleans, Louisiana, and enrolled at Tulane University on a full scholarship for his master's degree in design. After college, he worked for three years for the New Orleans Opera House designing sets. He also worked for a company that designed Mardi Gras floats. Zhang believes that these positions gave him an opportunity to learn about American culture. He also discovered there were many fine art galleries in the city of New Orleans, which attracted him because he always wanted to be an independent artist.

The Zhang family then moved to Dallas in 1993 because he wanted his daughter to attend the school system there. He worked for a commercial art company for more than two years before deciding to take the risk and try to do his own art for a living. He found encouragement after winning a national park competition in Jackson Hole, Wyoming. He also won the purchase award at the Bosque Art Classic in Clifton, Texas. In New Orleans, Zhang had been creating figurative paintings of the world around him, but after winning these competitions, he became interested in painting cowboys and Western images. A television reporter in Dallas asked him if he ever painted cowboys. He thought that was a wonderful idea since he was living in Texas, a cowboy state. In this manner, Zhang began his new direction in art.

Zhang met Dr. Glenn Blodgett, veterinarian and horse division manager at the 6666 Ranch, who invited him to come out to a branding and watch the cowboys at work on the ranch. Zhang visited other ranches in Texas, New Mexico, and Colorado and found the lifestyle fascinating. Zhang began to study the types and body shapes of horses along with the tack and gear used by cowboys, in the current time and in the past. He bought a small ranch and began raising his own horses.

I think the horse like I have in my paintings is a very loyal animal that works very hard. They are muscular, but their personalities are important also. They have been used for work for 2,000 years as transportation, farming, and ranching. They are beautiful, handsome animals. That's why I started drawing them even when I was little.

Zhang uses photographs, memories, imagination, and sketches to help him compose a painting. He likes to use images of working cowboys, horses, and cattle instead of trying to get someone or something to pose for him. He believes you can tell the difference when someone is posing and when the image captured is a natural, casual action.

Zhang has begun a series of bird's-eye view paintings where he shows the cowboys on horseback. This is a different angle than traditional Western art, but it shows the movements of the horse and rider in a unique manner. The background is eliminated, serving to highlight the other details of the painting. The saddles and the shirts are more prominent. The movement of the horses, almost snakelike, flows across the canvas this way.

Zhang used images of the land rush era to create a conversation about equality and freedom. Being raised in a communist country, he embraces the freedom he can depict on the canvas. The story of the American West is of people who are free and unrestrained by class or background. Zhang has spent hours sitting on fence railings watching cowboys work in Texas. He picks up the dust and drama of brandings and roundups that he depicts without the modern conveniences of the work such as pickup trucks and cell phones. He combines his observations of working cowboys with the landscapes and big horizons of the West: "Movement is important for Western art. The beauty is when [cowboys and horses] move. I just so enjoy when cowboys are moving. Most of the time their life is like that."

Zhang feels that Van Gogh, Rembrandt, and Sargent were very influential in his art but adds that abstract art has also had an influence on his work. He likes to try different approaches to creating art and to combine his historical studies of the West with his love of horses in his paintings.

Zhang describes his painting style in terms comparable to Chinese calligraphy. There are two ways to write in calligraphy: slow and formal or quick and casual. Zhang prefers to paint the quick way with simple lines and emotion. This allows for more originality but also conveys more action in the image. He says he can paint the horse with a "less is more" process. His work tends to be very impressionistic up close and more realistic from a distance. This does not mean that details are lost but that the mind can recognize the horse and rider and saddle and gear without every single facet of the subject being included.

Zhang's work has received international acclaim and is in collections in the United States, China, Canada, and Europe. He has exhibited in the Prix de West in Oklahoma City, the Autry National Center's Masters of American West Fine Art Exhibition and Sale, and the Night of Artists Sale and Exhibition at the Briscoe Western Art Museum. He has also shown his work at numerous one-man shows.

Zhang and his wife Lily live in Dallas, Texas.

Freedom

(Oil, 48" × 96", 2015)

"This is the first one I've done with just horses running free. The shading in the front adds to the movement of speed. Their hooves disappearing into the dust brings the horses forward to the viewer. You can feel the energy and strength of these animals as they run."

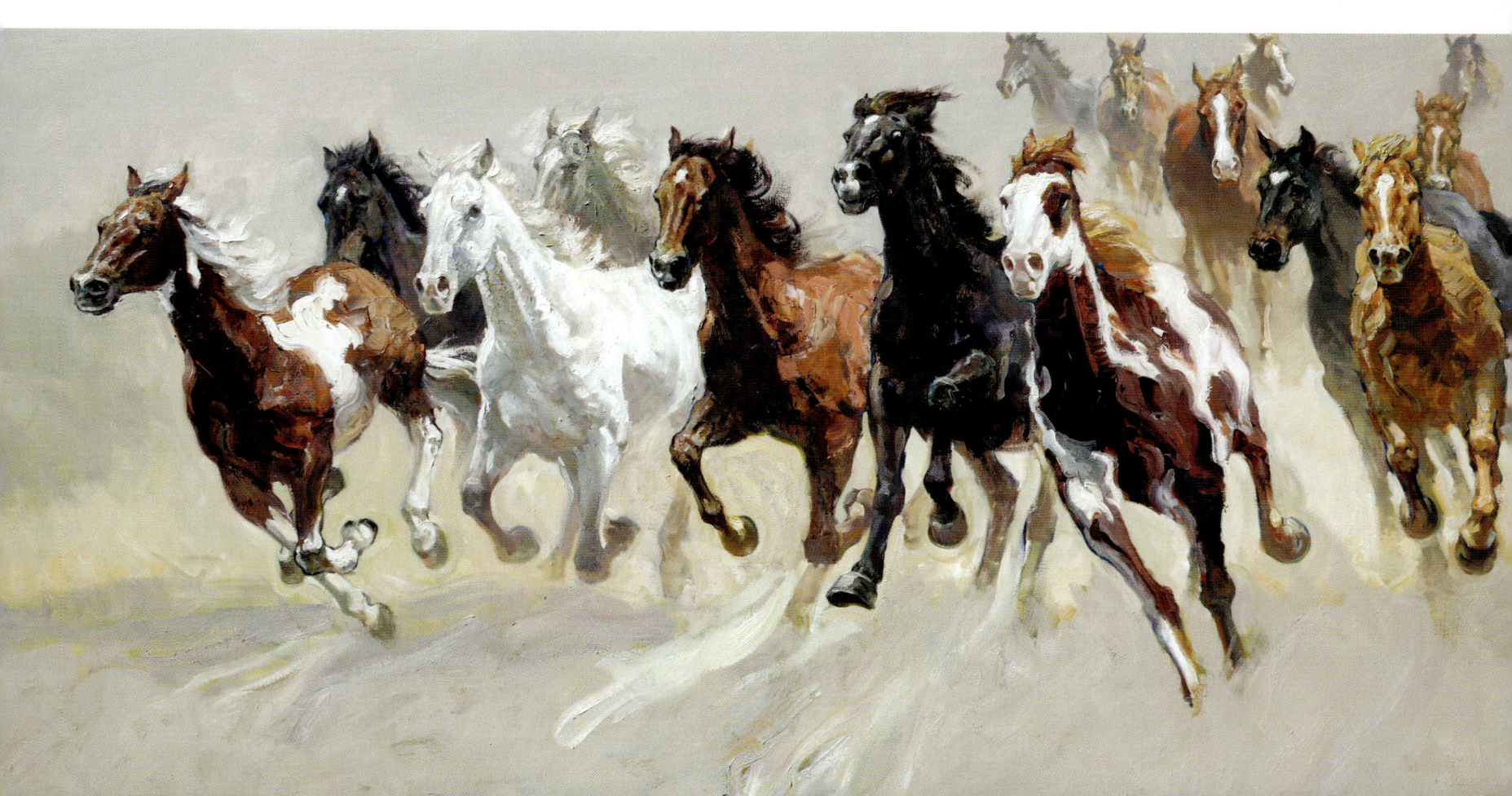

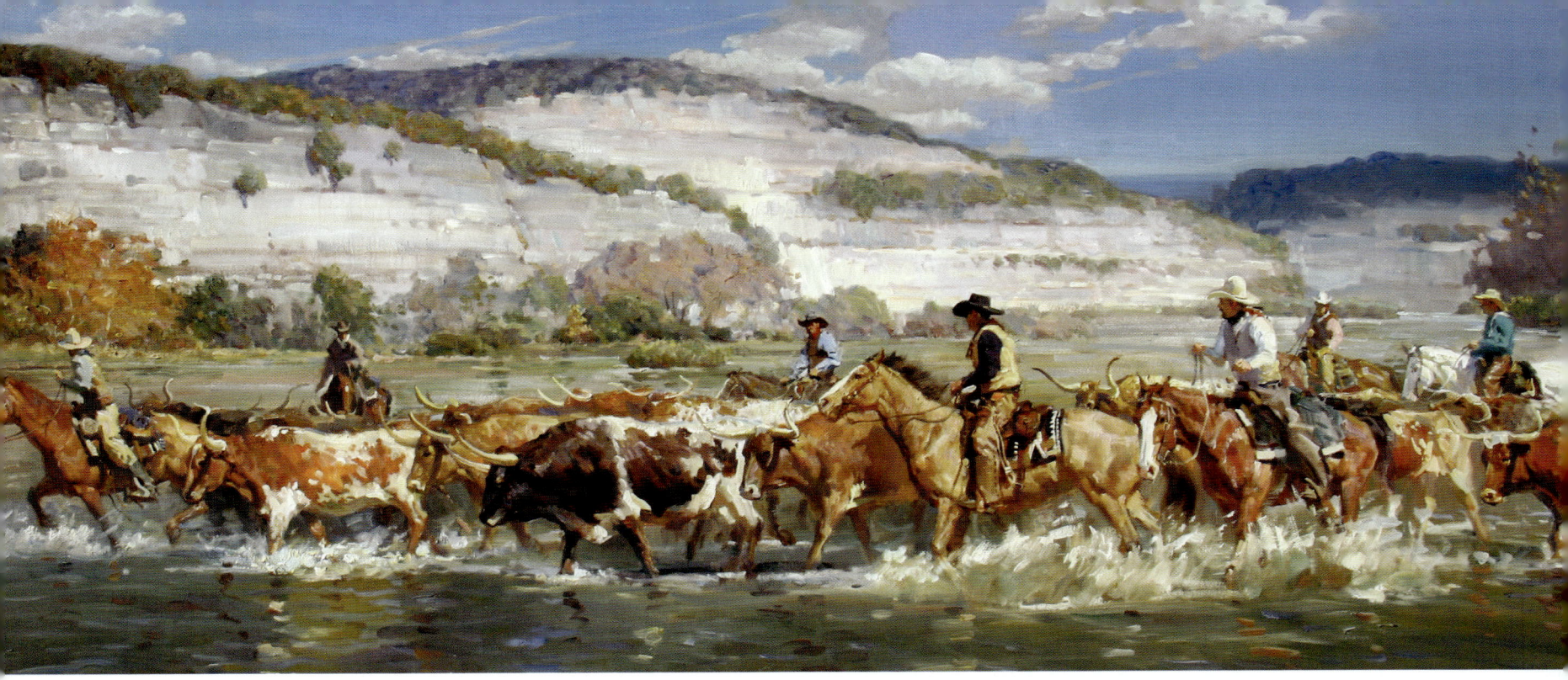

Brazos River Roundup

(Oil on linen, 36″ × 80″, 2015)

"This river crossing was done to put the cowboys and cattle in the water in front of the panorama of the rock mountains (actually modeled on some in Korea). The creek is wide and long. The Longhorns are still the main cattle on the trail."

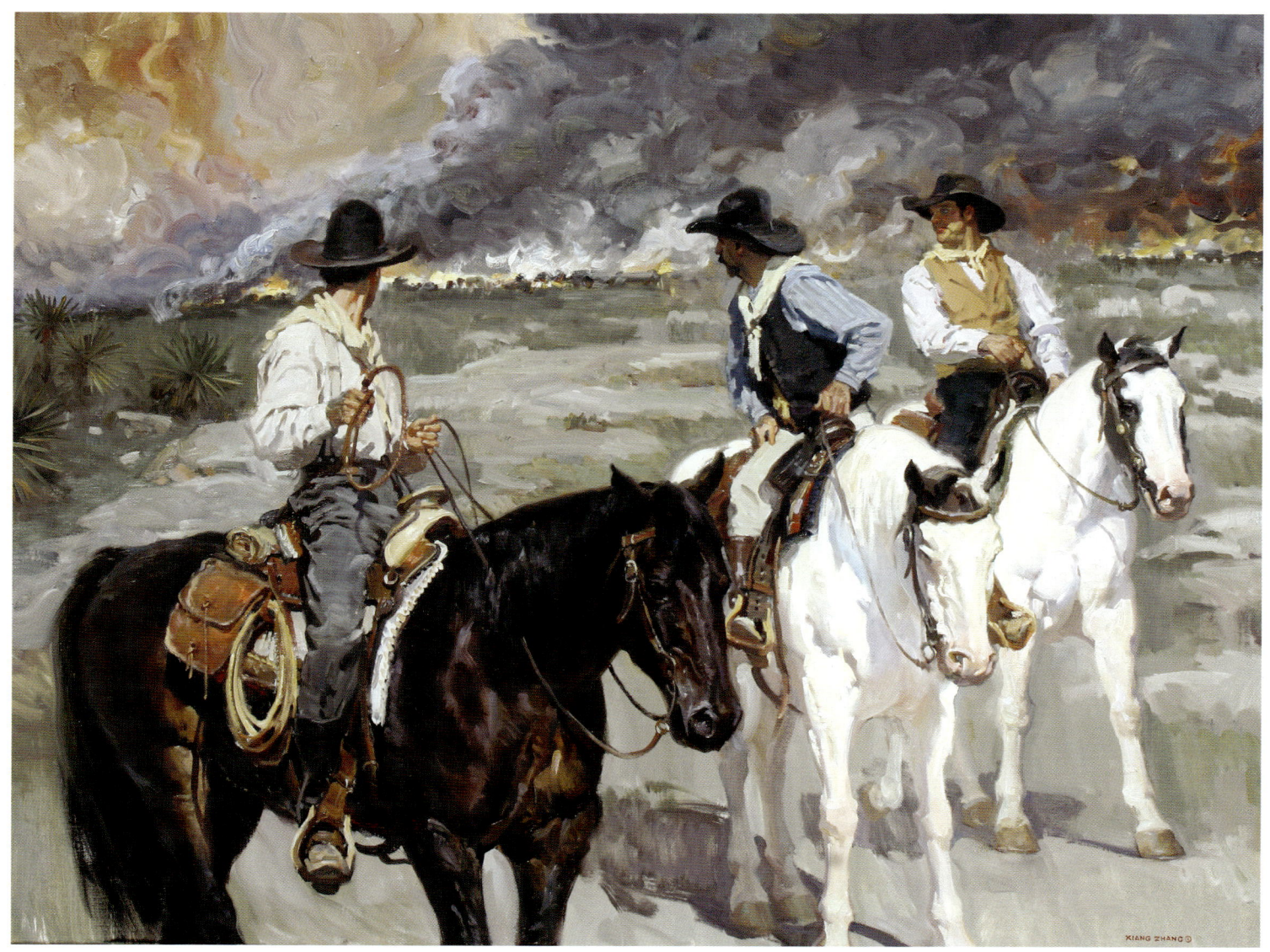

Wildfire

(Oil, 36" × 48", 2011)

"I read a lot of stories about the old-time cowboys who had to face wildfires while moving cattle. I got the inspiration from the big 2011 fire. I painted the mostly white paints into this because I think they are artistically pretty. The undertones of pinks really bring out the features of the horses. The cowboys are in period clothing and the saddles and tack are of the time period of [Charles] Goodnight and the JA Ranch."

Arriving Fort Worth

(Oil, 50" × 82", 2013)

"I created this one based on the stories of the cattle drives that stopped in the Fort Worth Stockyards. Whether they were on their way to Dodge City or Kansas City, they stopped to get supplies and to rest. I wanted to show the cattle driven through the hustle of a busy city with the vendors and the shops. This one has a more traditional cowboy look but with some contemporary elements."

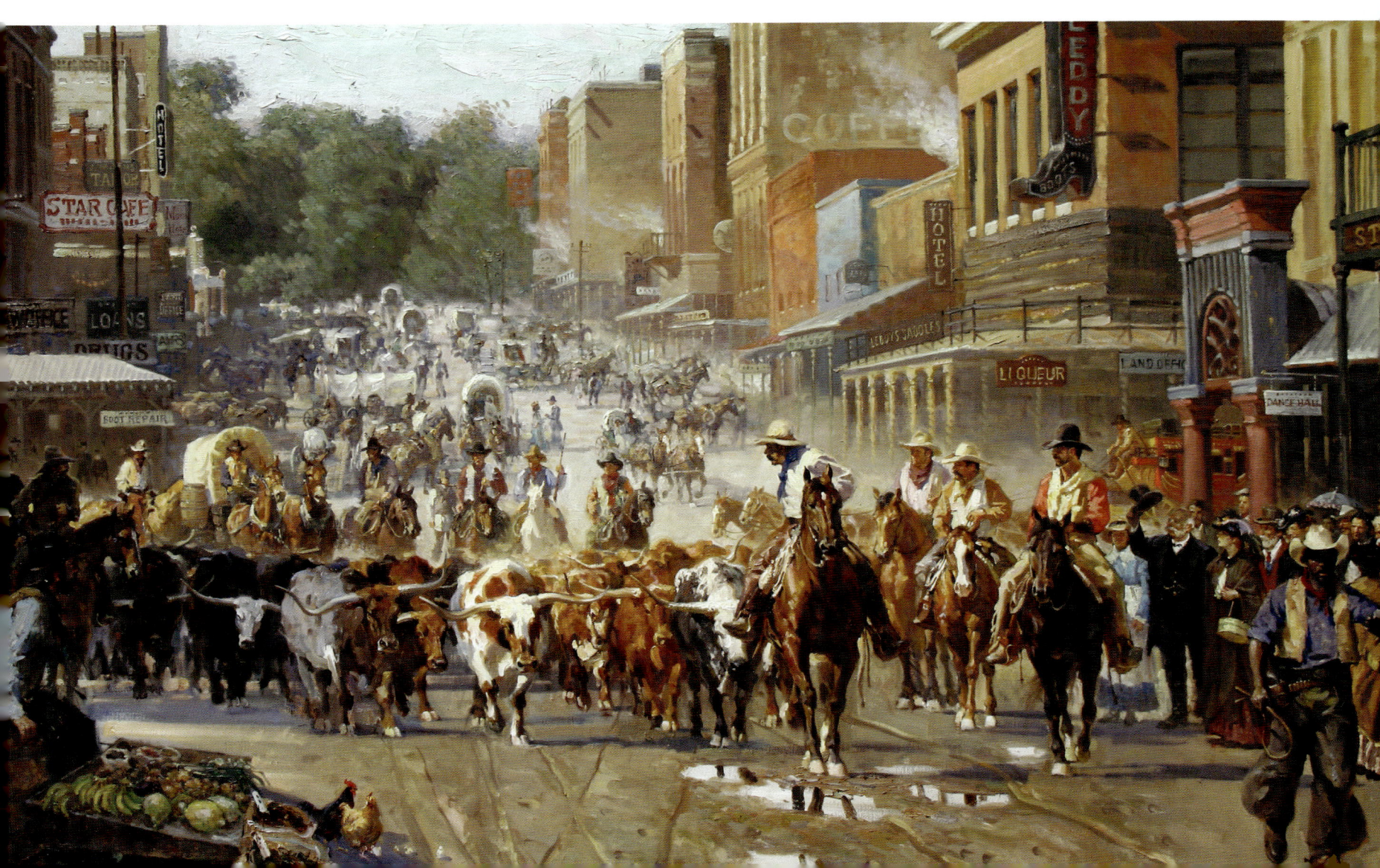

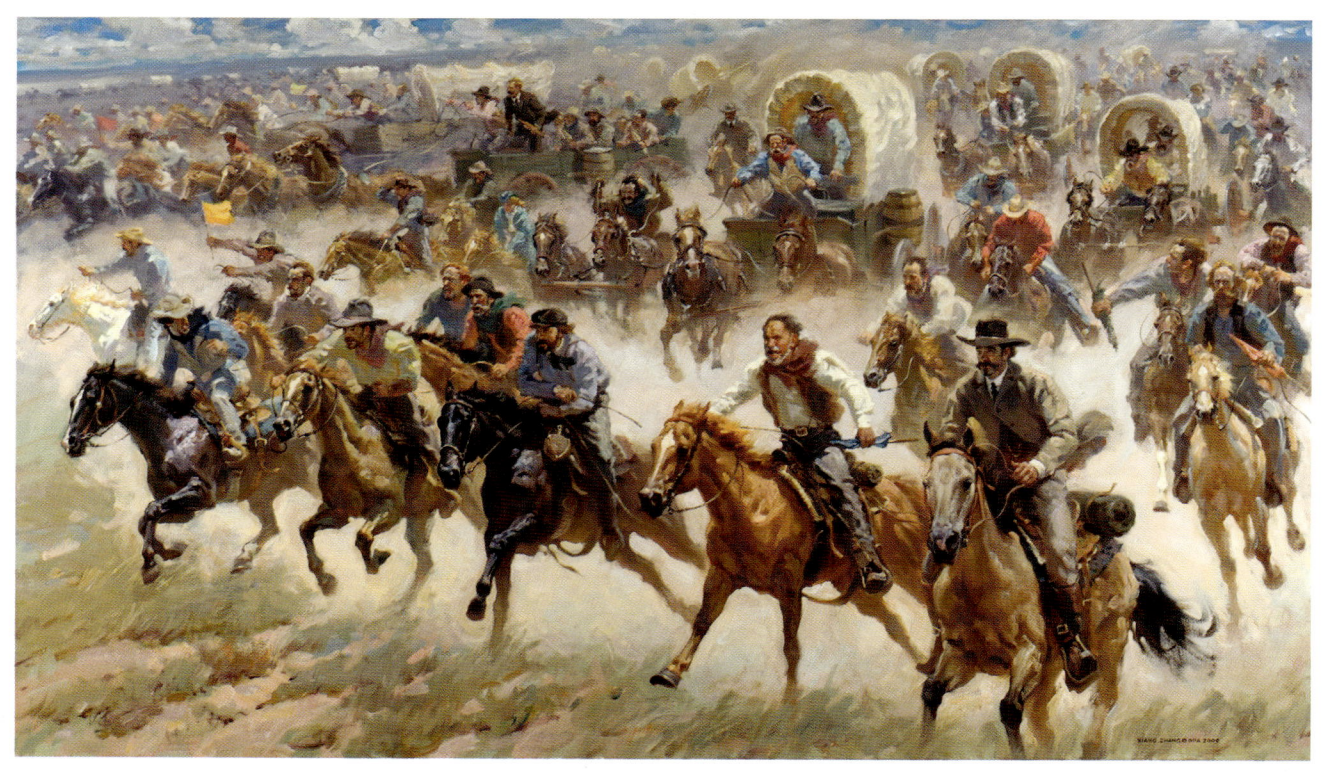

Oklahoma Land Run 1889

(Oil on linen 48″ × 84″, 2009)

"The Oklahoma Land Run is a very important event in Oklahoma history. On April 22, 1889, over 50,000 gathered for the first of several 'runs.' People came from everywhere in the world, mainly from European countries. There at the start line, when the cannon went off, they started to run on horseback, wagon, bicycle, even on foot for their dream land claim! To me, the start line symbolizes equal opportunity of the country. From the riders' facial expressions you can see how anxious they are for the dream to come true!"

Chisholm Trail 1867

(Oil, 40″ × 32″, 2019)

"This is a new type of composition for me, looking at the scene from the top. A bird's-eye view. The cowboys, and even the cattle, are done in a very traditional style, but this is a more contemporary view. No background or foreground, just the contrasting shadows to add some depth. Usually you see the front of the horse, but this view shows the powerful hindquarters. The same with the cattle, you see the backs and horns without looking at the traditional view of cattle."

Mikel Donahue

CHAPTER 5

Mikel Donahue

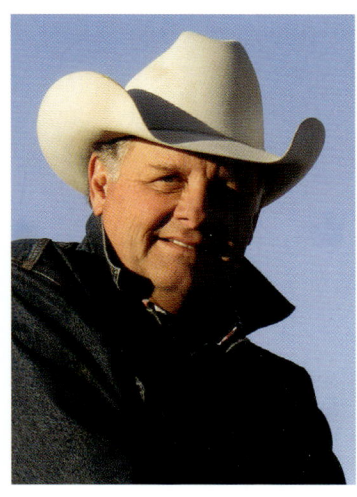

Mikel Donahue's family roots in Oklahoma go back to the Cherokee Land Run in 1893. His grandfather was one month old when Donahue's great-grandparents made the Cherokee Strip Land Run and settled in Wakita to begin a life raising Shorthorn cattle and farming wheat. Donahue's father and mother, Dean and Mary, moved to Tulsa in the early '50s. Mikel spent weekends and summers on his grandparents' ranch, where he learned to ride horses and "play cowboy," learning the cowboy way. He says, "I have photos of me up there either in front of or behind my dad and granddad on horseback. . . . I was six or seven the first time we moved cattle and Granddad put me out on point to go down and hold a corner at an intersection . . . so that was my very first drive."

On his mother's side, Donahue's family was from Central Oklahoma. His maternal grandfather first fostered Donahue's interest in painting Western scenes. She took him when he was a young boy to the Gilcrease Museum in Tulsa and the National Cowboy Hall of Fame in Oklahoma City. In these museums, Donahue was inspired by the images of the great Western artists. He also describes his grandfather as a "hobby painter" who copied Frederic Remington and Charlie Russell paintings from calendars and magazines. Some of these paintings were done on plywood, cardboard, or whatever was available, as the family was not well off. Several of these paintings remain in the family.

Donahue believes that he was privileged to be drawn into the Western culture and painting from exposure from both sides of his family. He remembers that he used to color, draw, and paint images at a young age. The only art classes he took when he was young were the ones that were at school. A family friend, who worked at a small art gallery in downtown Tulsa, took a few of Donahue's works to display and sell. He remembers that one painting in the sale was a portrait of Donahue's father as a young boy on his favorite horse Tony. Three out of the four paintings sold, creating a very exciting experience for a teenager.

While at his grandparents' ranch in Wakita, Donahue would always be sketching the horses and cattle and the daily working scenes of ranching life. Horses were, and still are, a focal point of Donahue's paintings. He studied the anatomy of the horse from technical textbooks loaned to him from a veterinarian who was a member of his church. In his view, it is essential that the study of the muscles and joints be combined with hands-on knowledge of how the horse actually moves: "I'm a big believer that you have to understand your subject to be able to paint it. You know, being able to see it in action in real life, how muscles work and move . . . helps you understand it a lot better."

Donahue studied commercial design at the University of Tulsa and became an art director in the advertising field for more than thirty years. He believes this training has helped him in emphasizing good composition and design in his works. Some of his influences in developing his style of art were Cowboy Artists of America (CAA) James Reynolds, Gordon Snidow, and Bill Owen and illustrators Norman Rockwell and Andrew Wyeth.

Donahue's process in creating his paintings is variable. He will often take photographs of scenes of ranching; however, he captures the scene with sketches as well.

I also do a lot of sketches and take a lot of field notes on color, shadow, and light. When I get back to the studio, I'll usually have some ideas in my head of things that I've seen that caught my interest or I really would like to look at and I'll go back and look at my sketches and photographs.

He says there were times when nothing gelled for several months, but an idea may be pulled together by an experience or catching inspiration from parts of several photographs.

It's trying to capture the essence of a moment. We have a mare that we've raised . . . and I'll let her out in our yard in the evening, watching how the light and shadows play across her and the trees and the grass. There's just a real sense of calm, a peace and serenity about the moment. How do you capture that?

Donahue says he was always drawn to attention to detail. He believes that detail brings a person into the painting and lends a sense of reality. He also believes that honesty is important in his paintings. He says, "Something I try to do is to be honest about the cowboys and the horses and be realistic about it and not try to put a facade on something. I don't use models—everybody's real."

Within his career, Donahue also knows what makes a good ranch horse and portrays each one as an individual in his detailed works: "I would say a good horse to me would be like a good person—to work with somebody that you can count on day to day. They're very steady, quiet-headed, with an innate sense of . . . cow. They know what they're there for."

Donahue has earned many awards in his art career for both drawing and painting. He was invited to join the Cowboy Artists of America in 2016. To date, his awards at the Cowboy Artists of America show include the Ray Swanson Memorial Award, the Gold Medal for Mixed Media, the Silver Medal for Water Solubles (2022), the Anne Marion Best of Show, and the R. Watson Boots True West Award as well as thirteen Gold and Silver Medals for painting and drawing.

Donahue and his wife Christie live in Broken Arrow, Oklahoma. They have been involved in Quarter Horse racing for many years and have bred and raced their own horses.

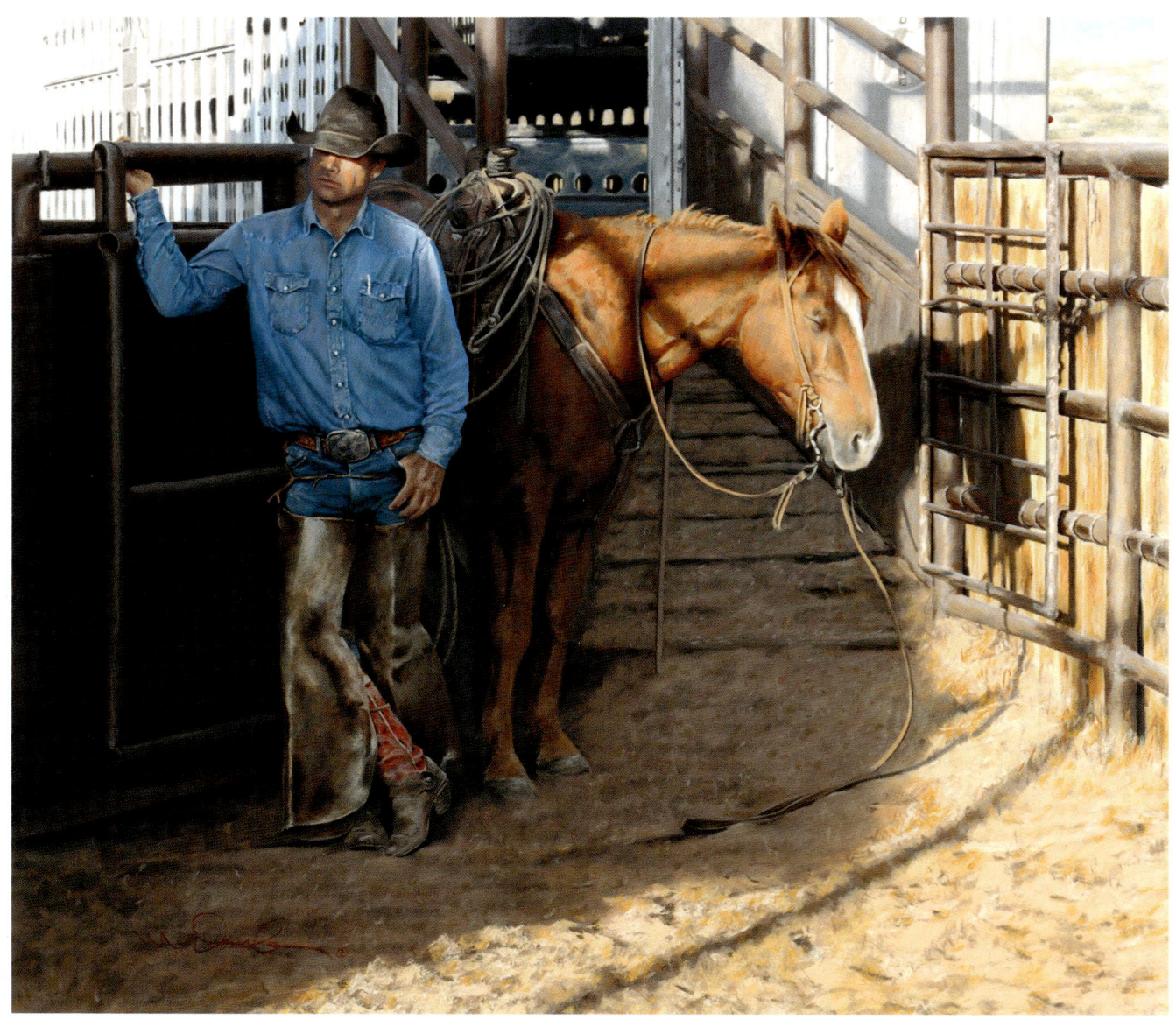

Shipping Day

(Mixed media, 19″ × 22″, 2013)

"Early morning finds the trailer in place
to begin loading yearling steers."

Still Waters

(Mixed media, 20″ × 30″, 2011)

"Taking a break for a drink at a cool spring while headed back to headquarters."

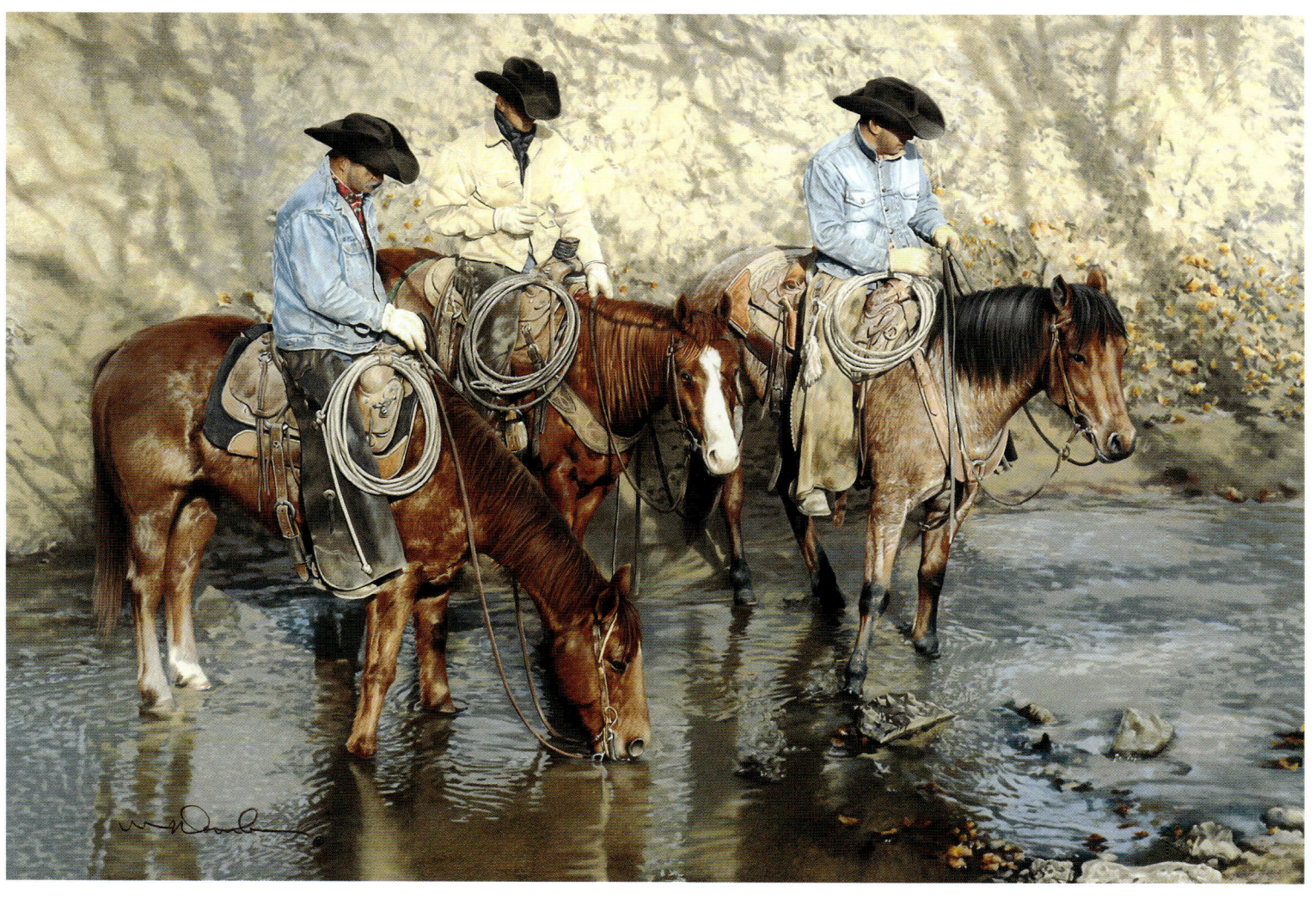

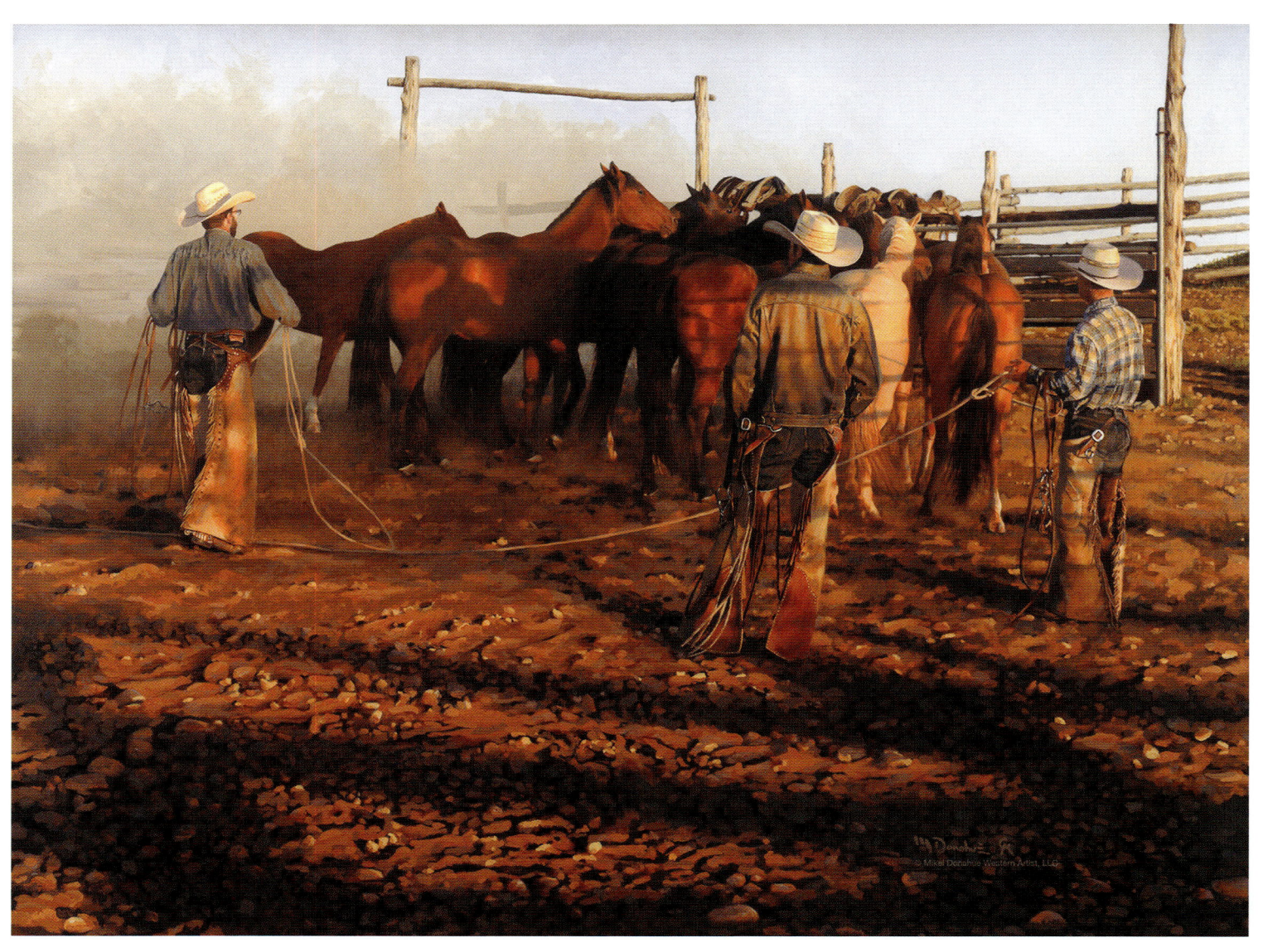

The Catch Hand

(Acrylic, 20″ × 30″, 2022)

"The early morning sun finds the catch hand getting ready to drop
the houlihan on a mount for the day's work ahead."

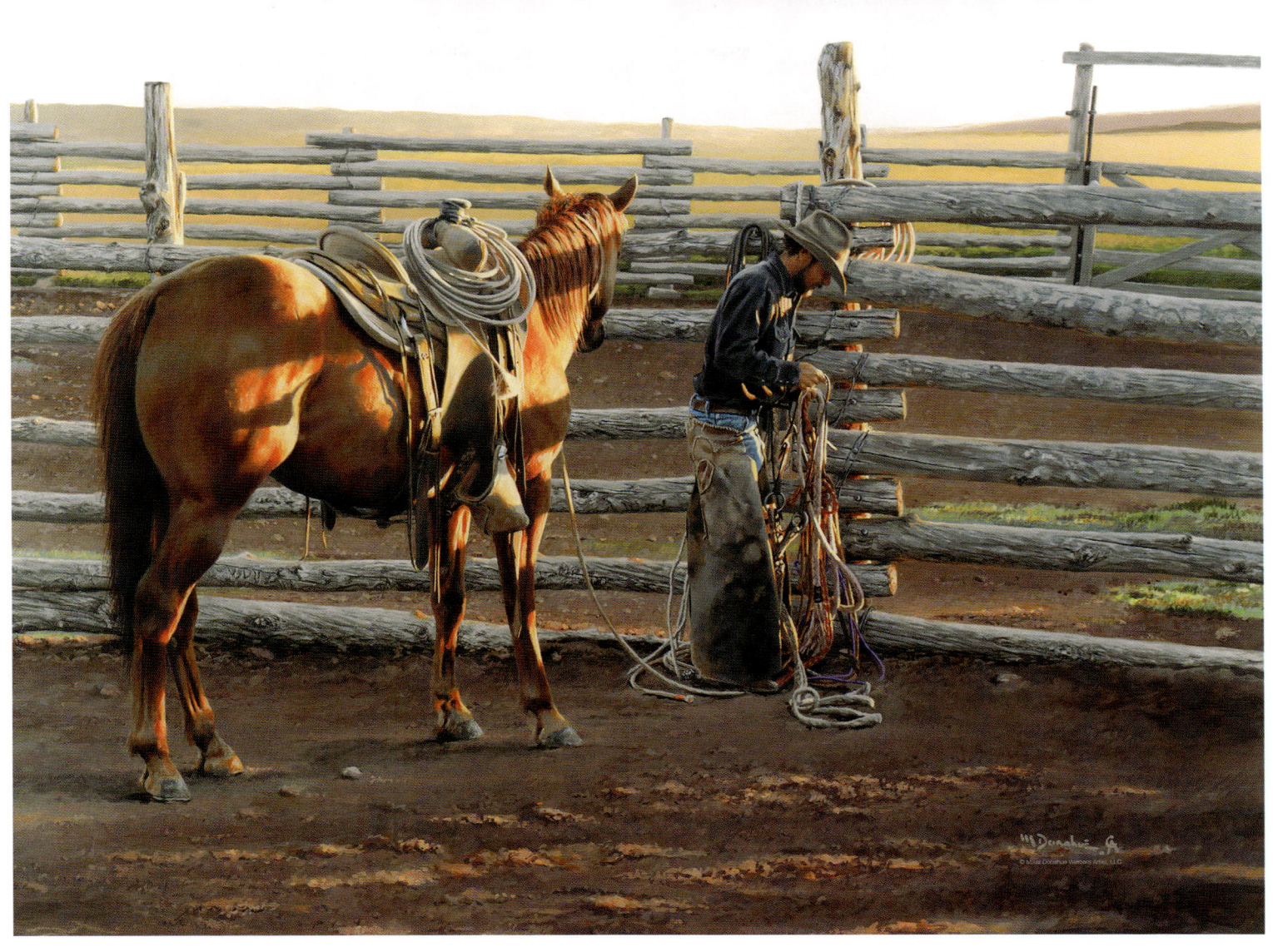

Burning Daylight

(Mixed media, 20″ × 26″, 2021)

"Getting a late start seems to put an urgency to the day's work ahead."

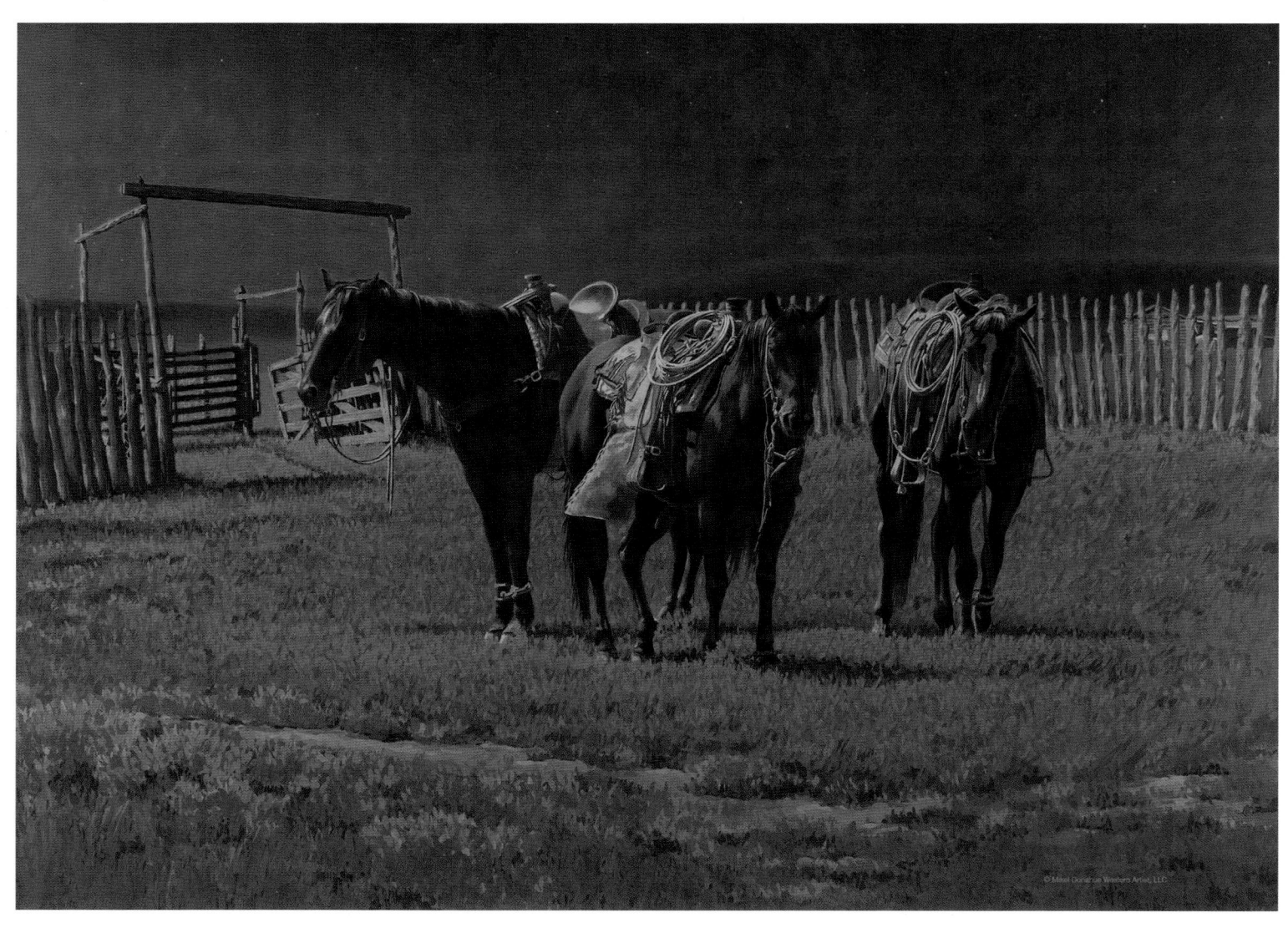

Poker Night

(Water solubles, 22″ × 32″, 2021)

"Cowboys entertain themselves with a game of poker
while the horses rest in the soft moonlight after a long
day of ranch work.""

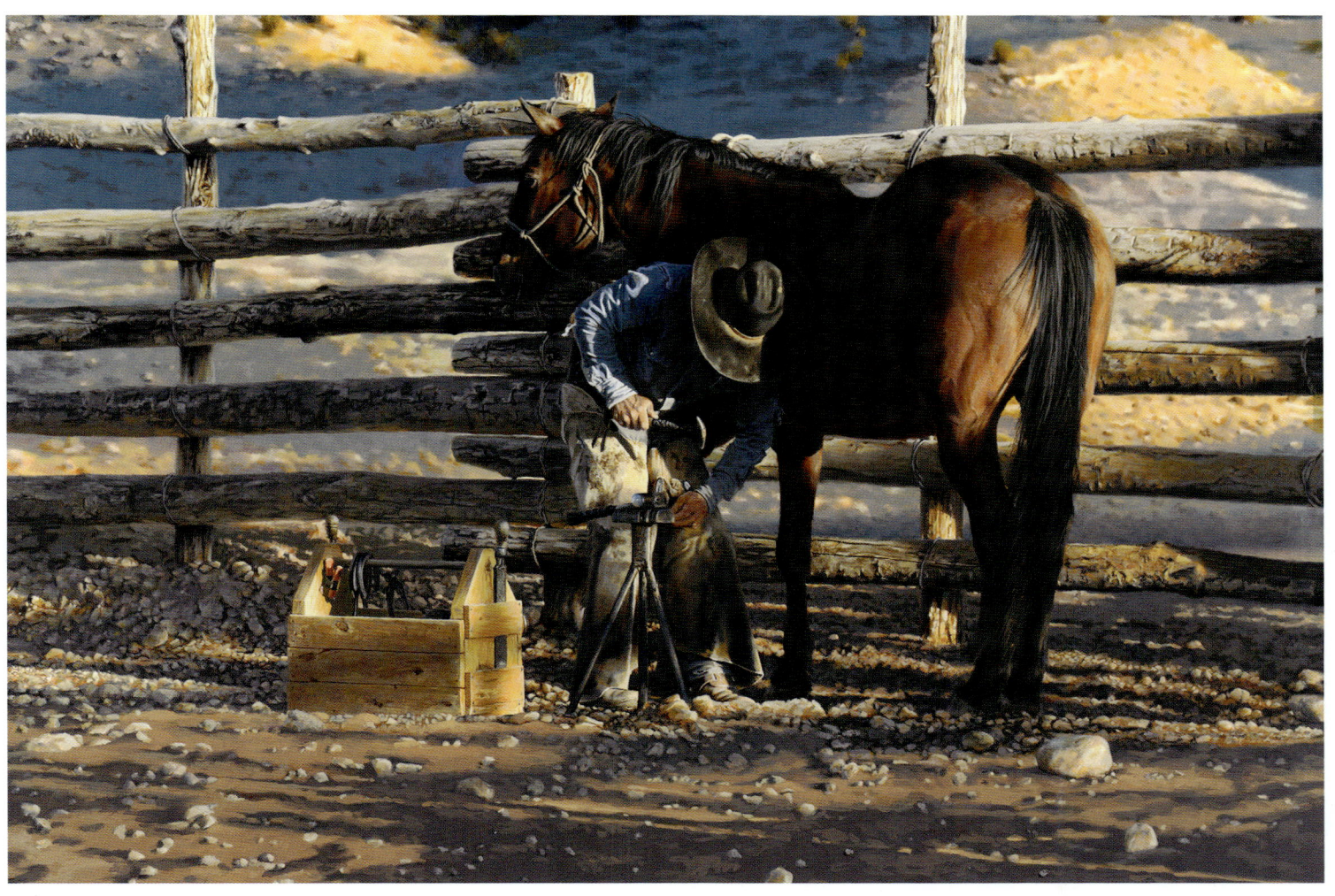

For the Want of a Nail

(Mixed media, 22" × 30", 2022)

"For want of a nail, the shoe was lost.
For want of a shoe, the horse was lost.
For want of a horse, the rider was lost.
For want of a rider, the battle was lost.
For want of a battle, the kingdom was lost.
All for the want of a nail."
—Proverb

Shawn Cameron

CHAPTER 6

Shawn Cameron

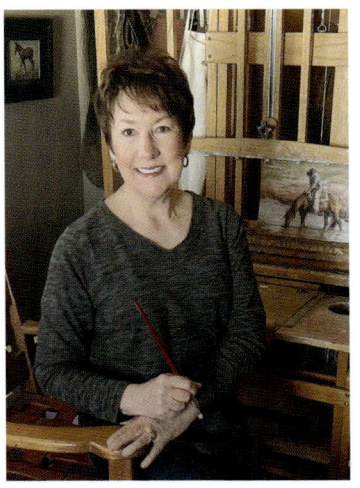

"A lot of people have said I should write a book about my family. Both my parents were pioneer Arizona families and came into the state 1860s and 1870s—one in the northern half and the other in the southern half."

Western artist Shawn Cameron's father's family, the Wingfields, traveled the Oregon Trail in a covered wagon, settling in Oregon as ranchers for several years. Her great-great-grandfather Edward could not endure the cold winters, so the families travelled south with 200 head of cattle and settled in the Verde Valley region of Northern Arizona, which provided both summer and winter ranges for the cattle and horses. Eventually, a family member bought the Sutler store, naming it the Wingfield store, which they ran for more than seventy years. This store provided goods and food that the settlers and ranchers in the valley needed. The business even included a bank and a post office.

Cameron's mother's family came from Texas and settled near Globe, Arizona. Her grandmother, Mary, was born in Geronimo, Arizona, and married John Osborne, the foreman of the Chiricahua Cattle Company, which was then the largest ranch in Arizona. They ran over 10,000 head of cattle and a large remuda. John went on to become one of the most prominent cattlemen in Arizona.

Cameron's grandmother, grandfather, and mother were very involved in raising horses for racing, ranching, and rodeo. At three years of age, Cameron was given a young horse from the rare Gila band of mustangs that an employee of her father's broke and trained for her. The horse became her best friend and knew many tricks including lying down, dancing, and drinking strawberry pop from a bottle. Cameron went to school in Arlington, Arizona, close to the feedyard her grandfather built. While she was growing up, she was able to spend summers riding and working at different ranches the family owned, including the Valle Ranch south of the Grand Canyon and their ranch north of Phoenix called the Horseshoe Ranch.

Horses were the most important thing in the world to young Cameron, so it was natural that she started to draw them at a very young age. She credits her fifth-grade art teacher for motivating her when she won her first art award in a contest. Cameron's mother was artistic and wanted to pass on that creativity to her children. She purchased oil painting kits for Cameron and her brother, showing them how to create an image. Cameron was a shy girl, and on the ranches in the summer, her favorite pastimes were riding horses and painting. Still not comfortable around people, she was not motivated to pursue a formal career in art because of her apprehension about taking her art to show and talking to people.

Cameron was nineteen years old when she married her husband Dean, and the couple moved to the Horseshoe Ranch, becoming an integral part of the various family ranches. She drove many miles attending night classes to obtain a teaching certificate, but Dean was a source of encouragement for his wife to pursue a career in art. He staged a practice art show on the ranch to make her more comfortable in talking about her art.

Eventually, Cameron decided to focus on art and show her artwork because deep down, she felt that she was given a talent from God and believed that He would help her learn. Although she did not have any formal art education, she learned from people who came into her life and helped to open doors for her. Artists who influenced and encouraged her included Robert "Shoofly" Shufelt, Joe Beeler, and Bill Owen. She credits Bill Owen for her

understanding of the color wheel and how to mix these colors in various lighting. Cameron's love of horses has remained key to her artistic expression, and the working ranch horse and the culture of ranching have always been the focus of her art: "I never get tired of looking at the horses. I think they're one of the most magnificent [animals]. Even the ugly ones are magnificent . . . with the Roman noses and all the scars. They're the workhorses with a story to tell."

Cameron has worked in several media in depicting ranch cowboys and their horses at work, including graphite pencil, bronze, and watercolor, although her current work is mainly in oil. In her oil paintings, Cameron prefers to concentrate on the details of certain areas and to leave others to a quick brushstroke that comes off like Impressionism. The result is a contrasting style that pulls the viewer in to the depth of the painting. She feels that it is important to engage and draw a person into the painting. She never wants a viewer to just look at a flat image. She says, "I want people to feel that dust and to know what it was like when the sun came up over the top of all these animals. I've got to remember that that's what I want them to feel."

Cameron has earned many accolades and awards in the art world including the Lifetime Honorary Membership in the Mountain Oyster Club (2013) and the Will Rogers Award for Artist of the Year (Academy of Western Artists, 2019). Her paintings have won numerous awards in prestigious shows. Cameron was named Co-Featured Artist with fellow artist Martin Grelle at the C. M. Russell Auction and Sale. She has also served as an executive board member of the Phippen Museum of Western Art in Prescott, Arizona.

Today, Shawn and Dean live on some acreage in Pine, Arizona, where she has built an art studio and where they keep horses for Dean to help their Arizona son and daughter who also are involved in ranching. A daughter and her family in Texas are also very involved with agriculture and horses. Cameron has a rich source of material gleaned from taking pictures and working on the family ranches. Her artwork captures the working Western ranches, a culture she loves to share.

My motivation is glorifying God while enjoying the culture that He's given me and sharing it with others. . . . I think that's beautiful. I'm motivated by the life I've lived, the horses and the peoples that are riding them. I have such admiration for people around me— their integrity and their morals—and I thought I would be remiss if I didn't share what I see.

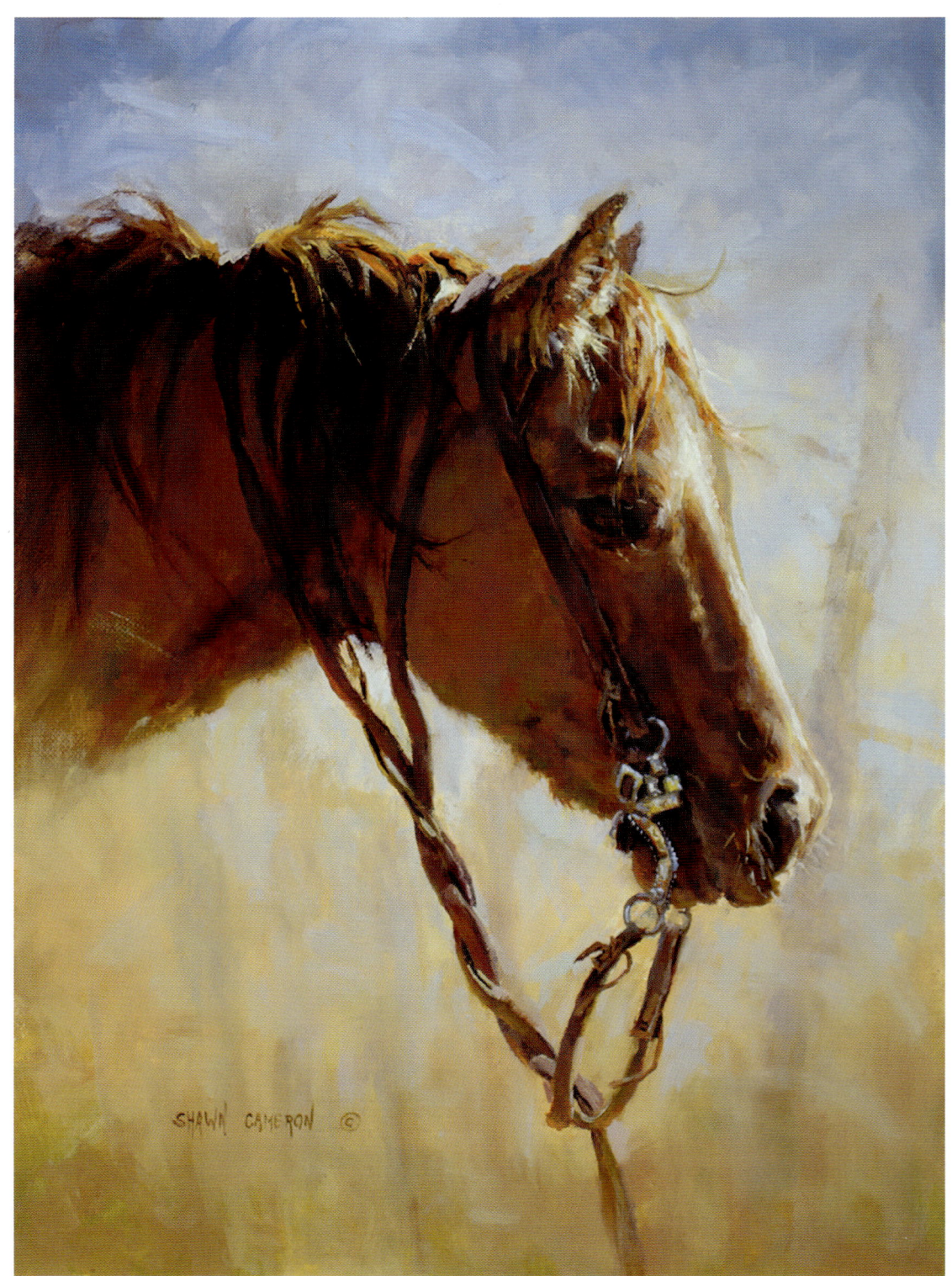

Forty Winks

(Oil, 16″ × 12″, 2013)

"This is another scene from the Valle Ranch when the horses were relaxing after gathering. I love the light on the bit in his mouth. I saw action even though the horse was just standing there because of the twist of the reins and the wind in his mane. It's cool. He's hobbled of course and that's what they did with the reins."

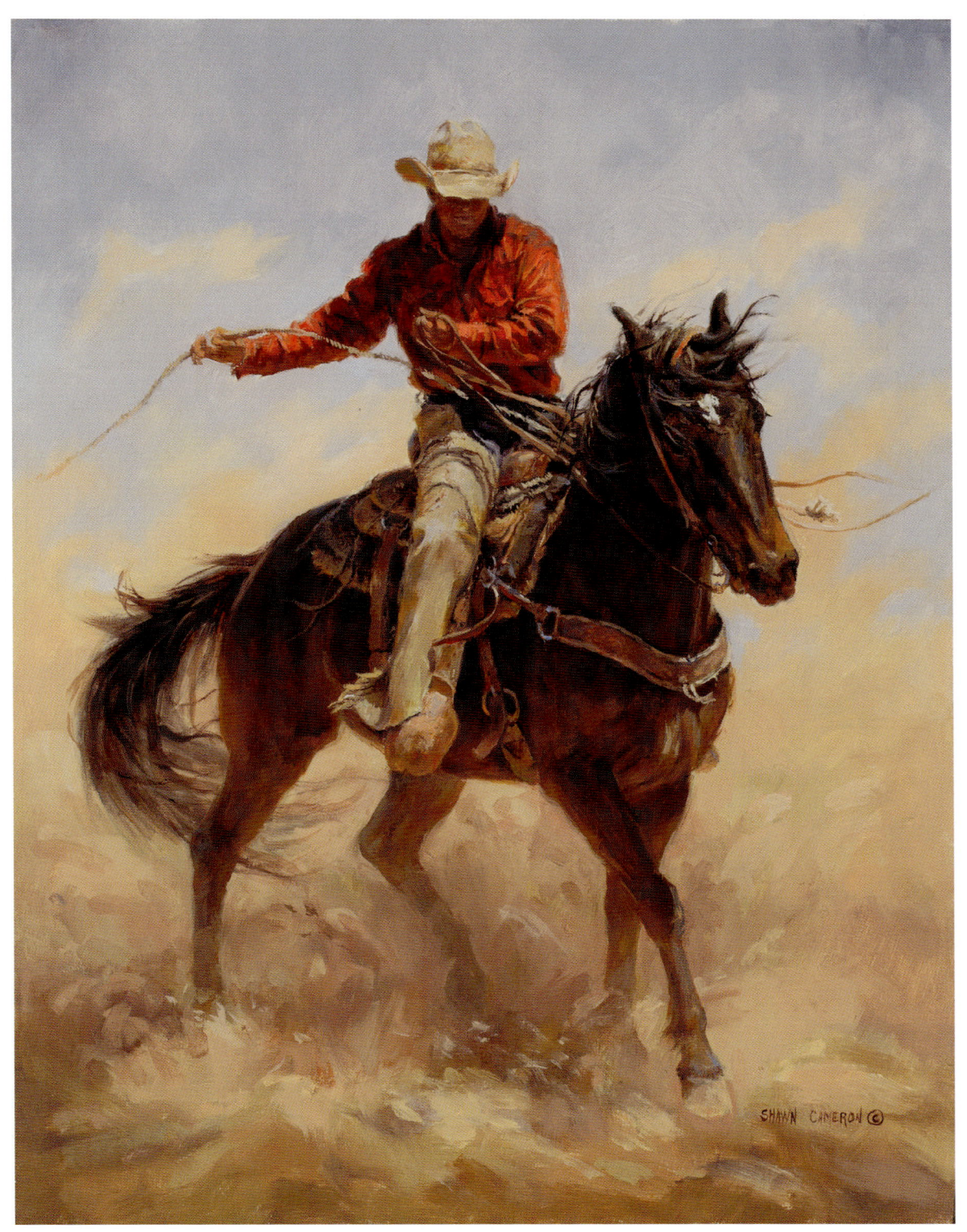

Contrary

(Oil, 14″ × 11″, 2015)

"Most of my scenes are from the ranching theatre. The cowboy's name was Clancy Goswick. There is a calf at the end of the rope and . . . for some reason this horse started acting up. My goal was to capture the action I saw happening there. There are certain things like the horse's face that I get into the detail . . . but for the background and the dust, I tend to make looser strokes and it gets a lot more impressionistic."

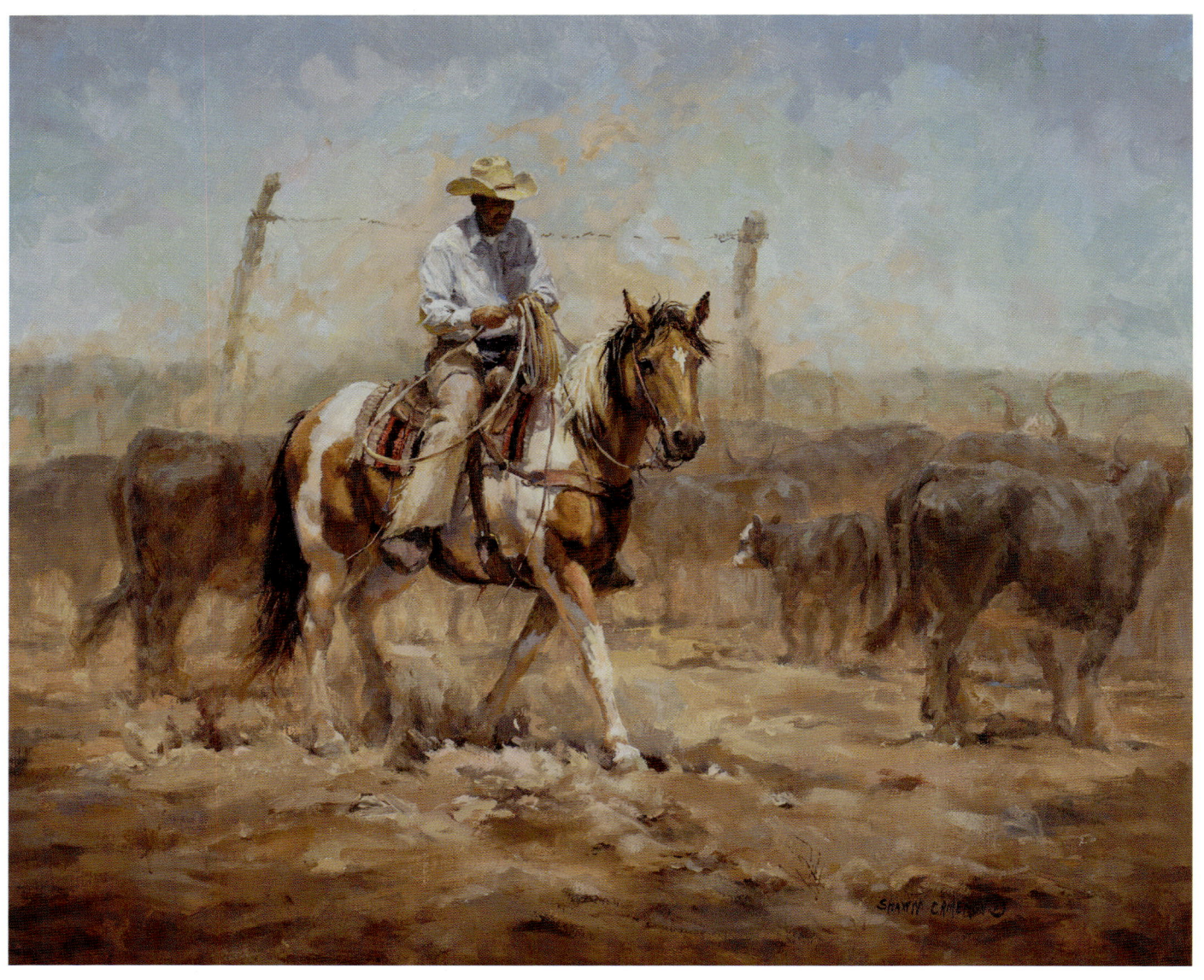

Corral Dust

(Oil, 16″ × 20″, 2020)

"Pinto used to be in the bronc string in the rodeo, but I don't think he bucked hard enough. This is Dean riding at the Valle Ranch. I loved painting Pinto—when he is dragging calves to the fire, he was just like a freight train. He didn't care how big the calf was. This was an experiment in directing the viewer's eye with color . . . for the horse to stand out in all that dust. That's kind of the way it is."

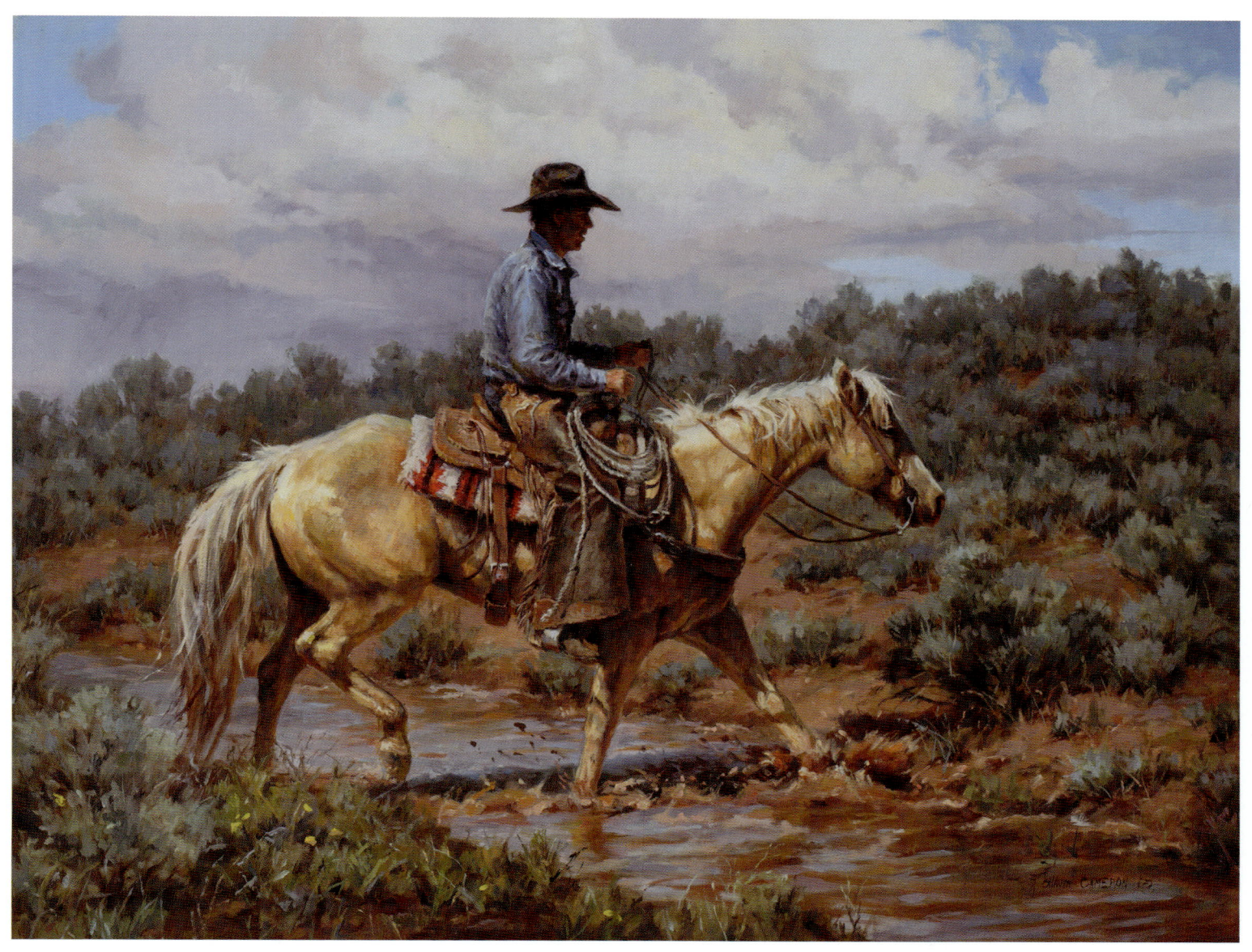

Clearing Skies and Muddy Draws

(Oil, 18" × 24", 2015)

"We were helping our son gather cattle after monsoon rains had come . . . mud was everywhere . . . on the horse and in the draws. I loved capturing our son, Brooks, in the middle of this situation."

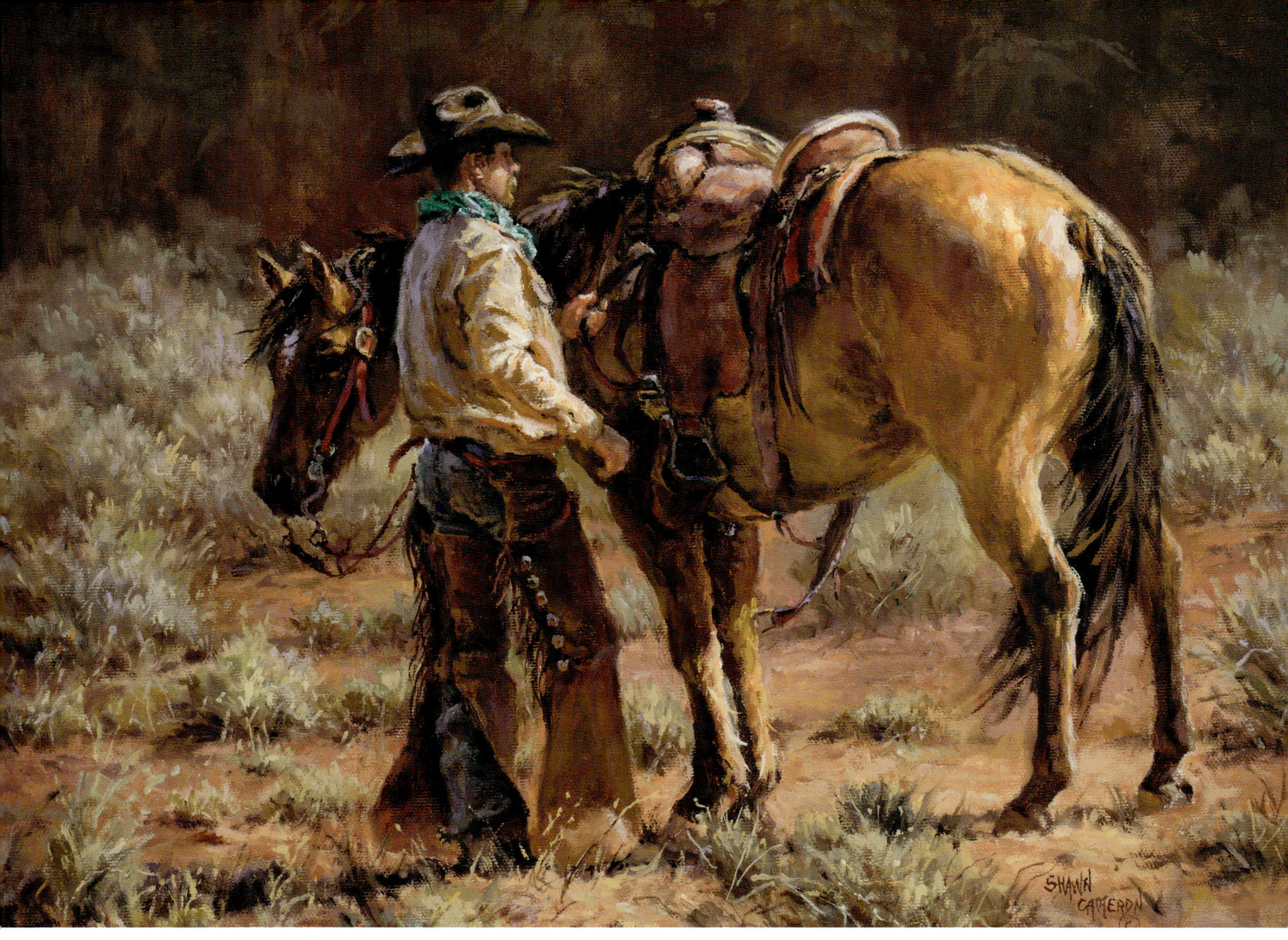

Mid-Morning Adjustment

(Oil, 12″ × 16″, 2022)

"We were helping our daughter Kacie and her husband Dan with their cattle when I saw Dan in the mid-morning light adjusting his cinch. I couldn't resist this scene."

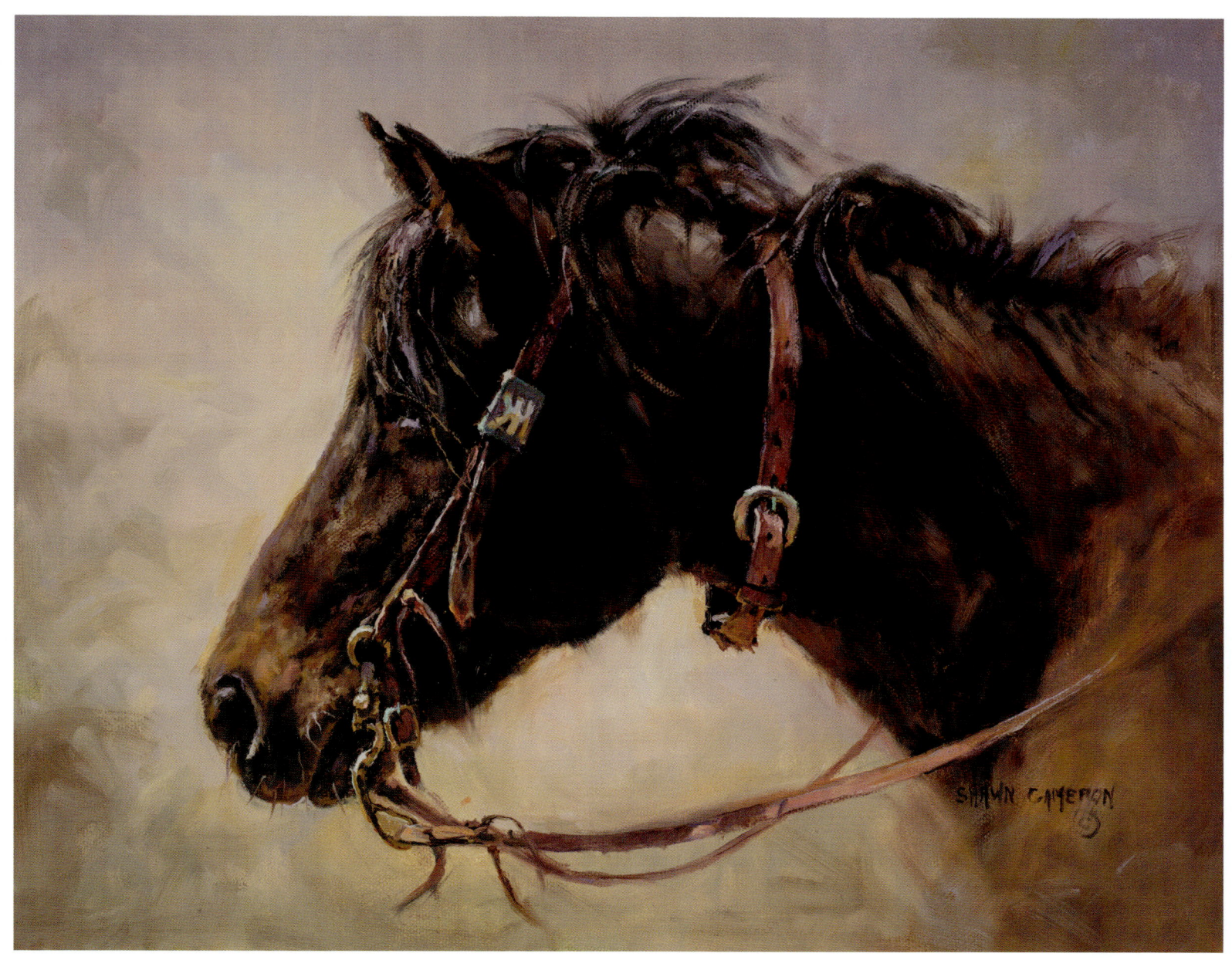

His Day Job

(Oil, 11″ × 14″, 2022)

"This was a horse ridden by a cowboy day-working for our son. I loved the seasoned character I saw in this face."

Tom Browning

CHAPTER 7

Tom Browning

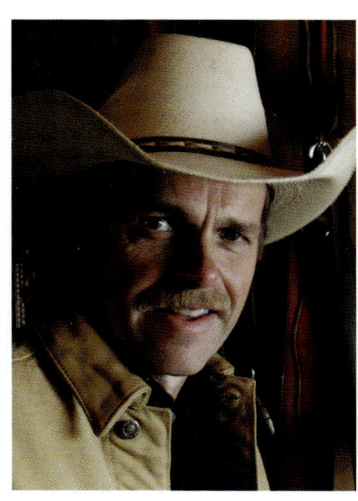

om Browning was born to Charley and Cleo Browning and raised in Ontario, Oregon. This area is a farming and ranching community in the eastern part of the state, which lies along the Snake River and borders Idaho. From a small child, he always had a strong interest in both horses and art. When Browning was in the fourth grade, he and his best friend shared these interests, and they would sketch and draw together. Although his family did not have horses, Browning had plenty of opportunity to ride horses at his friends' ranches and always jumped at the chance to do so.

He took as many art classes as he could in school and chose art over sports in high school. He was immersed in art, painting mainly horses and wildlife in nature. It was during this period that he began moving from drawing to painting: "I never really considered anything else as a future career or anything. I always knew that I wanted to be an artist at some point. I had no idea how that was ever going to transpire."

Browning attended the University of Oregon and majored in art, where he took as many classes focusing on painting as he could. A visit during his college years to Montana introduced Browning to the paintings of Charlie Russell, which he felt changed his life and gave him a sense of direction.

I took a trip to Montana and was introduced to Charlie Russell's work. . . . I had never been exposed to his work, and after seeing that, it was one of those "fire in the belly" moments [that] just kind of took over everything that I thought about. I realized that what I wanted to create was Western art. And that was at the ripe old age of 21.

Browning left the university early in the spring term of his senior year to pursue an art career. He began by working closely with a taxidermist with the goal of learning as much about animal anatomy as he could. Later he took a horse anatomy class, which went into detail on equine structure, muscles, tendons, and bones of the horse. This class had a great impact on his painting. A gallery in Portland soon began to take Browning's drawings to sell. He also began to paint more, based on the influence of Charlie Russell. He said, "I knew that's the direction I wanted to go."

Horses have always been the focus of Browning's work. He describes the horse as being so important to the development of the West that representing the horse in his works is "just part of the narrative for me." He seldom paints cowboys or Native Americans when they are not riding a horse. He enjoys adding Paint horses to his images because they stand out among the other horses. He feels that the most difficult thing in painting horses is to capture their gestures. He says, "In two minutes of watching a horse, you will see 1,000 gestures, and some of them will stand out and really grab me—I love it when that happens."

Browning's style in painting tends to be loose, without every detail depicted in the works. He feels that in depicting the horse, less is better, and he trained himself early on to try to see how much information he could convey in his works with very little paint on the paper. He says, "As long as everything is accurate, everything's in the right place and it's got nice light on it, it just seems right. It's amazing what you can come up with, with very little detail." Browning describe this process as simplicity of line and mass.

Backlighting is prominent in many of Browning's paintings, and he enjoys painting with this creative feature. In describing backlighting, Browning says that it is crucial to get the drawing accurate because "the light, the backlighting is essentially creating an outline of everything it touches." His oil paintings often show light reflecting off dust, creating beautiful effects.

Early in his career, Browning did a great deal of painting from life. He feels it helps to determine what is most essential quickly. In looking at photographs, he can edit them quickly and does not try to re-create the photo. According to Browning, photographs can be distorting, causing foreshortening and awkward movement in the horses. He feels it is important not to reproduce the image exactly and that the artist must correct problems in the photographs. Prior to painting, he works out the details by sketching the idea of the painting on paper and then transfers this onto the canvas. This presents him with a guide to his painting; however, using his looser style, he does not adhere to the lines but blends everything together.

In addition to Charlie Russell, Browning has been artistically influenced in his works by British artists Alfred Munnings and Lucy Kemp-Welch. He fell in love with their work and was inspired by their knowledge of anatomy and how light would fall across the muscles of the animals in their images. He took a break from Western art for a period and followed both American Impressionists and American illustrators; however, he has always returned to Western art. Browning studied under and became friends with noted Western artist James Reynolds, who was influential in the development of Browning's style.

Throughout Browning's career, he has been invited to prestigious shows across America. He is a member of the Northwest Rendezvous Group, earning the Award of Excellence in 1994 and four Jurors awards in their shows. He is also a member of the Portrait Society of America. Browning was invited to become a member of the Cowboy Artists of America in 2009. He has won numerous awards for his art including the prestigious Prix de West Award at the National Cowboy & Western Heritage Museum in 2009 for his painting *Dawn of a New Day* and the

Silver Medal for Oil Painting in 2010 at the Cowboy Artists of America Annual Exhibition at the Phoenix Art Museum. He has also written an acclaimed instructional book titled *Timeless Techniques for Better Oil Paintings*.

Browning and his wife Joyce currently divide their time between Scottsdale, Arizona, and Bend, Oregon, where their son Michael and his family also reside.

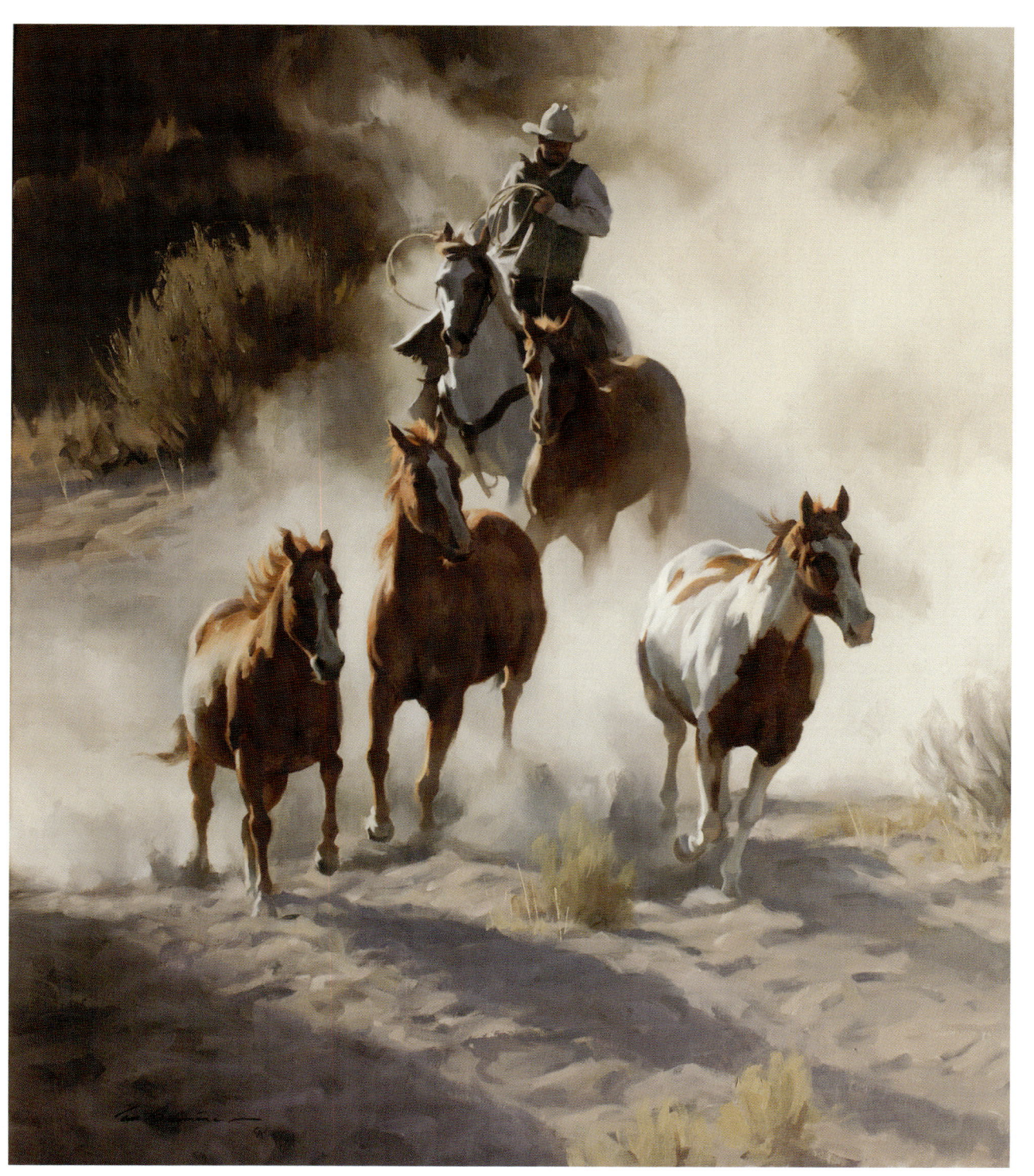

Downhill Run

(Oil, 34" × 30", 2018)

"One of my favorite Western subjects to paint involves action and a combination of interesting light and dust. It was fun placing each horse to come up with the best design, then adding the dust to help simplify the overall painting and let the rider and horses really stand out."

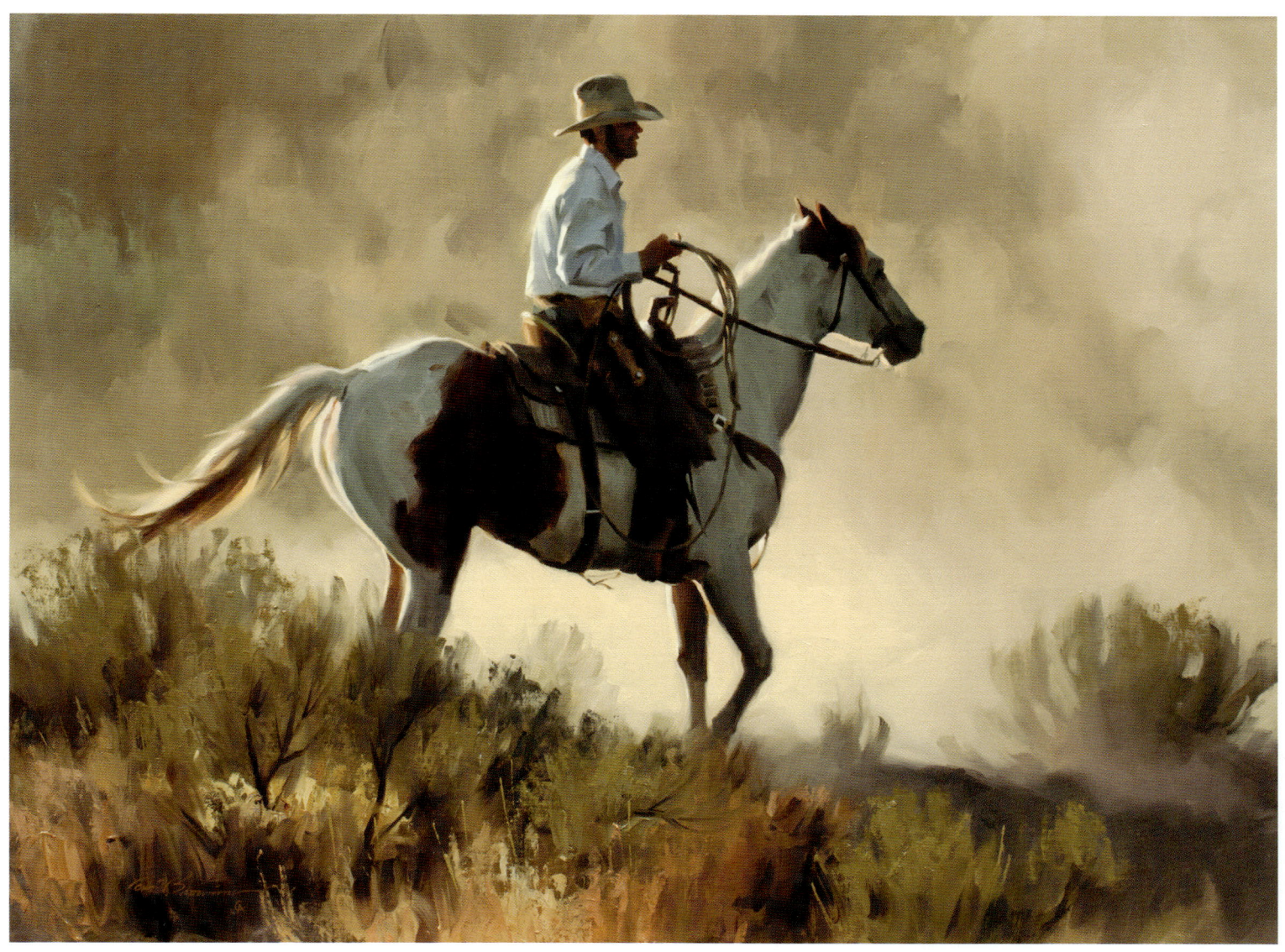

Stirrin' It Up

(Oil, 22" × 30", 2015)

"This painting turned out to be one of my favorites. Once again, backlighting provided all that I needed to express this moment filled with light and dust. We had a sunny evening, and in this particular area the dirt had been ground to a fine powder. As this wrangler drove the horses through, a veil of dust made an amazing backdrop for the scene."

When the Hills Are Kissed by the Sun

(Oil, 14″ × 24″, 2019)

"I never like to let a good sunset go to waste. If I can't paint it I just enjoy it. But since I love painting them, I'm always looking for a good story to depict this glorious time of day. Here a Blackfoot scout reflects on that magical moment when the sun leaves the sky and disappears behind a distant hill."

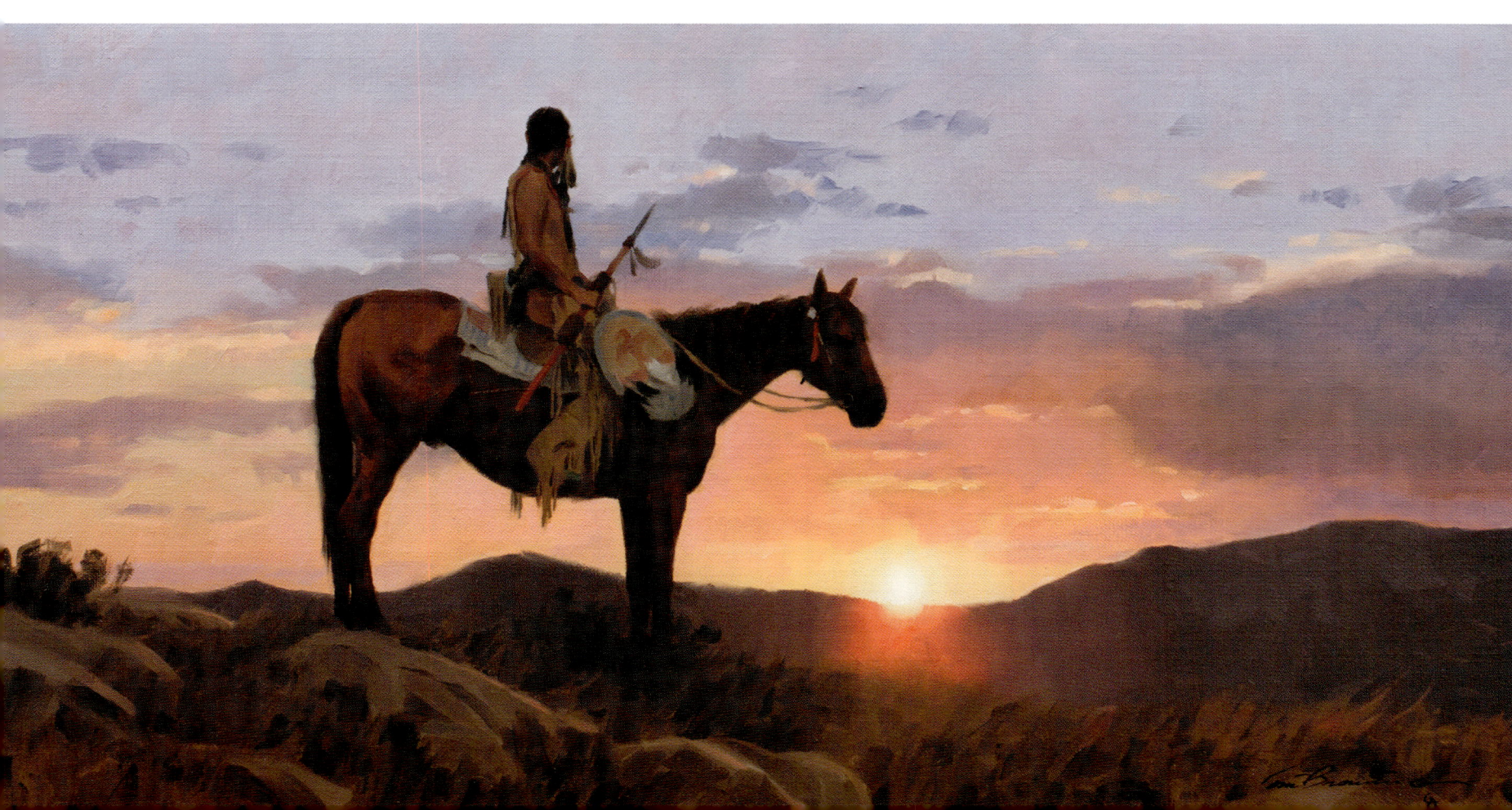

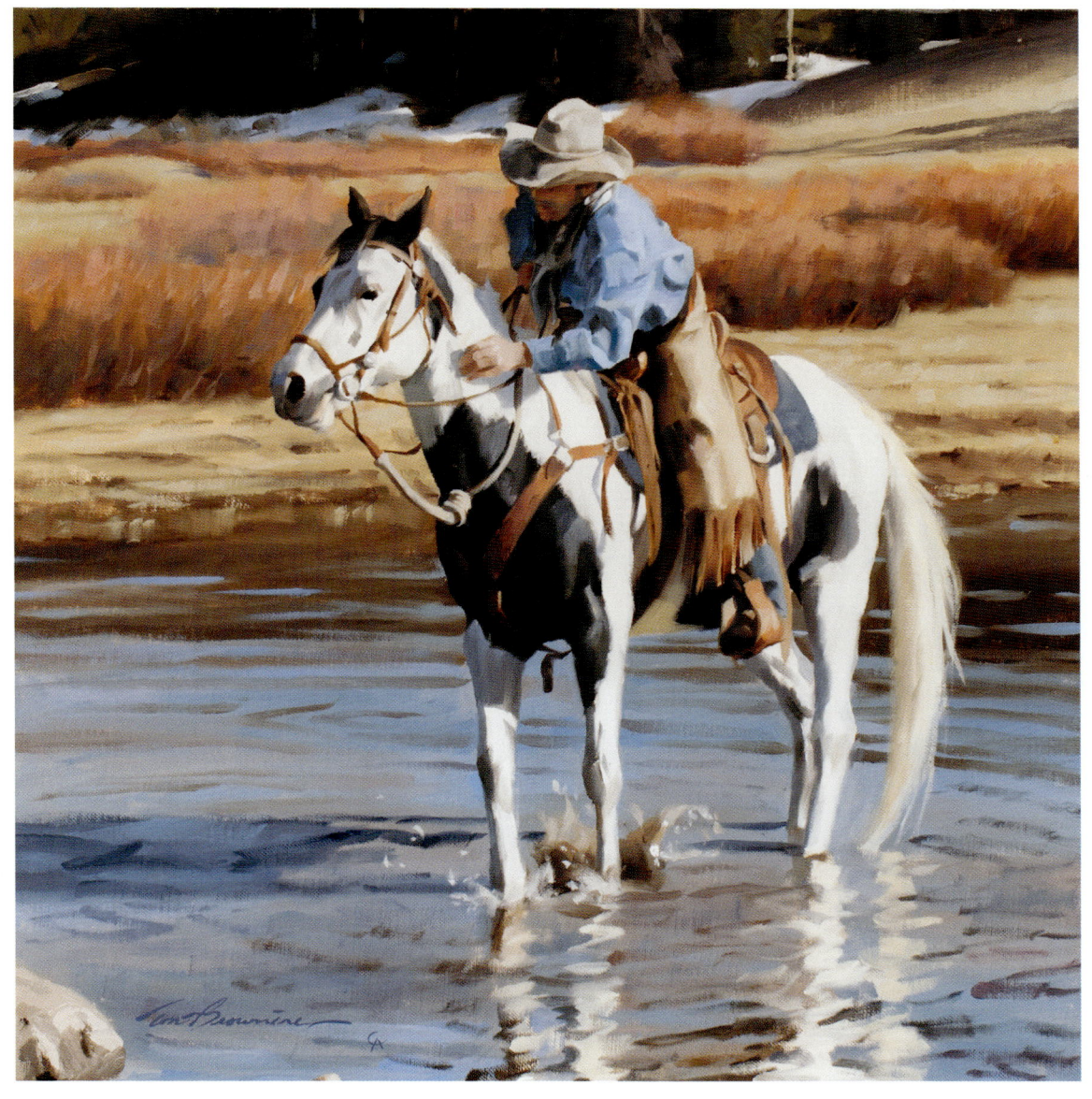

A Calming Hand

(Oil, 18″ × 18″, 2021)

"When this wrangler's horse became uneasy about crossing a flooded pasture, the rider stopped and began talking gently to his mount and stroking his neck. This had a calming effect that surprisingly worked. Within a minute or two, we continued on to many more crossings."

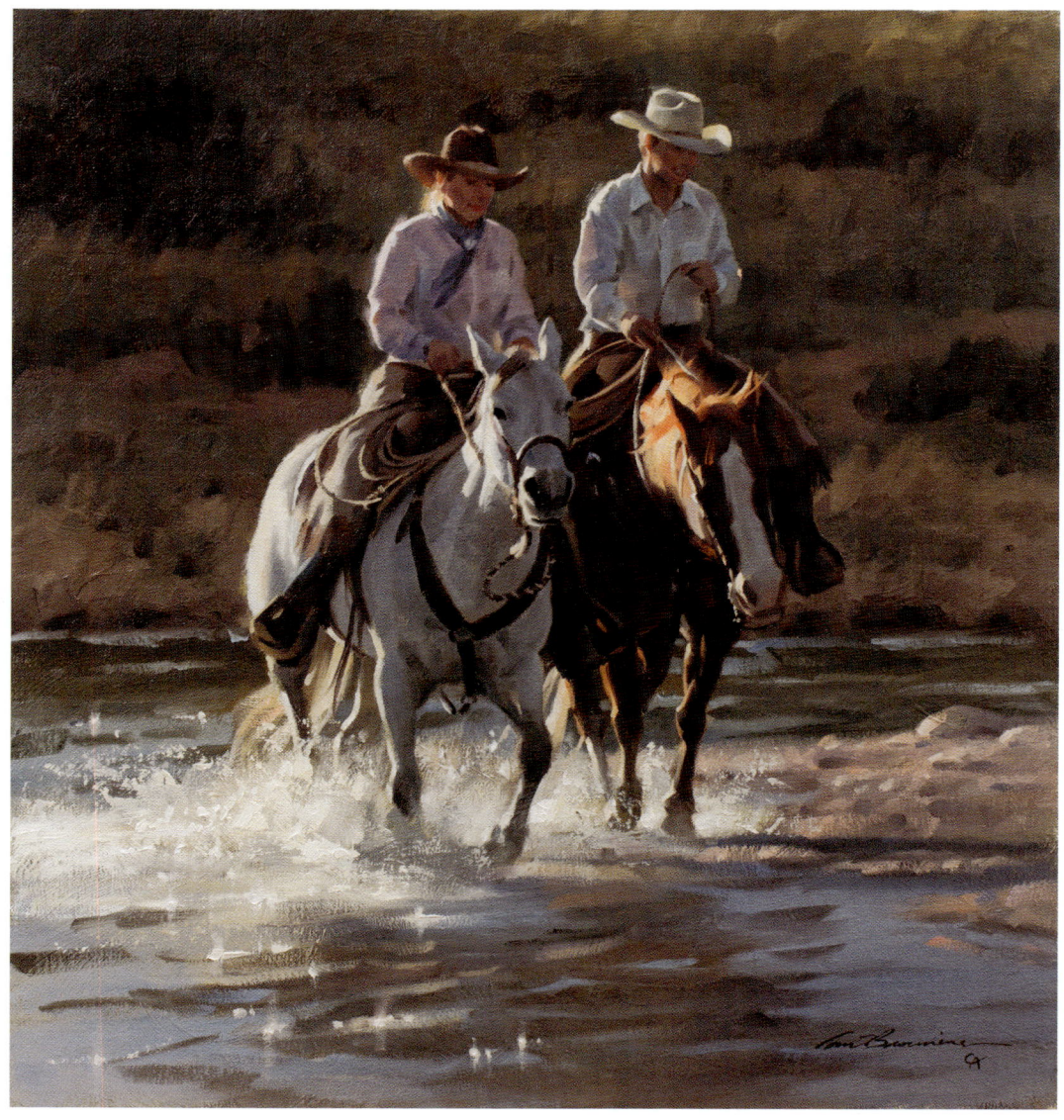

Evening Ride

(Oil, 19″ × 18″, 2019)

"With a beautiful evening sun setting behind this reservoir, I had a couple pass through the shallow water over and over again. I came up with several interesting compositions from this one spot and never tire of painting this theme. The backlit splashing water always seems to provide a pleasing painting."

The Rough String

(Oil, 20″ × 36″, 2020)

"In this painting, the most common scene on any ranch, a wrangler gathers up the horses he's going to use for the day. This particular ranch, Rock Springs, in Central Oregon, has provided me with a lifetime of ideas and Western paintings. I've painted this particular cowboy many times since he always looks good on a horse and fits the role of the 'real deal.'"

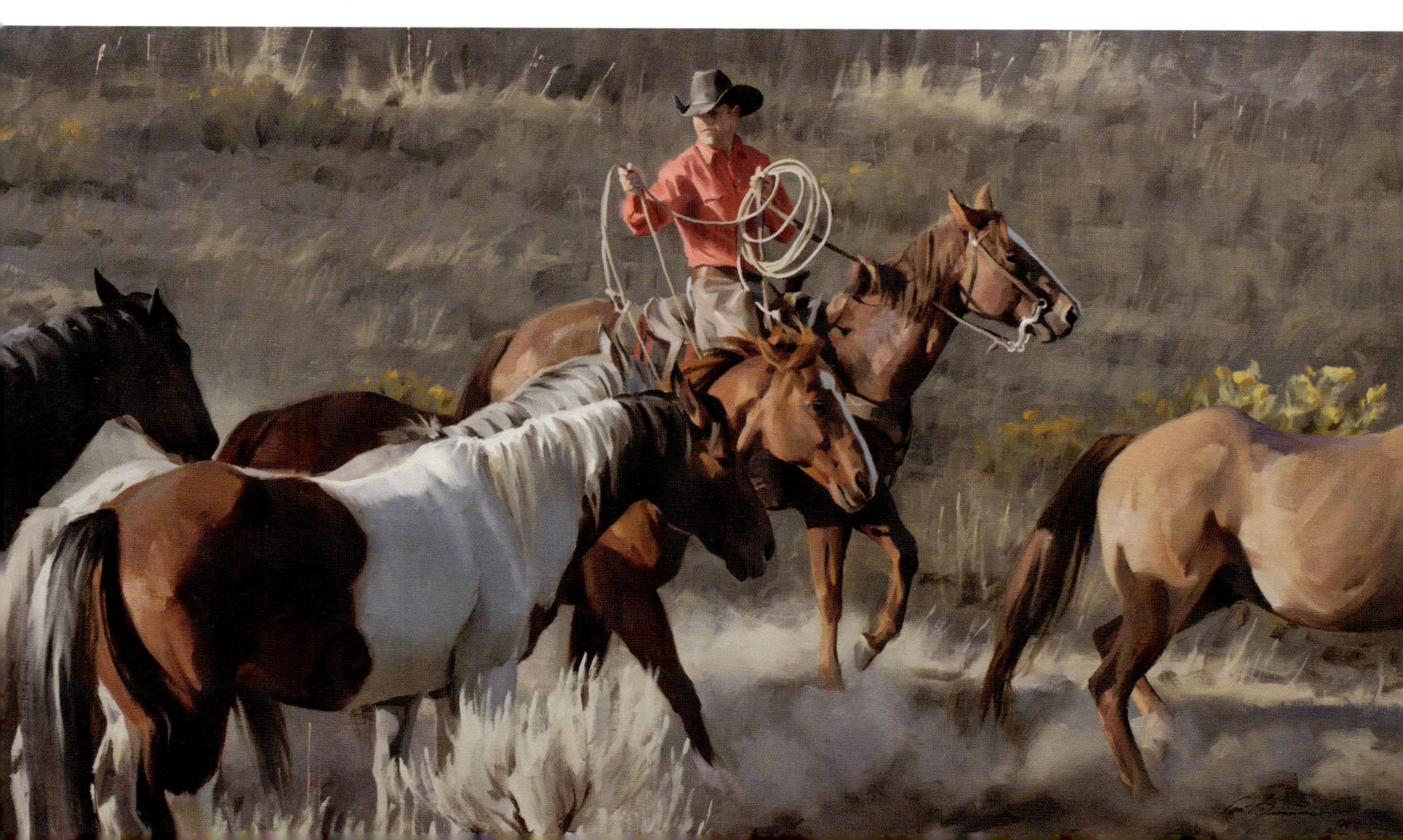

Rosie Sandifer

CHAPTER 8

Rosie Sandifer

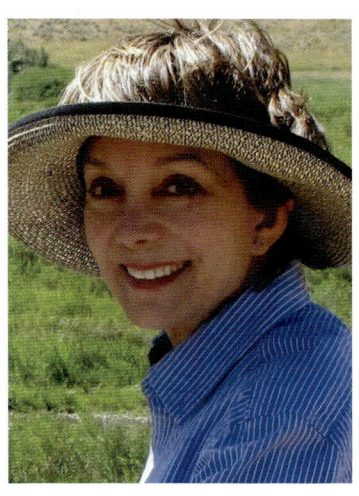

Rosie Sandifer's art career began with the Norman Rockwell images found inside the *Post* magazine that came to her house every Saturday. At the age of seven or eight, she started drawing them, trying to copy Rockwell's illustrations. Sandifer would try to draw other famous people whose photographs appeared in a newspaper or magazine. During church services, she would draw the people she observed around her. One of her most cherished childhood works was a pastel drawing featuring young Sandifer with her little sister in bed on Christmas Eve with the dog at the foot of the bed, with Santa coming through the window with his gifts: "I just had the bug early, and I've been so influenced by things along the way that that's how this career was built."

Her parents moved to Lubbock, Texas, when she was two years old from Columbia, South Carolina, where Sandifer was born. Her father was in real estate, a business that brought the family to Texas. She started art classes in eighth grade at Hutchinson Middle School.

I had a girlfriend whose parents would take us on horse rides. So, it started there. That was the most exciting thing we got to do then. I love horses. Part of it was to figure out how to draw them.

After graduating from high school, Sandifer attended Texas Tech and studied to become an English teacher. Circumstances caused her to transfer to Southwestern Oklahoma State University in Weatherford, Oklahoma, where she studied commercial art.

She took 18 hours of art and painting classes per semester. She returned to Lubbock to re-enroll in Texas Tech University to study art education.

Sandifer began doing some shows and then went with a group of artists to see a big art show. She saw the artists there selling artwork for impressive profits and realized that to do that she needed to be trained by a professional painter. She went to Cloudcroft, New Mexico, and studied under Ray Froman, who specialized in portraiture. In the class, the students painted three portraits a day: one in the morning, another in the afternoon, and one in the evening. Sandifer says, "My challenge has always been to be able to create something that expresses the vision I have in a work of art."

At the end of the 1970s, when her children were little, Sandifer's studio was the crowded utility room with the washer and dryer. When the children were napping, she would go there and work using a makeshift stand-up easel mounted on the washer. Sandifer sketched her children at home and at their school functions. She even gave them drawing lessons before school each day.

Sandifer accompanied several Lubbock artists on a trip to Santa Fe and visited Bettina Steinke's studio. Although Steinke advised the group that a career in art could not be done if they wanted to raise children and have a conventional marriage, Sandifer persevered and returned to see her several times to show her latest paintings. Steinke would critique them and offer advice. As Sandifer improved, Steinke became convinced Sandifer could earn a living as a portrait painter and pushed her to begin. Sandifer's career took off after she painted an image of her son and displayed it at the country club. And she kept studying.

One day a friend showed me a sketch of a horse. I have always loved horses and wanted one. I learned that if I drew one, I had that beautiful horse. I used photos, models, and anything I could find to help me do better sketches.

Sandifer really never intended to sculpt; however, she reached a point where she wanted to see if she could draw all the way around a sculpture just to see if she could. She painted portraits and figures so extensively that sculpture seemed a natural step. She went on a trip to paint in Spain, and due to an unplanned layover in New York, she was able to go to the Metropolitan Museum of Art. There, a sculpture by Edgar Degas, *Little Fourteen-Year-Old Dancer*, so impressed her that she set up her own sculpture studio upon her return to Lubbock. Sandifer then went back to Texas Tech and enrolled in a sculpture class. To her amazement, she found that after she was taught how to build a maquette of clay and with the model there in front of her, she just started building. Sandifer believes that came from having painted from life, over and over and over.

Sandifer then was drawn to do larger lifestyle pieces. She built one of her favorite pieces, *Freedom of Youth*, modeled after her daughter on a rope swing in the backyard of their home. This work is now an installation at Texas Tech in the courtyard of Holden Hall. Sandifer continued to paint, and as her paintings sold, she began sculpting in earnest. She began creating life-size works and monuments. Her creations can be found at locations from Texas A&M University to the Special Olympics' Tribute Park in Normal, Illinois. However, sculpting eventually wore Sandifer out and in 2006, she returned to sketching and painting.

Sandifer found renewed interest in sketching and painting Western landscapes. Many of her landscapes focused on the horse. She sought to paint the anatomy of the horse accurately, so she sat in on an equine anatomy course in Illinois. In the class, Sandifer studied equine cadavers to become familiar with the muscle structure below the skin.

I had several anatomy books. I also attended equine anatomy studies in Illinois. I told the professor I was trying so hard to learn, could I join his class? To me, the muscles used in whatever the representation of the horse is, are very important to me.

Capturing the correct gait and stance of the horse is also fundamental to Sandifer. If one or the other is off, she believes, it really shows. When she is painting a horse, the figure must represent a natural stance or gait.

> *That painting,* River Crossing. . . . *Did you see all those horse legs in there? I had legs coming out from everywhere. So . . . It was very much of a challenge. I had to leave and go to another painting and come back because it was a really a tough painting.*

Sandifer spends a lot of time coming up with new ideas of what medium to use. She likes working in pastel very much because with pastels, she found, you can put one color over another. However, she found the pastels were hard on her fingers so she would have to wear gloves. This inhibited her drawing patterns because she couldn't blend with her fingers gloved. These days, she narrows her primary medium of art to oil paint. In her oils, she uses a great deal of backlighting that contributes to the overall feeling and atmosphere of her horse paintings.

Sandifer is nationally recognized in sculpture and painting. She is a Fellow in the American Artists Professional League and a Fellow in the Natural Sculpture Society. Her numerous awards include the Anna Hyatt Huntington Award from the American Artists Professional League, the Vincent Glinsky Memorial Award from the Audubon Artists, and Best of Show in Oils at the Texas Cowboy Artists Show in Amarillo, Texas.

Sandifer summarizes some thoughts about the legacy of art:

> *I had the good fortune to meet Electra Waggoner Biggs at her ranch near Lubbock. She told me about working on her sculpture of Will Rogers. After completing the clay sculpture, she went to Europe for a rest. Upon her return, she destroyed the clay piece and started again. She told me, "When you are dead, they won't remember your name. All that will be remembered is if the work is good or bad."*

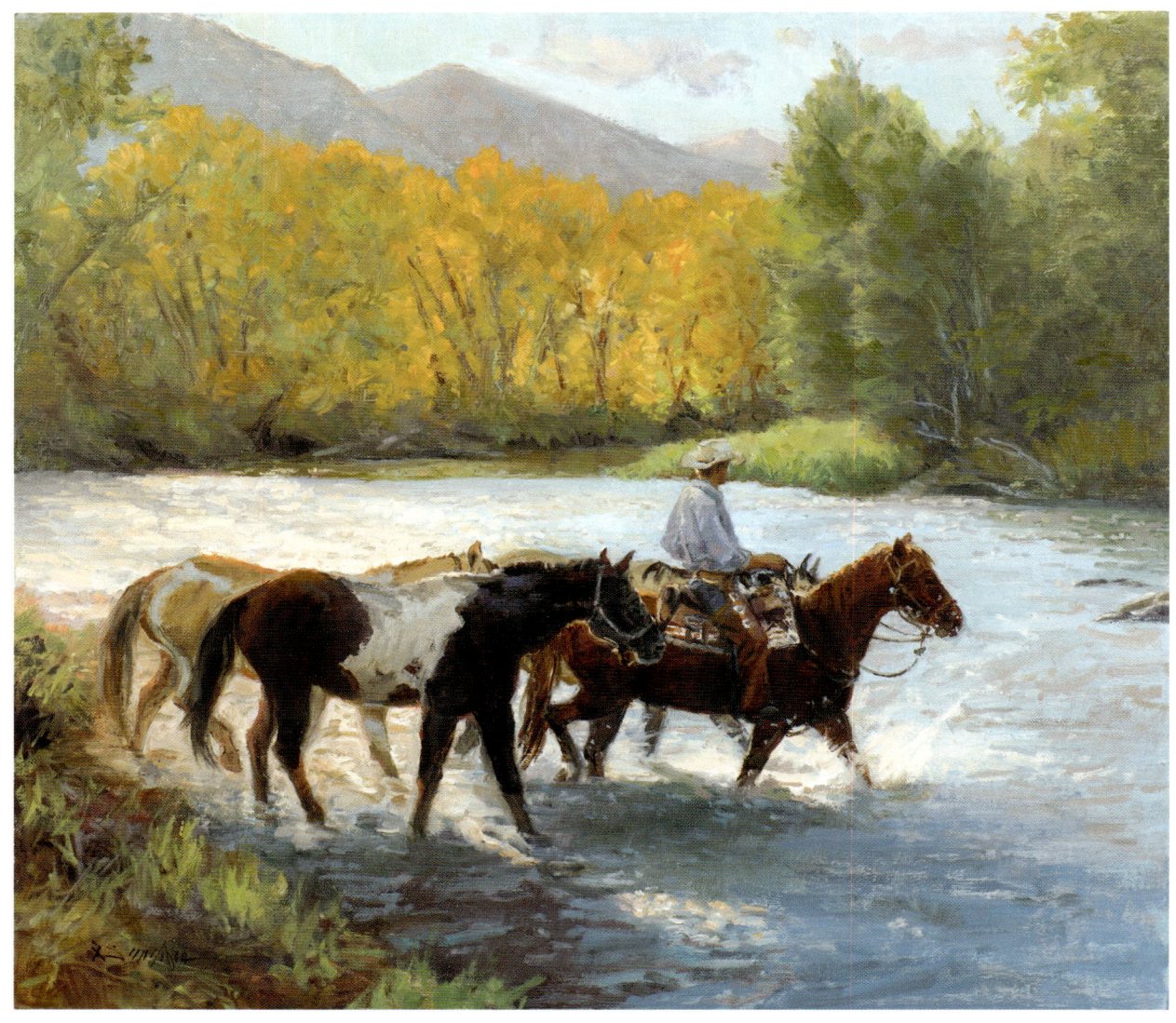

Aspen Gold

(Oil, 14″ × 16″, 2022)

"My *Aspen Gold* oil painting of the cowboy leading the three horses to the other side of the Colorado River features the dramatic green-golden color of aspen leaves as they turn during the fall season. I keep a glass bowl of fallen leaves replenished each autumn on our kitchen island. The design is a circle from the water splashes to the trees leaning up and left to the branch heading down to the grass on bottom left and back up to the splash."

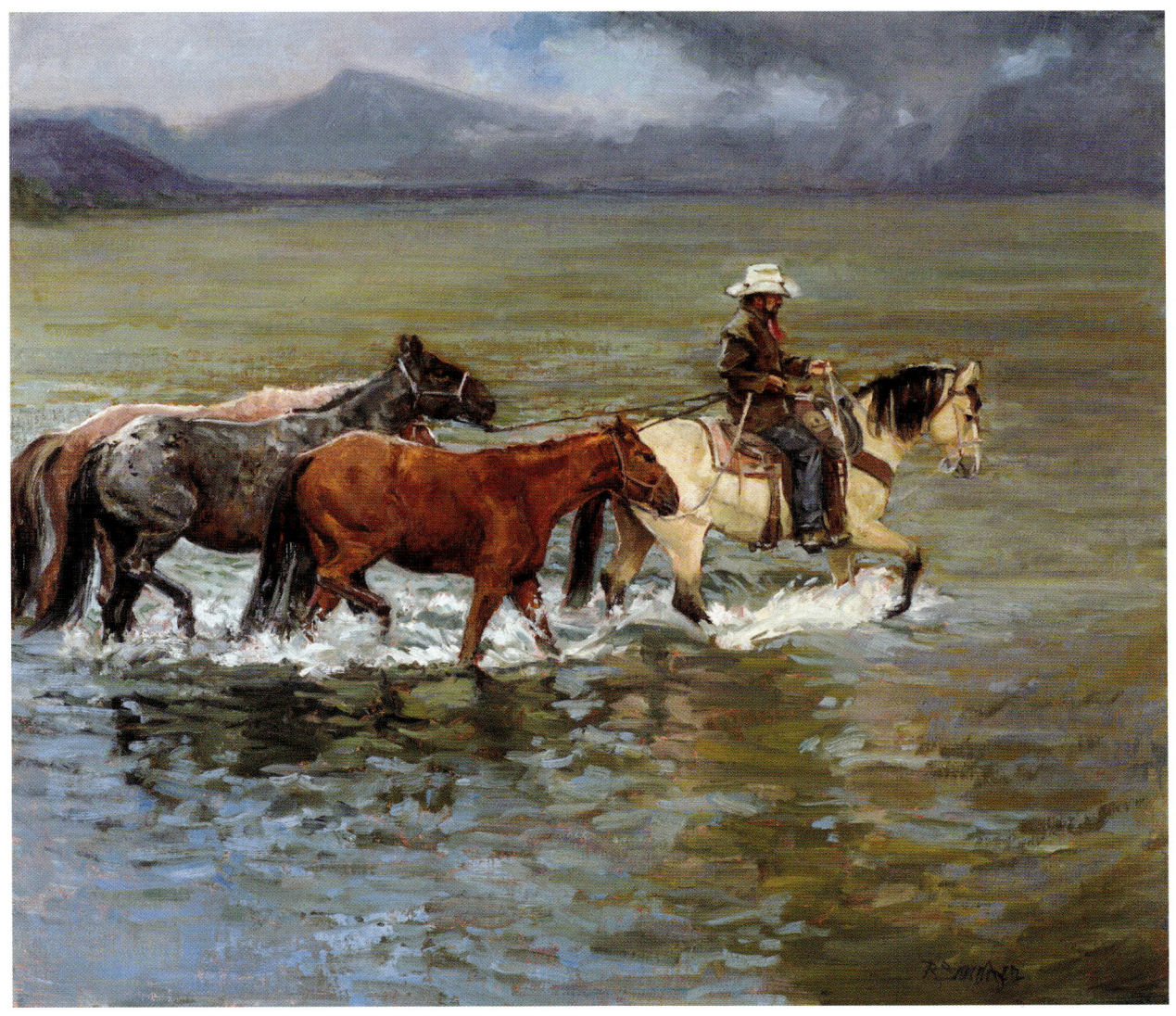

Lake Storming

(Oil, 16" × 20", 2021)

"The oil painting *Lake Storming* was inspired as a storm approached over Lake Abiquiu near Ghost Ranch in New Mexico. I hurried to get my small plein air piece finished before loading up my gear and myself into the car just as the storm landed. It seemed to me the perfect background for four horses to be splashing through. The storm clouds lead the eye down to the red roan's back highlights, down to the water shadows, creating an S design."

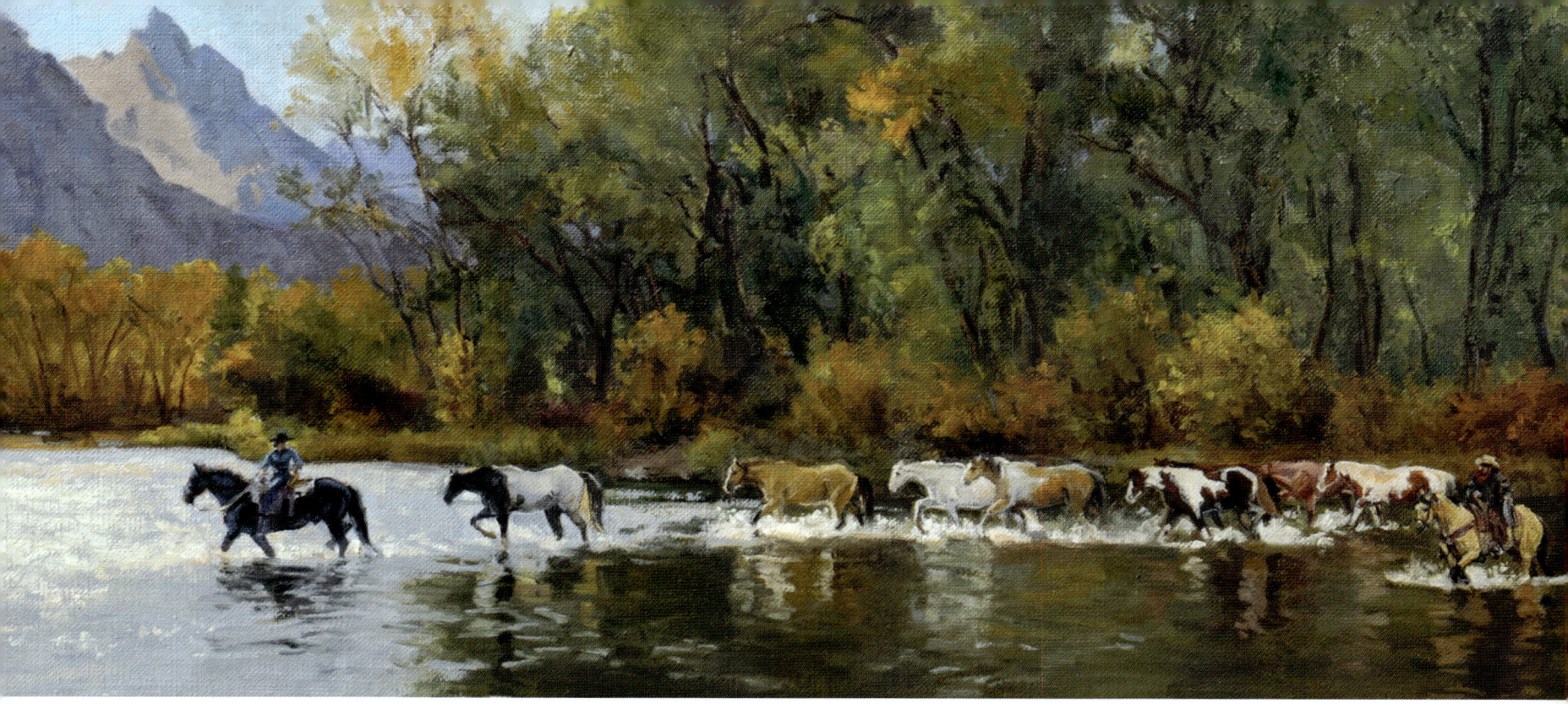

River Crossing

(Oil, 12" × 24", 2021)

"The oil painting and giclée print *River Crossing* features horse wrangler Ali Briggs on her horse Dually leading eight horses across the Colorado River with wrangler Kache Kearney bringing up the rear. The background is taken from a plein air painting of the peaks along Trail Ridge Road in Rocky Mountain National Park. Here the mountain light leads your eye down to the water's highlights, to Ali and Dually, to the water shadow, up to Kache on his buckskin, to tree branches leading back to mountains."

The Dozen

(Oil, 12″ × 24″, 2022)

"*The Dozen* oil painting is from a scene I saw on my way up from Arizona through Utah and on into the Tetons and Yellowstone areas. I loved these colts' natural gathering, creating a coordinated shadow as well. This design takes the eye up the neck of the right horse, over to the upright tail on the brown horse, back down the neck of the horse standing next to it, and back through the shadows between."

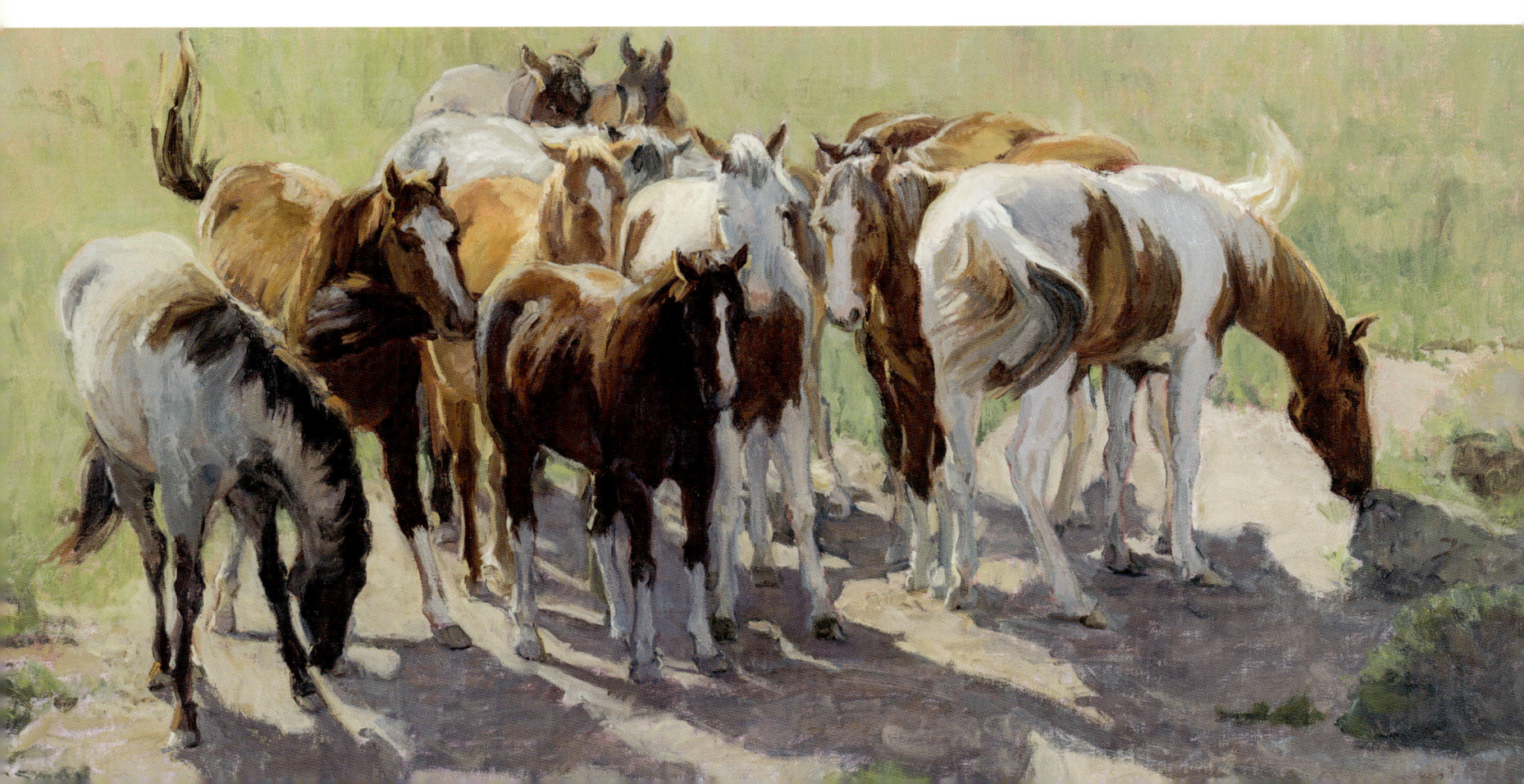

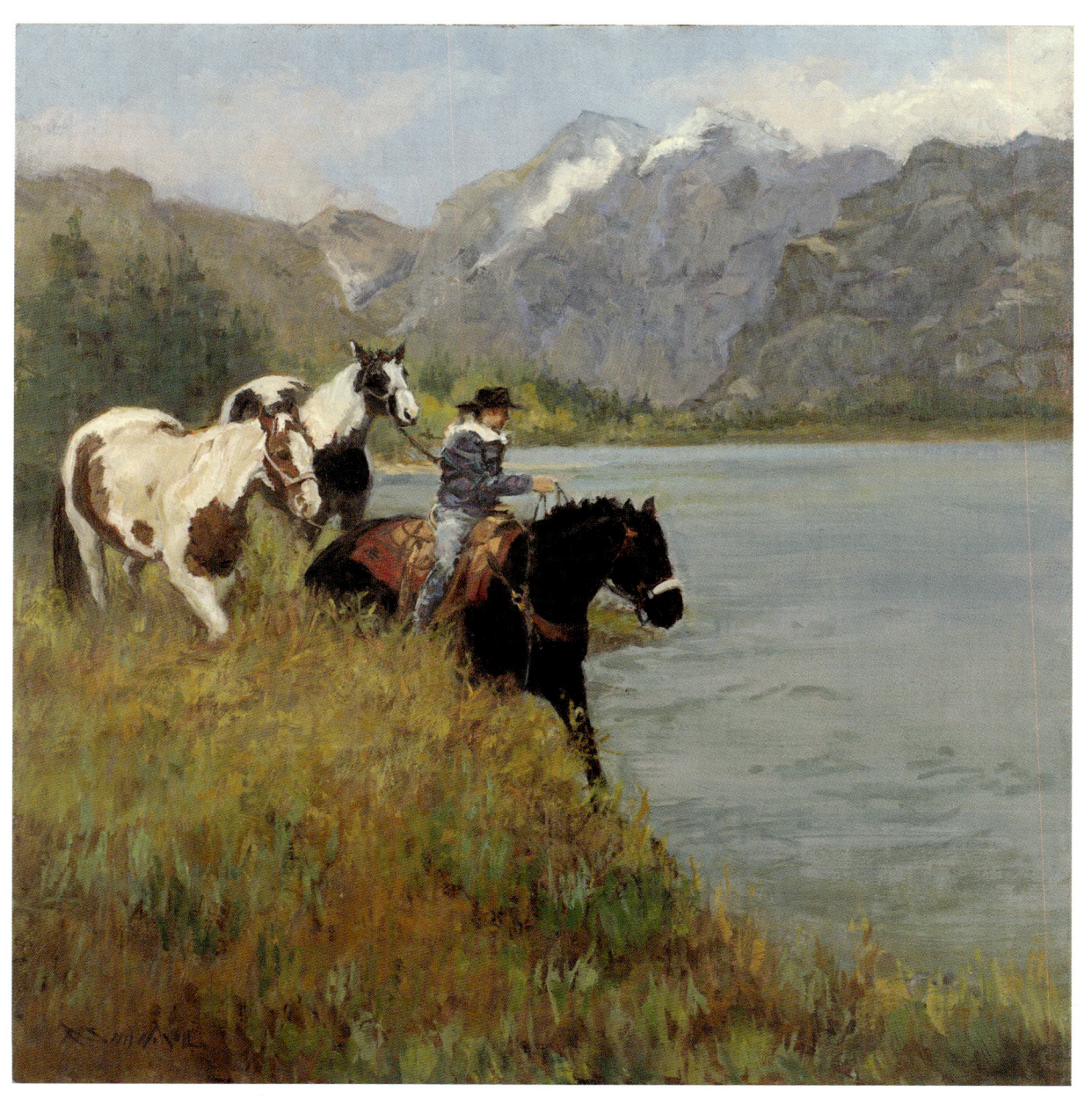

Trio

(Oil, 9" × 12", 2023)

"The oil painting *Trio* evolved from my watching horse wrangler Ali Briggs on her horse Dually lead the two paint horses down to cross the Colorado River. From my plein air paintings, most of which I keep as reference, I choose different mountain backdrops to go with the various Western figures. Clouds lead to snow caps, to the horses, down to river's edge, to light grasses leaning left, taking you back to the front darker mountain, to Ali and Dually."

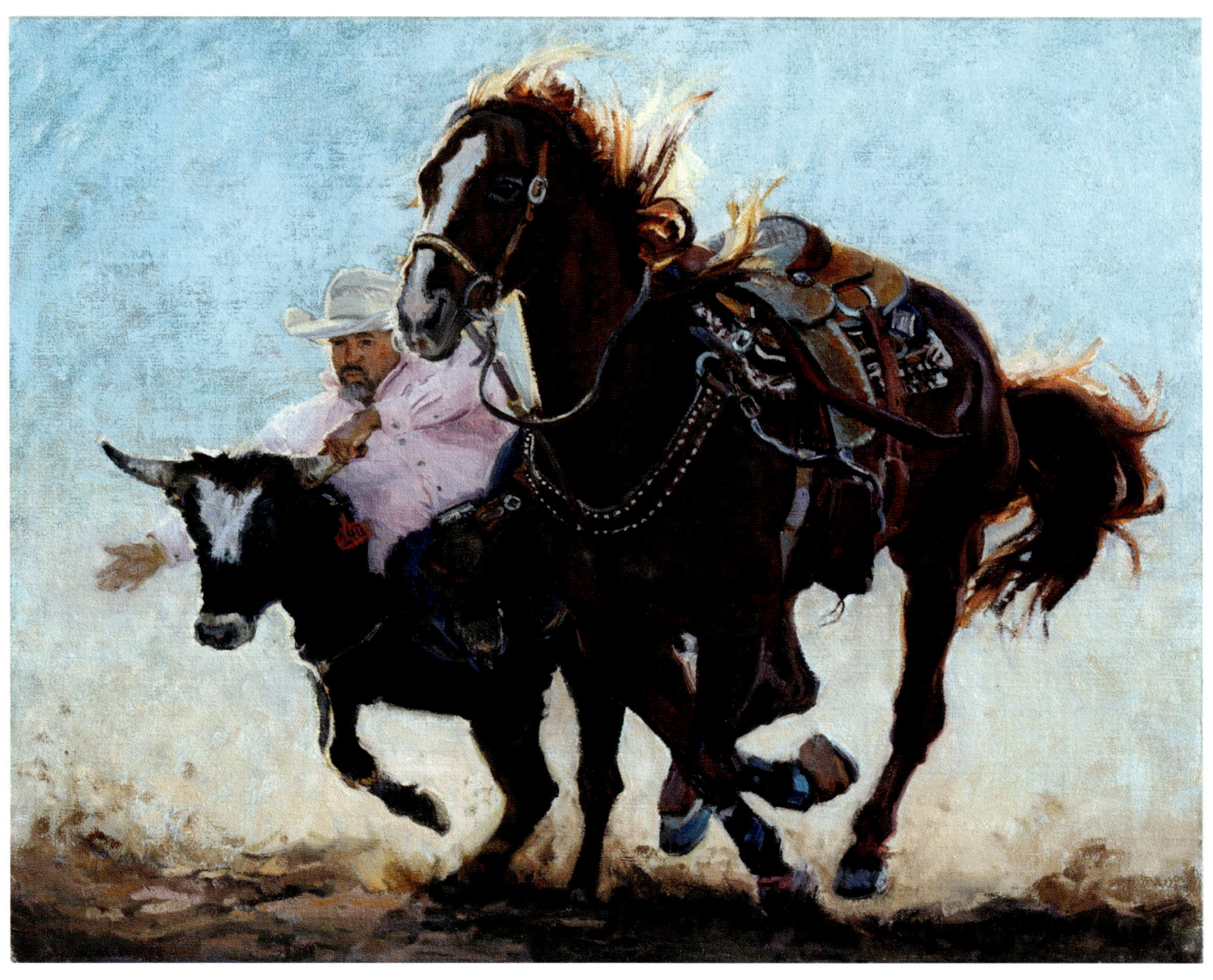

Sport Rodeo

(Oil, 16″ × 21″, 2020)

"The *Sport Rodeo* oil painting is a triangular design from the cowboy's outstretched hand up to his horse's flying mane to its tail and back down to the flat dirt. I watched this cowboy's ride at the Santa Fe, New Mexico Rodeo."

Don Weller

CHAPTER 9

Don Weller

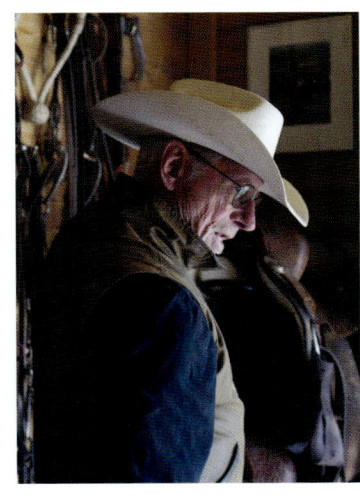

Photo by Williams

D on Weller grew up near Pullman, Washington, in an area with large wheat and dry pea farms among the rolling hills. The area was known for its long dry summers. His family home was on twenty acres about three miles from town. His father was an architect and professor at Washington State College (now Washington State University), where his mother also worked as a dietician.

Weller was drawn to the art and stories of Will James, enamored with the cowboy life. He found himself always drawing horses and cowboys. His mother saved some of this early work, which Weller described as "pathetic imitations of Will James

adventures." All along, he dreamed of the cowboy life and imagined a life on the range.

I explained to my folks that I needed a horse, and the whining actually paid off when I was about seven or eight. I got a horse and rode country roads, through wheat fields and dry peas, and down the rivers looking for cowboys, pretty much unsuccessfully.

One day, in junior high, Weller was riding the familiar roads and discovered a group of cowboys riding and roping in a pole corral. Weller returned on practice days to watch and eventually the cowboys, who were members of the Washington State College rodeo team, showed him how to rope first bales of hay and later calves. He then participated in rodeo in high school and subsequently at Washington State. "I had many friends on the rodeo team, so when I got to college, of course that was the first thing I did," he says. Besides calf roping, Weller liked the action of the wild cow milking events, where all the ropers and muggers (cowboys who hold the cow still) participated in the arena at once. He shared, "I often did better in that than I did in the calf roping because there, luck was as important as skill. I think I was a rather slow calf roper. I don't just think that, it was proven many times." His long, hot summers were filled with harvesting wheat and rodeoing on the weekends.

Weller planned to go to the veterinary school at Washington State after graduating from high school but instead found himself gravitating toward art classes. He soon changed his major to art, although the department at the time was focused on abstract art. Weller said that "drawing is drawing, whether it is horses, or the model in class at the university and I enjoyed it. And though I learned a lot from painting classes and art history, I knew I'd never be an abstract expressionist, all the rage at that time." All along, however, he was anxious to leave Pullman and "go somewhere with no wheat, and where the real cowboys were doing work."

After college, Weller sold his horse trailer and his horses before he headed to Southern California to try to find a job in the art field. With no money, he slept on his uncle's couch until he eventually landed a job in graphic design. However, he soon was transferred from the Air National Guard to active duty during the Berlin Crisis, a Cold War conflict between the United States and the Soviet Union concerning the status of the divided German city. After this, he returned to graphic design, moving from job to job with advancing responsibilities before going into business for himself. Weller developed many high-profile clients and painted album covers for Angel Records, posters of the NFL, art for the Olympics, and a cover of *Time* magazine featuring an iconic image of Elton John.

Weller was also teaching at UCLA at the time, where he met his wife Cha Cha. The couple eventually "had all the palm trees and cement we could take" and picked up and moved to Park City, Utah. There, Weller saw a small ad for the National Cutting Horse

Association (NCHA), which sparked his interest. While roping calves at a country fair in late 1969, he watched a cutting contest and was so impressed that he approached the NCHA with the idea of producing a book for them. In the process of producing this book, Weller started riding cutting horses and began to compete successfully in shows. He shared, "It became an addiction. . . . It's the adrenaline rush of a good horse working a fresh cow, and it's still what I do for a hobby nowadays."

Much of Weller's art is known for its action and the explosiveness of the horses. He calls on his experiences and adventures with friends and cowboys at cutting events, rodeos, roundups, and brandings. The majority of his paintings are done in the winter, when it is too cold and snowy for riding. Much of his inspiration comes from the photos taken over the summer months, but he stresses that "it just doesn't end there—repainting a photo is not interesting to me."

Weller specialized in watercolors for most of his career but began working on some oil paintings, believing that a good painting is based on composition and value, although "color and subject matter get the glory." He said, "I like the watercolors to look fresh and to look like they were fun to paint. They look slightly spontaneous, even though they're not at all."

Weller explains the process as trying to figure out how to take an image and tell a story, while at the same time making a composition that has all the right elements. Integral to his work in watercolor is the contrast of light (white of the actual paper) and dark (black paint) values. Before beginning to paint, he often does a value sketch of his reference photograph, including the detail he wants to stress while eliminating the extraneous elements of the work.

I start with a person's face or the horse's head. I have the reference of where the shadows are, so I may or may not sketch it in, but I know where I'm going to put the dark parts. When I start painting, I usually begin with one little part and then it grows across the page.

As for subject matter, horses are what most interests Weller. He says, "Probably the first thing I ever drew was horses and cowboys, and I'm back to it after years of doing football players, Elton John, and Hollywood Bowl subjects." Weller particularly likes to paint different colored horses for different reasons. For lighter horses, there is a great deal of artistic opportunity to paint shadows. For darker horses, he states that "you can explain the top line, the highlights on the hips, shoulders, a couple of places on the legs, the faces, and then a lot of stuff you can just paint black."

Weller captures the action and emotion of rodeo events by exaggerating the gestures of the action. He explains:

In the process of drawing a horse or rider, I try to analyze where the action is and what's happening and exaggerate it a little bit—not enough to scare anyone but enough to increase the sense of the action. If that horse is doing a certain part of the bucking, I might exaggerate whatever that is. This creates a sense of tension for the viewer.

Weller's favorite event is saddle bronc riding, which he believes is iconic of rodeo, due to its long tradition in the West. Portrayals of ropers both in the rodeo and at ranch brandings are also common themes in his art. Gesture and tension are highlighted in his watercolors.

Weller and his wife Cha Cha currently live in rural Oakley, Utah, where they bought a small ranch to keep their cutting horses. His artworks have won numerous awards, and he has been featured in exhibitions across the country. He has published seven books, including *Tracks: A Visual Memoir*, whch received the Westen Heritage Award in the Literary category. His most recent book is *The River Flows: Watercolors of the American West*.

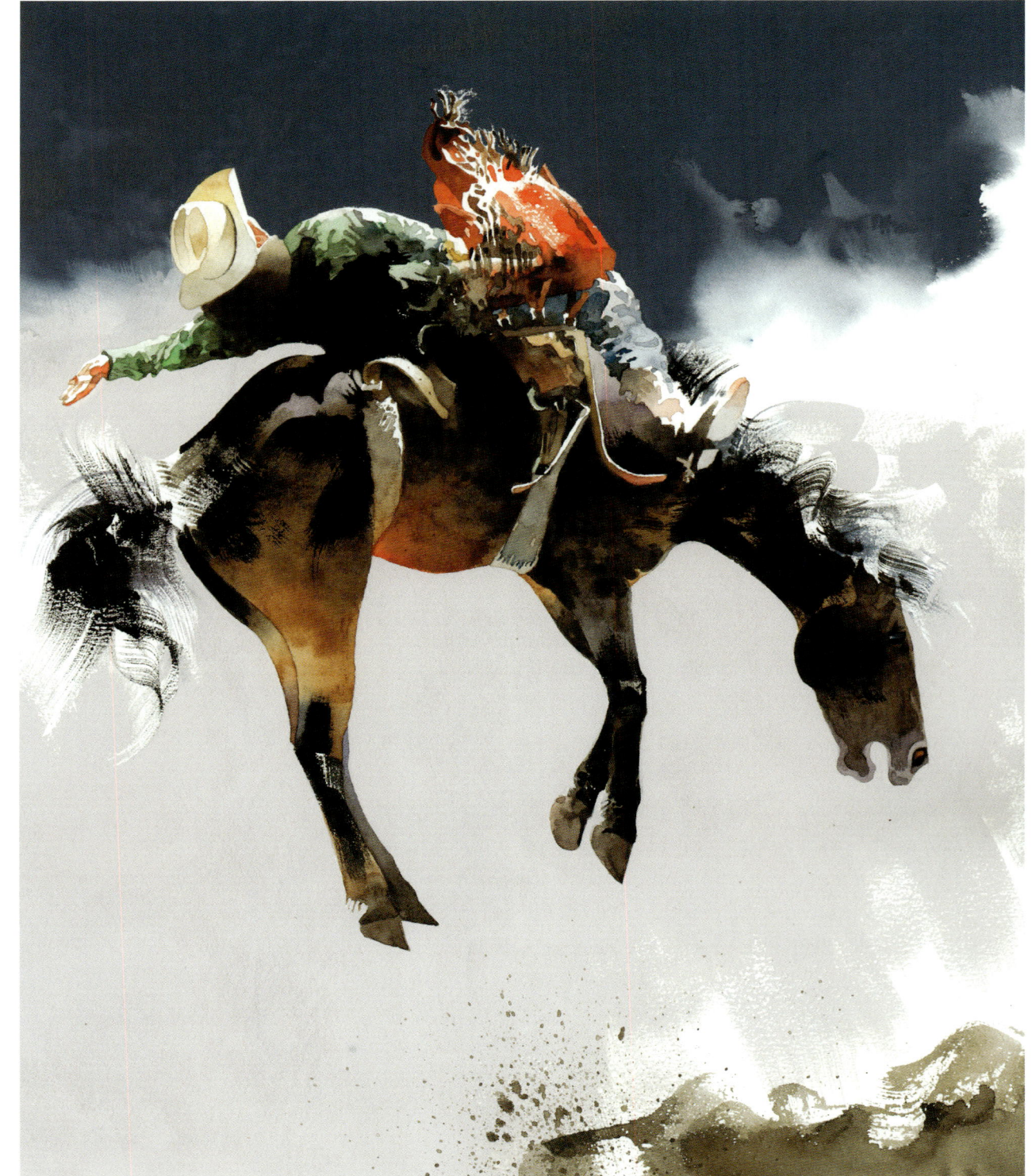

One Hand in the Riggin'

(Watercolor,
16″ × 13.5″, 2011)

Weller used the ground level vantage point from the press pit in the Cheyenne arena. "[It was] great to get immediacy and the lower angle. I tried to get across that the horse was really bellowing." Of most interest to Weller is the horse's face, bellowing mouth, and stiff front legs, so this is where he uses the greatest contrast of darkness against the light gray background.

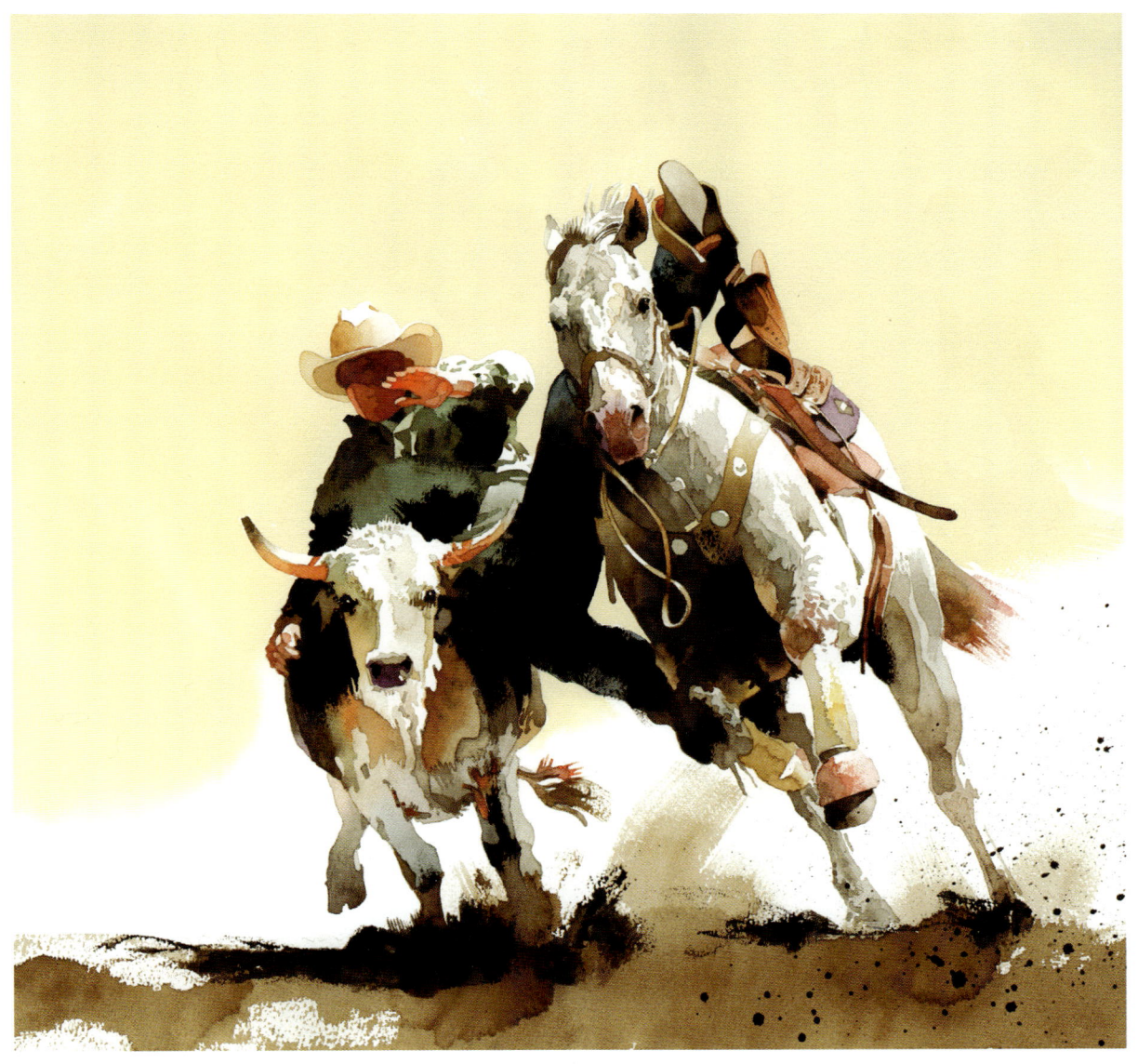

We Called It Doggin' (Cheyenne Frontier Days)

(Watercolor, 15″ × 15″, 2011)

"It's right at the instant where you commit. [The horse] has put the bulldogger in a good position to wrestle the steer down, showing the partnership between the two athletes. The shape [of the work] is a strong shape and it's not meant for the eye to wander—I want the eye to keep coming back to the head of the steer and the cowboy."

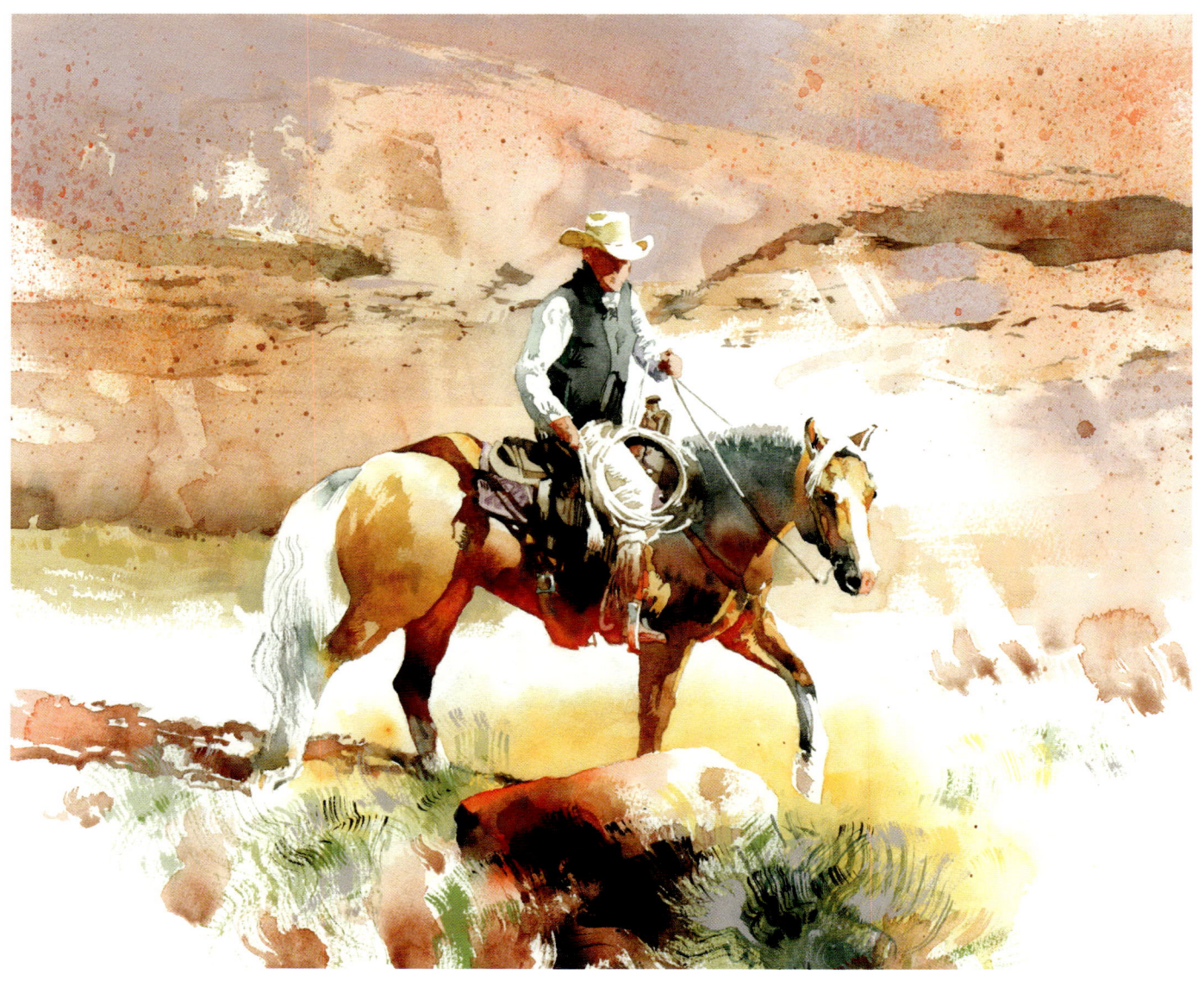

Red Rocks

(Watercolor, 14″ × 18″, 2017)

"We go visit our pals in Moab, Utah, most every year. It is spectacular red rock country, and my paintings from there seem to exaggerate the red. Even the shadows under the horse's belly are red. The red spattering on the rocks behind was done with a toothbrush."

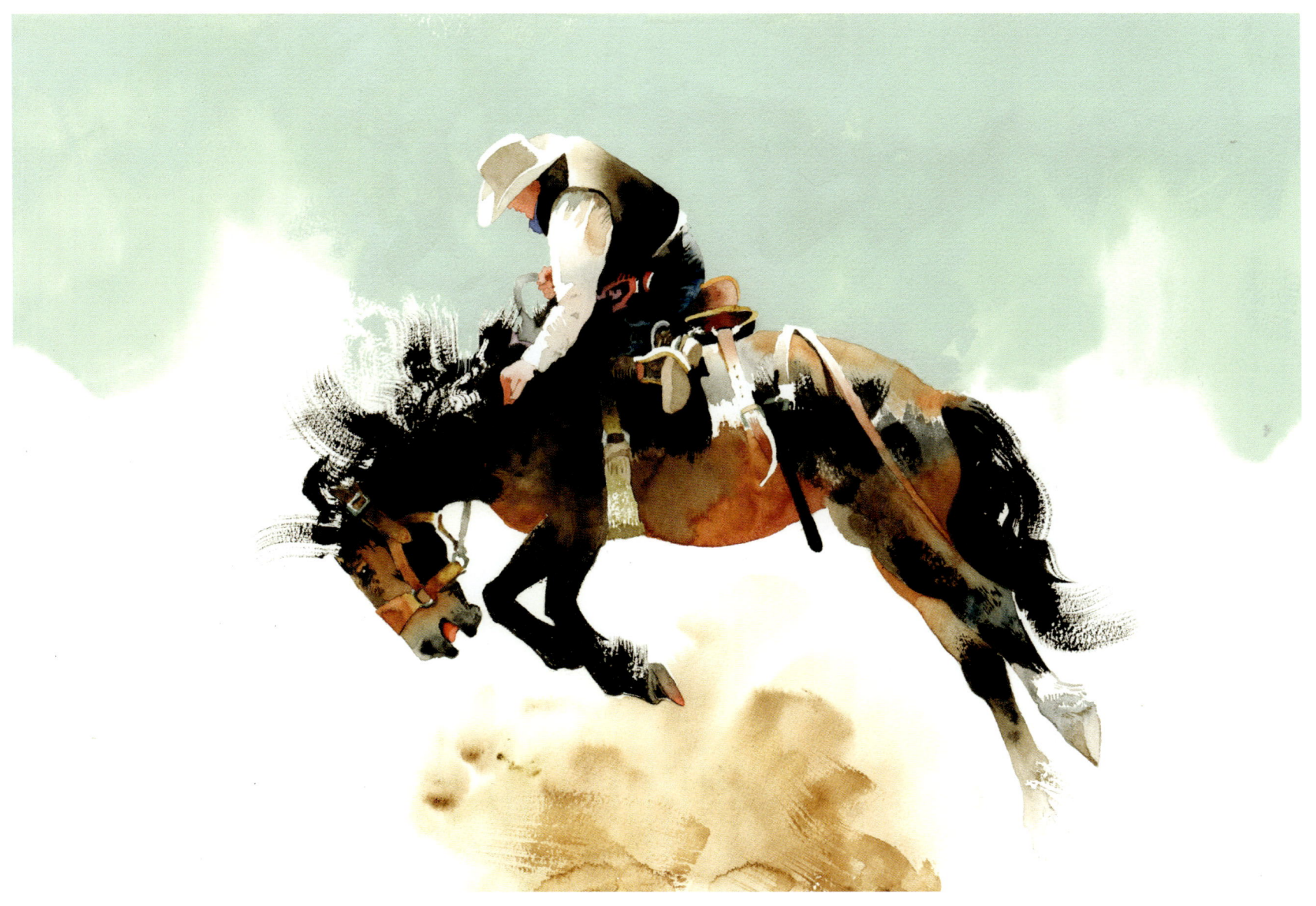

Rodeo Icon

(Watercolor, 14″ × 18″, 2016)

"The rider's position is correct for the high part of a jump, since his spurs are in the cantle of the saddle. As the jump comes down, his position would have the rider's legs straight, toes out, spurs at the horse's shoulders and the rider stretched out, free hand reaching for the stars. Those are the two classic positions for the saddle bronc rider, the icon of rodeo. Those are my two favorite positions to paint."

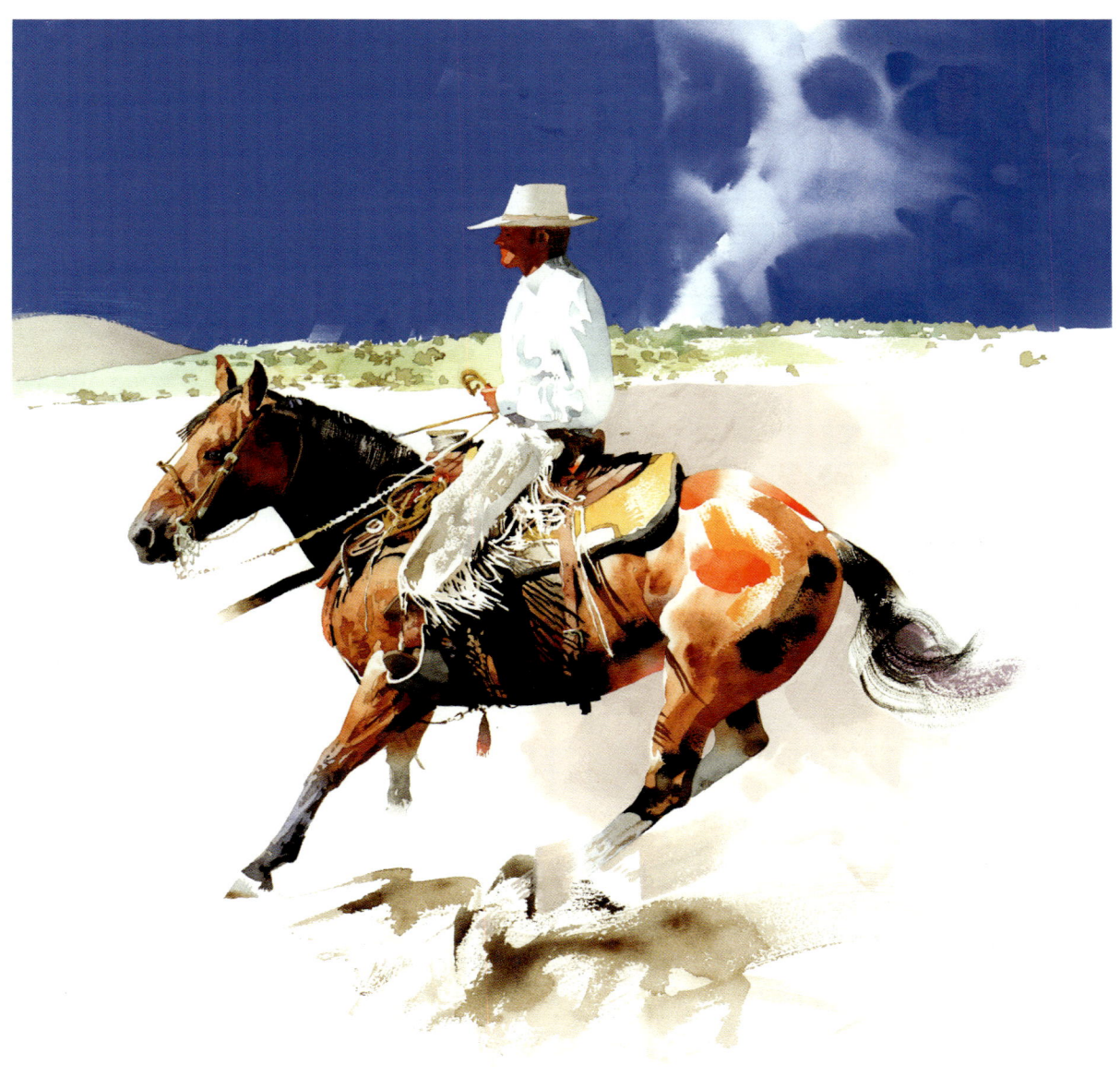

Wade and Spade

(Watercolor, 20" × 20", 2013)

"It really is a spade bit, and of course it is a Wade saddle. His hat and gear suggest he is in the Great Basin, Nevada or Utah. The horse is spinning, his nose is tipped slightly in the direction he's turning. The tassel at the center of the cinch hangs vertical; it's at the center of the rotation. The tail blowing to the right and the latigo flying left show the centrifugal force of the action. Even the shadow suggests drama."

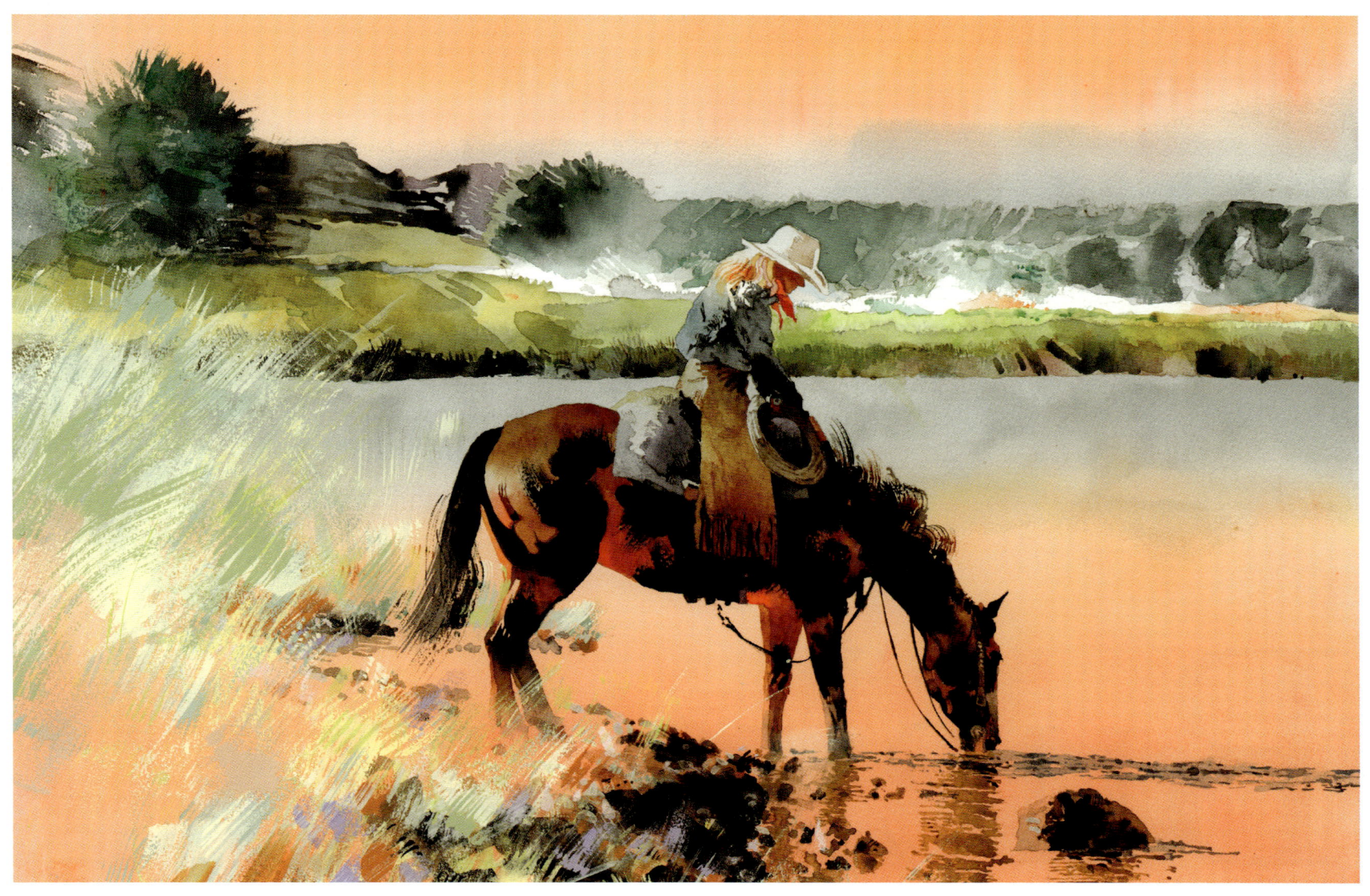

Evening on the River

(Watercolor, 13.5" × 19", 2015)

"This was on a ranch in South Dakota on the Cheyenne River. Although it started with the rancher's wife offering a drink to her horse, the painting is much more about mood than it is about the cowgirl. Sunsets can be crisp, but some, like this one, are thick, heavy, quiet, and all-encompassing. The composition is rather straightforward; the painting is really about the mood and color."

Buckeye Blake

CHAPTER 10

Buckeye Blake

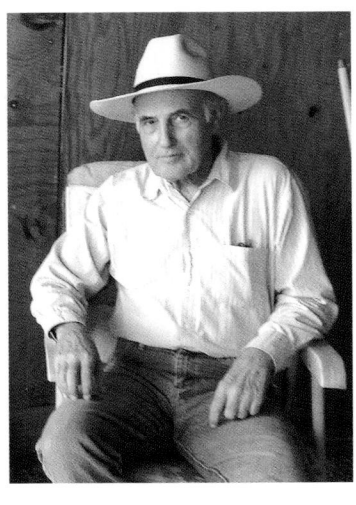

James Cole "Buckeye" Blake grew up around horses and cowboys. His grandfather bred some of the early Quarter Horse ranch horses, roping horses, racehorses, and polo ponies on a ranch in Oklahoma in the early 1900s. The family left for California during the Dust Bowl to try to find a better life. Blake's father was a rodeo cowboy and, like many of the cowboys, he was able to get a job in the early Western films. Blake's mother was from England and met Blake's father at a rodeo in Hollywood. Her family had moved to Whittier, California, when she was a teenager. She came from a family of artists and was herself artistically talented.

The Blakes moved around frequently because of the Depression and did whatever they could to make a living. Blake's father got a job as a United States Border Patrol agent, moving the family around to small US-Mexico border towns, including Tecate, Campo, and Jacumba in California and Ajo, Arizona. They continued to move around looking for better jobs. They owned a hotel in Los Angeles, built horse trailers, and raised livestock. Blake's mother painted portraits and dance hall murals. They were hired on various ranches as they moved, and Blake remembers he was always around livestock and cowboys. Along their travels, he picked up his nickname "Buckeye" when the family passed through Buckeye, Arizona, for a rodeo.

The Blake family moved to Carson City, Nevada, when Buckeye was in his early teens. He began showing his art in various locations and selling what he produced. Blake showed his artistic talent in school, where he won many of the art contests. He left school in his junior year, moving to Hollywood for employment in the movie studios. He had a connection there because his sister lived in Los Angeles with her husband, who was a movie producer. In the studios, he learned lettering and design and acquired a new knowledge of color and shapes. Blake said that Hollywood was his art school because he got to work with a movie studio that designed a great deal of animation and images for cartoons.

While in Hollywood he drew cartoons and scenery for several years before moving to Nevada to pursue his own art. In 1979, he moved to Montana to produce large sculptures of Charlie Russell's funeral. Unlike many of his contemporaries, he never favored a single medium. Instead, Blake works in oil paint, watercolor, sculpture, pen and ink, leatherwork, and screen prints. He did the posters for the Cowboy Poetry Gathering in Elko, Nevada, for years and gained a reputation for his use of color and design.

Blake has a unique style that reflects the old rodeo posters of the 1920s and '30s. His paintings and sculptures are exaggerations of Western realism. He presents a scene in his paintings that is mindful of the old Western movies.

So it's fun. I'm from a family of artists and I always created stuff. I think it's a difference in the bloodstream. I would grab a piece of clay and start to make it into a figure or something and my mother painted. My dad was really good but he wouldn't do it. He was an old cowboy and he thought it was feminine. Anyway, so I come from a long line of creative people but you have to practice it. I didn't go to art school or anything, but the artists I admired—I would go meet them and find out who they were and . . . if they would share their knowledge.

Blake said the horse got tangled in his family tree and they have never moved away from that. Because of his grandfather's

role of raising horses and his father's experience of being a rodeo cowboy, it was just natural for him to paint and draw what was around him daily. He used his lifelong experiences with horses to accurately create the horse in everyday life on ranches and in motion on the rodeos.

Art is not a kind of exact science. There is just not some standard rule you go by at all. The guidelines are transparent, and it is however you want to approach it. But to do art, you have to have an understanding of movement in different situations. With the horses you ride every day, you see how the muscles work. It's like watching ballet. You study the dance and you study what those motions are and how that feels, and the rhythm of it. That line you make on a page is merely a mark from the rhythm of your arm. If you imagine what it feels like to be riding a horse, you are putting what you learned into the stroke of paint on your canvas.

Blake found inspiration in the work of Will James and Charles Russell. Today, his style is still based on James's view of the West. Blake also substantially drew inspiration from the Taos artists who had European art training and showed him how to create content based on real and imaginary life. But to Blake, it is important to stay humorous while telling a story of Western history. The artistic style of Maynard Dixon shows up as an influence in his paintings and drawings.

His art career began to build while Blake was living in Nevada. Scripps Howard Publishing commissioned him for artwork. Collectors discovered him and began buying from him. He moved to Montana with his wife, Tona, and their son, Teal, where he continued to excel. He created the life-size bronze of Charles Russell (*Kid Russell and Monte*) that stands in Great Falls, Montana, and the *Kit Carson* life-size sculpture at the Carson City, Nevada, capitol grounds. Broadmoor Galleries in Colorado Springs, Colorado, carried his art and described Blake as "an artist whose experience as a working cowboy gave him firsthand knowledge of Western subjects. His paintings exhibit a fanciful graphic style mixed with a taste for pop culture interpretations of Western figures, especially cowboy and cowgirl iconography. He approaches traditional themes with humor, strong sense of design, and a sunny palette all of which give his work a lighthearted flavor."

Says Blake:

The more knowledge you have has everything to do with creating artwork. You have to be interested too so that you have the enthusiasm to give it that little bit of magic we are trying to create for the viewer. If you are not enthused, then the art becomes boring and drab and all the things we don't want it to be. You've got to do something that's appealing.

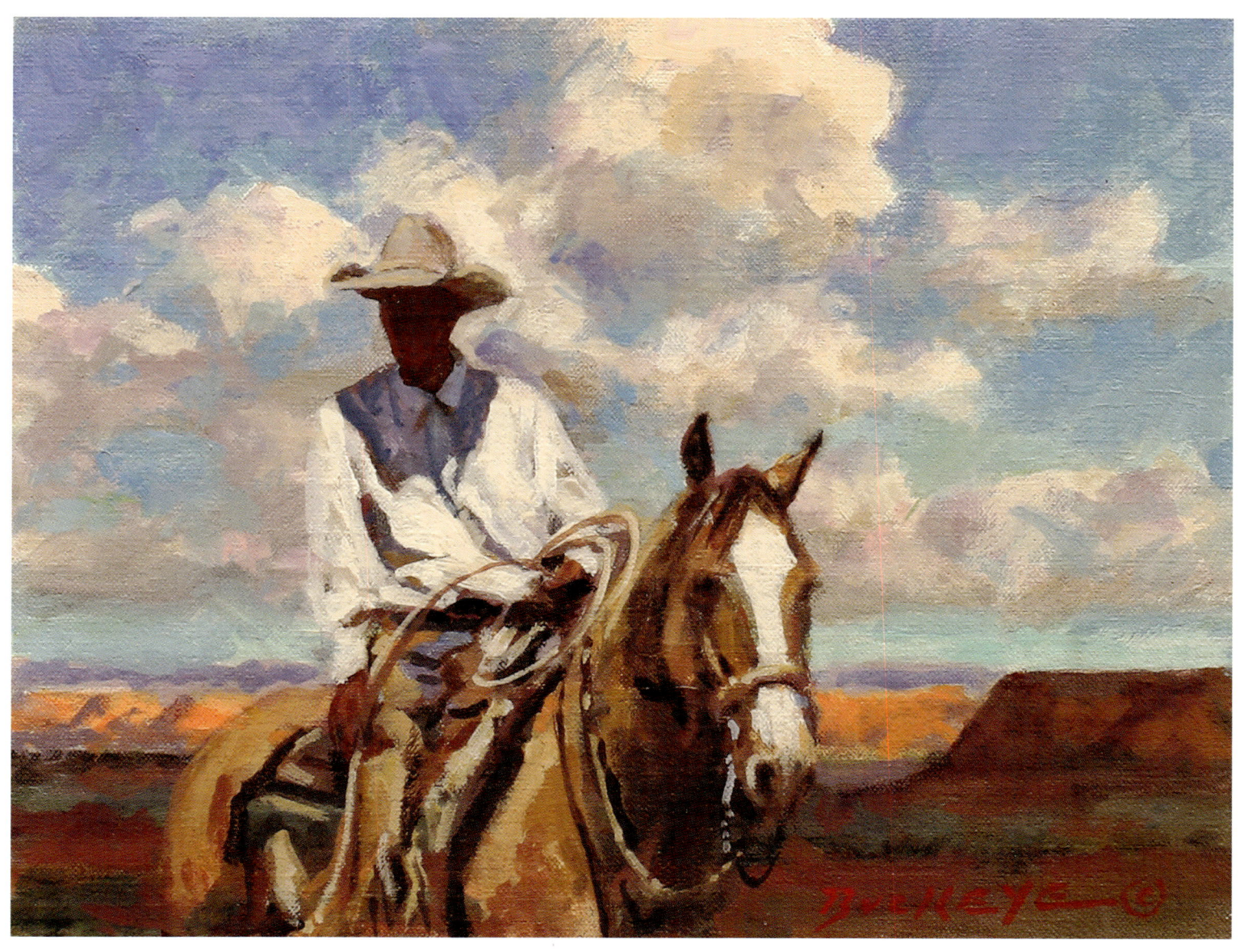

Big Sky Buckskin

(Oil on panel, 9″ × 12″, n.d.)

"If you put the right lines, you know. It's like if you make a portrait of a person standing outside and their hair is blowing. You know the winds blow, so you can put these obvious gestures in there. And that's where the secret lies about art. It's not just having the right clothing, period clothing, on this certain individual. It's, it's putting everything around."

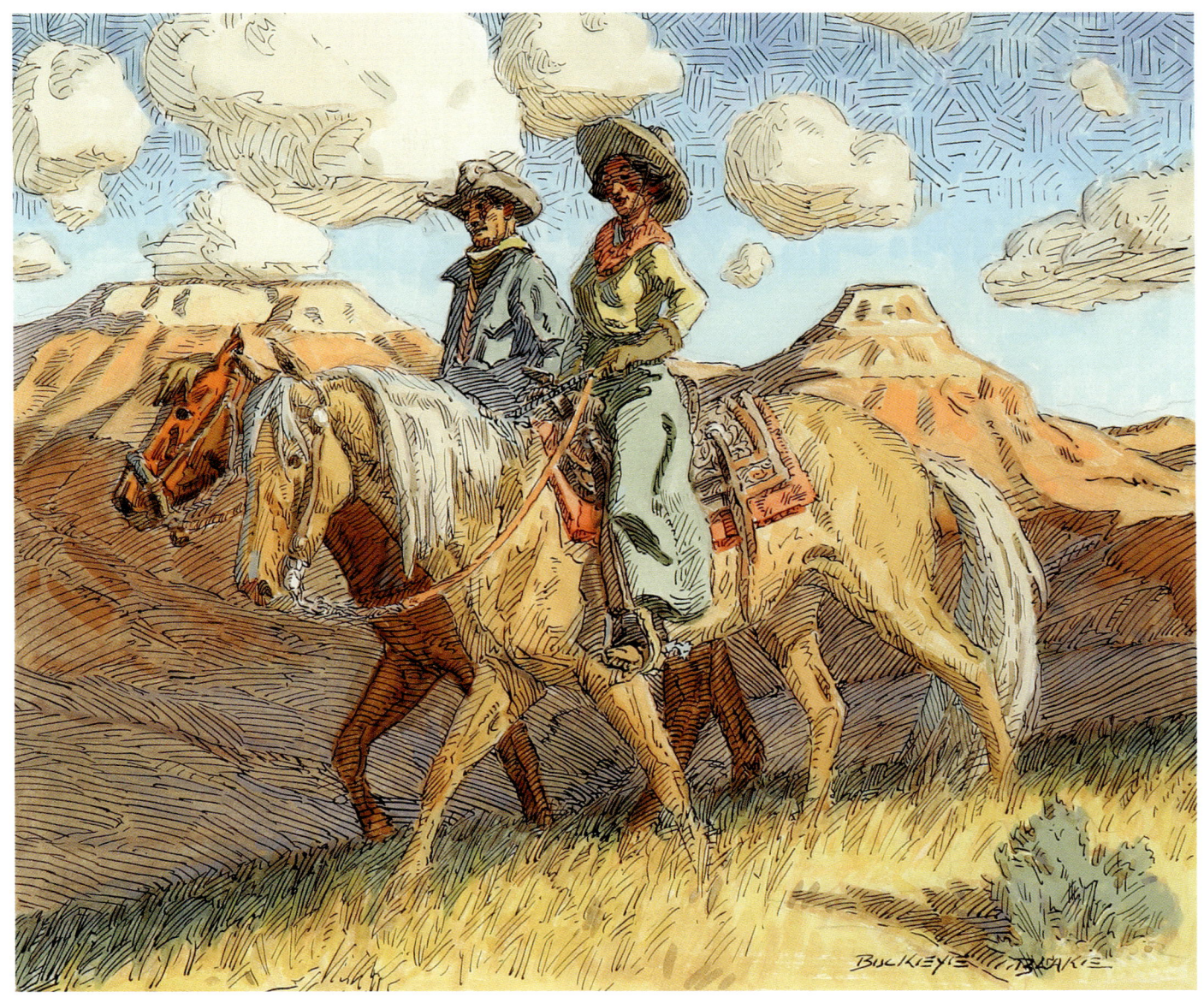

Arizona Romance

(Watercolor, 8" × 10.25", n.d.)

"I'm from a family of horse people. I've been around horses my entire life and it shows in my art. I still want to present the images I know so well from ranching and rodeo. And I want to show that courtship and love are part of that life too, as with these two in this picture."

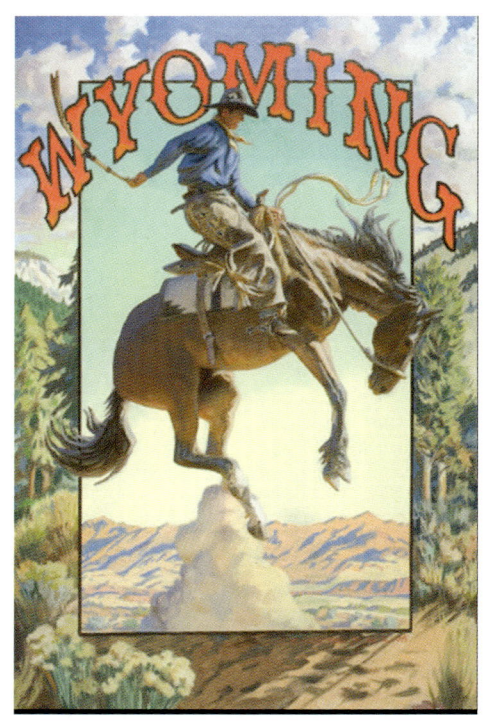

Wyoming

(Oil, 30″ × 40″, n.d.)

"If you've got a bucking horse exploding in front of a beautiful, big open landscape with pretty colors, you're trading a lot of stuff right there. No matter who's on the horse. That's why you want to put it on that wall by the icebox at home."

The JA Cavvy

(Oil, 15" × 30", n.d.)

"You see the motion, the action, and it's based on your whole life of being around horses and animals. There is a symmetry that you present to the viewer and it's all these horses turning and running together. The colors are mixed and muted by the dust and sun. And it's a moment that cannot be repeated in life."

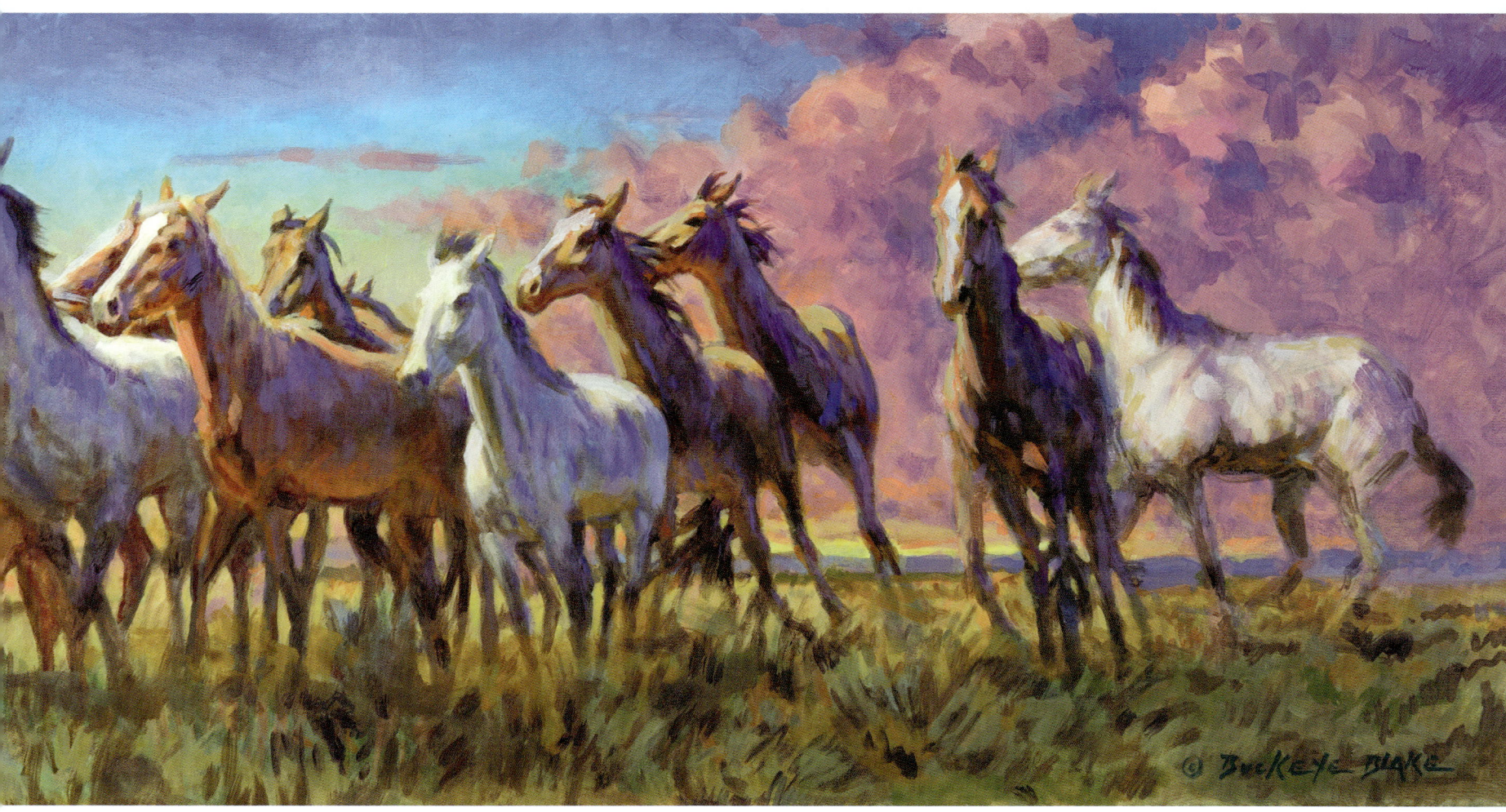

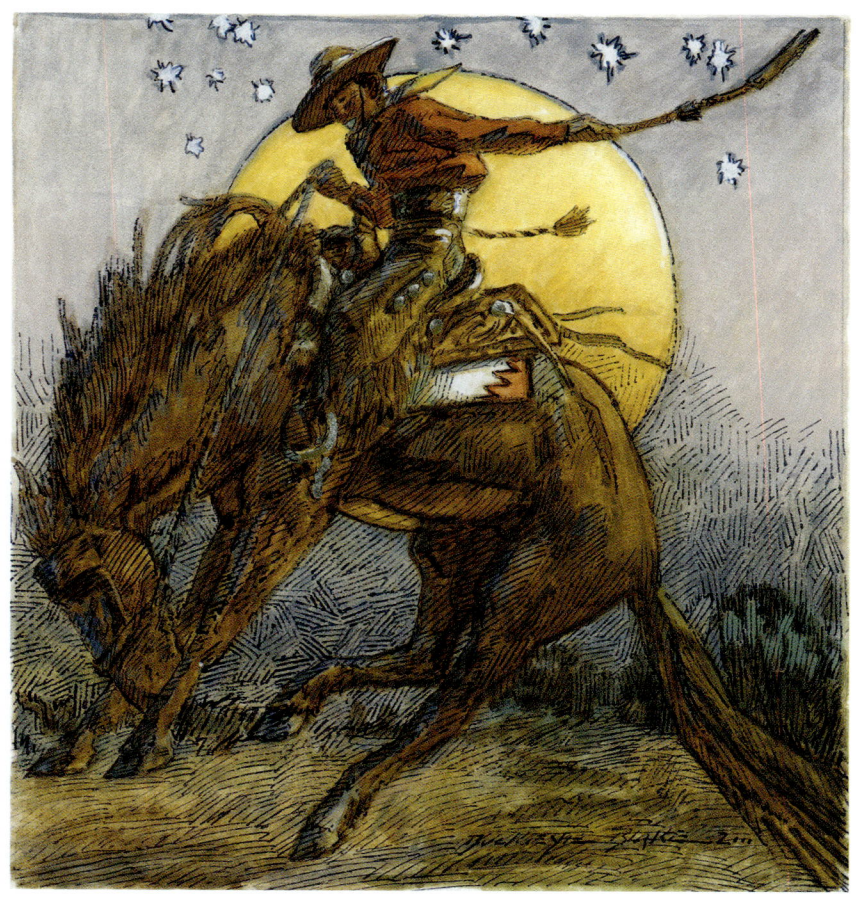

Cowboy Kid

(Watercolor, 10" × 9.75", n.d.)

"Being a horseman you put in that, you use that knowledge with each mark you make or each brushstroke. Your own emotions become part of the artwork. If you are feeling good and are interested in the story you are creating, then you end up with something that almost has a life of its own."

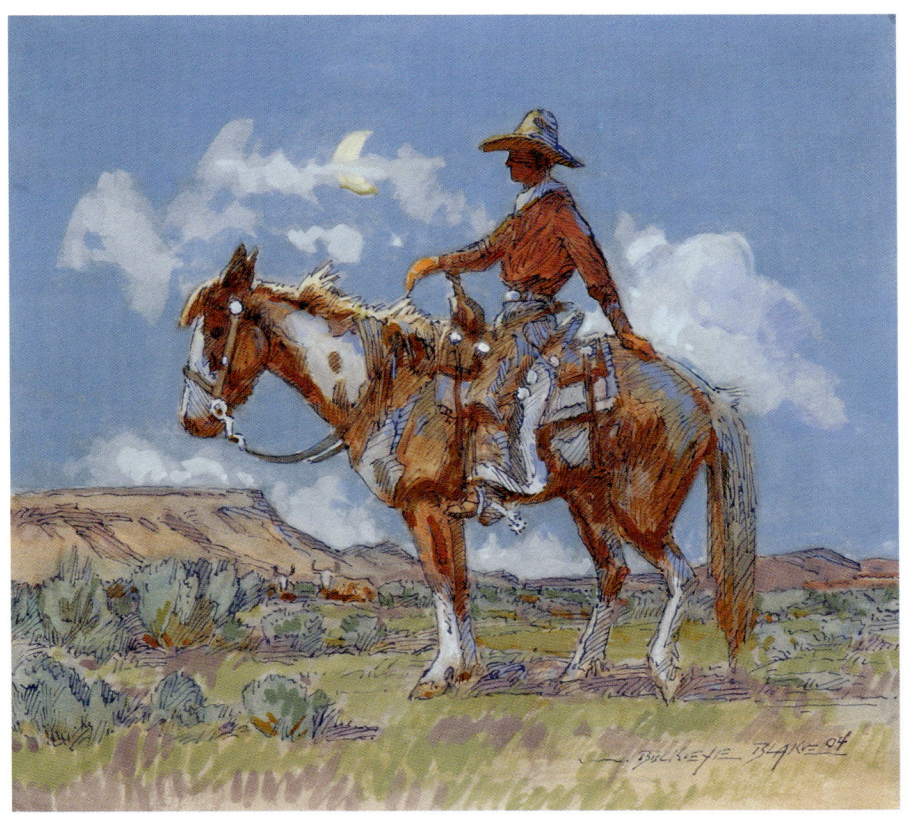

Pinto Moon

(Watercolor, n.s., n.d.)

"There are certain shapes or certain colors you use to set the scene, just like in a theater. Except you are the entire theater company, creating the characters, finding the emotion, making everything fit into something that draws in the audience."

Tim
Solliday

CHAPTER 11

Tim Solliday

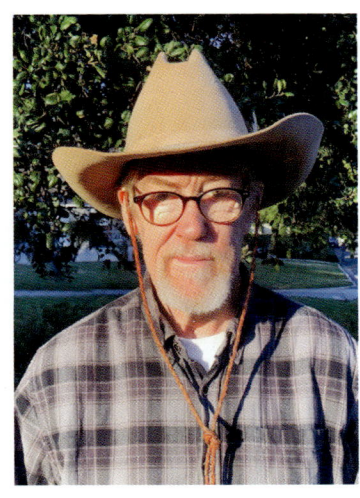

Tim Solliday's father was a technical illustrator for Douglas Aircraft in Southern California and was an inspiration for his son to pursue art. That job moved the Solliday family from Ottumwa, Iowa, Tim's birthplace, to Palos Verdes, California. He says his mother was also artistic but never really pursued art. Solliday grew up in the 1960s and found there was little traditional art training available to him. At the time, the art world was embracing anti-traditional and abstract avant-garde works, what he calls art that is not really art.

Solliday won an art competition when he was fourteen and later went on to study art at Long Beach City College. He dropped out of college when he found the courses did not teach the type of art he wanted to create. He was told that the works of artists such as Rockwell, Sargent, and others he admired as a young man were out of style and overshadowed by conceptual art.

Solliday wanted to learn to paint like Western artists Remington and Russell and many of the Taos artists who came later. As a result, he turned to illustrators and learned from that training. When he was in his twenties, while working as an apprentice at a billboard company, he met Theodore Lukits, a traditional painter using Impressionist principles, who was the founder of the Lukits Academy of Fine Art in Los Angeles. The work Solliday did on the large spaces of a billboard (usually 14 feet by 48 feet) taught him how to handle paint to create texture and depth. He also developed a strong work ethic. Most of the work was done using photographs projected onto the billboards, which created new challenges of using outdoor light.

Solliday was introduced to Lukits by the billboard company that for years had sent their young workers to the Lukits school to learn how to refine their artistic abilities. Solliday studied at the private training school near Beverly Hills in the Palisades area, learning a method of drawing from life called "drawing from the antique," a technique of learning to draw by making charcoal or pencil images of plaster or marble statuary and traditional methods of art proportion. Lukits had trained at the Art Institute of Chicago before moving to California and became one of Hollywood's premier portrait painters, painting images of silent film actresses and modern movie stars. Solliday said Lukits introduced him to the works of traditional Western art, landscape art, plein air painters, and more who had been forgotten by the mid-twentieth century. It was during this time that Solliday developed an aim of achieving a style of painting like that of William "Buck" Dunton and Ernest Martin Hennings.

Lukits taught Solliday the use of light and color and instructed him on how to use devices to copy outdoor light at different times of day and in different weather conditions. He learned about using "broken color," a technique that uses adjacent colors to accent other colors, giving the illusion of dark and light. He picked up the practice of using gray colors in the manner of Frank Tenney Johnson to highlight the brighter colors. This led Solliday into a career of plein air landscape painting.

Solliday's first show was a plein air landscape show in Pasadena, which led to representation in galleries there along Colorado Boulevard and created a buying audience in San Bernadino, San Marino, and Beverly Hills. Solliday became an important artist in California landscape painting with his use of pastels and large canvases. This renown built a wealthy clientele for Solliday's landscapes, but he missed painting figures and horses. He produced California landscapes but always had an interest in horses and images of the American West. Solliday would eventually switch to the images that held his heart, the Western genre, with some

misgivings. He thought he might lose his clientele from the plein air market, but they stayed with him.

I love the West, so I always wanted to do [it], but I had a good training in anatomy, and if you can understand human anatomy, [you can] understand horse anatomy even [though] the horse anatomy is difficult. It is no more difficult than the human anatomy—human anatomy is actually . . . the most complicated anatomical knowledge that you can have.

Solliday's work was accepted into some noted Western art shows and he began taking home first and second prizes. He was able to establish his work in galleries in Arizona, particularly Scottsdale, which was the focal place for Western art at the time. He had quit the billboard business by then to design posters and book illustrations and to create art for film companies while trying to pursue his own art full time. Art magazines noticed his talent, which made him known to a much larger audience of art lovers and galleries.

The good thing about collectors is that they introduce you to other collectors, without you knowing it, and other collectors come into their homes to see your paintings there and then they want to become a collector. So, I'm always adding collectors and it seems to still be happening, to a certain degree.

Solliday realized that collectors trust the gallery owners and they will look online to see recent acquisitions. He shares that some of his sales have happened this way, with people checking online to see new pieces. He believes he has a reputation to which his work continually measures up.

Solliday looks at the works of other horse painters and photographers to study movement and color. He considers what makes a horse look stiff or seems to have an awkward movement. He believes he has learned more about the movement of horses from the artworks of Hennings than from other images. Solliday has gained a thorough knowledge of human and equine anatomy and believes—as do most artists—that the better an artist knows the anatomy of a horse and uses that knowledge, the better the image and the better the composition. He claims, "I had several horses for many years and rode like crazy. I was drawing a lot of my horses, my own horses from life."

Travel is important in the creation process for Solliday. He said he used to spend two to three months on the road gathering reference material and painting landscapes. He took annual trips to the Southwest or to forests. He visited rodeos, ranches, and cowboy gatherings. His notes were a combination of drawings and photography that eventually built up a backlog of material he still uses. He also collects books, magazines, illustrations, and prints for ideas.

Even though a lot of the stories and type of things have been done before, they are pretty universal and they last—they span through time. And if you are a good artist and you have a good sense of design and composition, you can take advantage of a lot of the old worn-out kind of stories, but you put them into your own way by showing them in a way that maybe somebody else would not do.

Solliday begins with a small blank piece of paper and a series of scribbled ideas. Using that beginning, he creates studies that he condenses to one-line drawings. There is usually very little landscape unless he has produced a strange or unusual piece of landscape. He begins putting the colors together in a color sketch, doing two to three sketches, and picking one as the main image. He creates a couple of painting thumbnails with small marks of color for reference. Everything exists in a context of tonal value of lightness and darkness.

The composition and design of each of Solliday's artworks relies tremendously on the clothing and costumes worn in the scene. That emphasis on apparel, combined with the landscape, is used to create scenes with depth and detail not only of the mountains and trees but also of the beadwork, boots, and hats. The people and horses set within the landscapes show an interaction of the magnetism of all the elements used in the artwork.

The storyline of friendship, injury, and love is universal, but Solliday tells these stories in his own style that permeates each brushstroke or mark of a pastel. He attributes this incorporation of natural elements into human stories to his training and work in plein air art. All details aside, it is Solliday's belief that showing movement really defines his style. He says, "I get most of my inspiration on horses from other artists, you know, seeing these other great artists, painting wonderful horses in movement."

Solliday's works are featured in the permanent collections of several museums including the Briscoe Western Art Museum and the National Museum of Wildlife Art. His works have received many awards including first place in the California Art Club Annual Gold Medal Exhibition and first and third place in the Laguna Plein-Air Invitational (2001 and 2000). Solliday is an invited artist at several prestigious Western art shows including the Masters of the American West Exhibition at the Autry National Center in Los Angeles and the Prix de West at the National Cowboy & Western Heritage Museum in Oklahoma City.

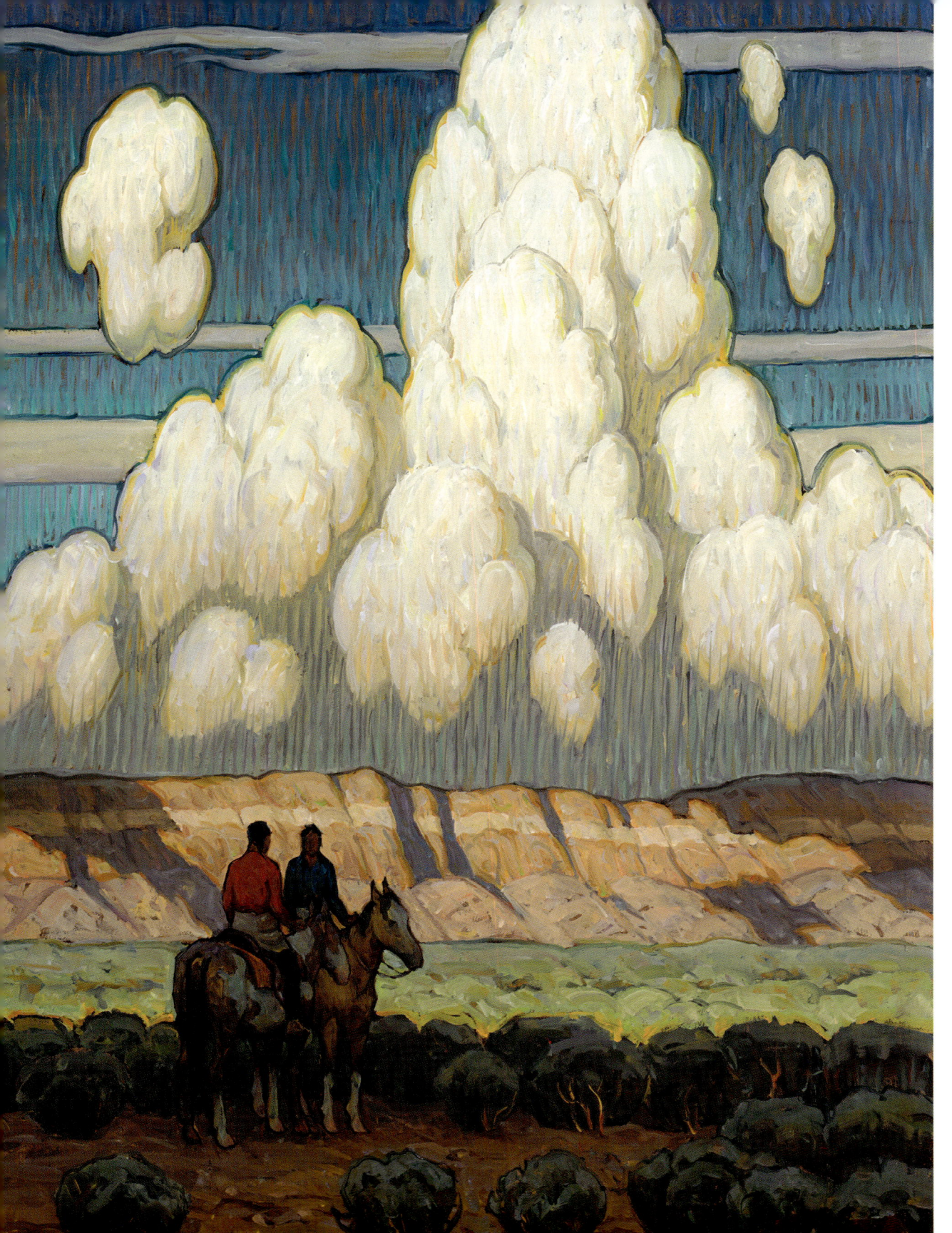

High Clouds and Shadows

(Watercolor, 24″ × 18″, 2015)

"I love the work of N. C. Wyeth and how he used clouds in so many of his pictures. Clouds can have a personality and that is what I wanted to show in this piece. It is a good Western subject and by adding two Indians in the shadows it gives it a mystery that adds interest to the whole scene. Clouds always give a chance for great light and shade. That's always a good element in this type of picture."

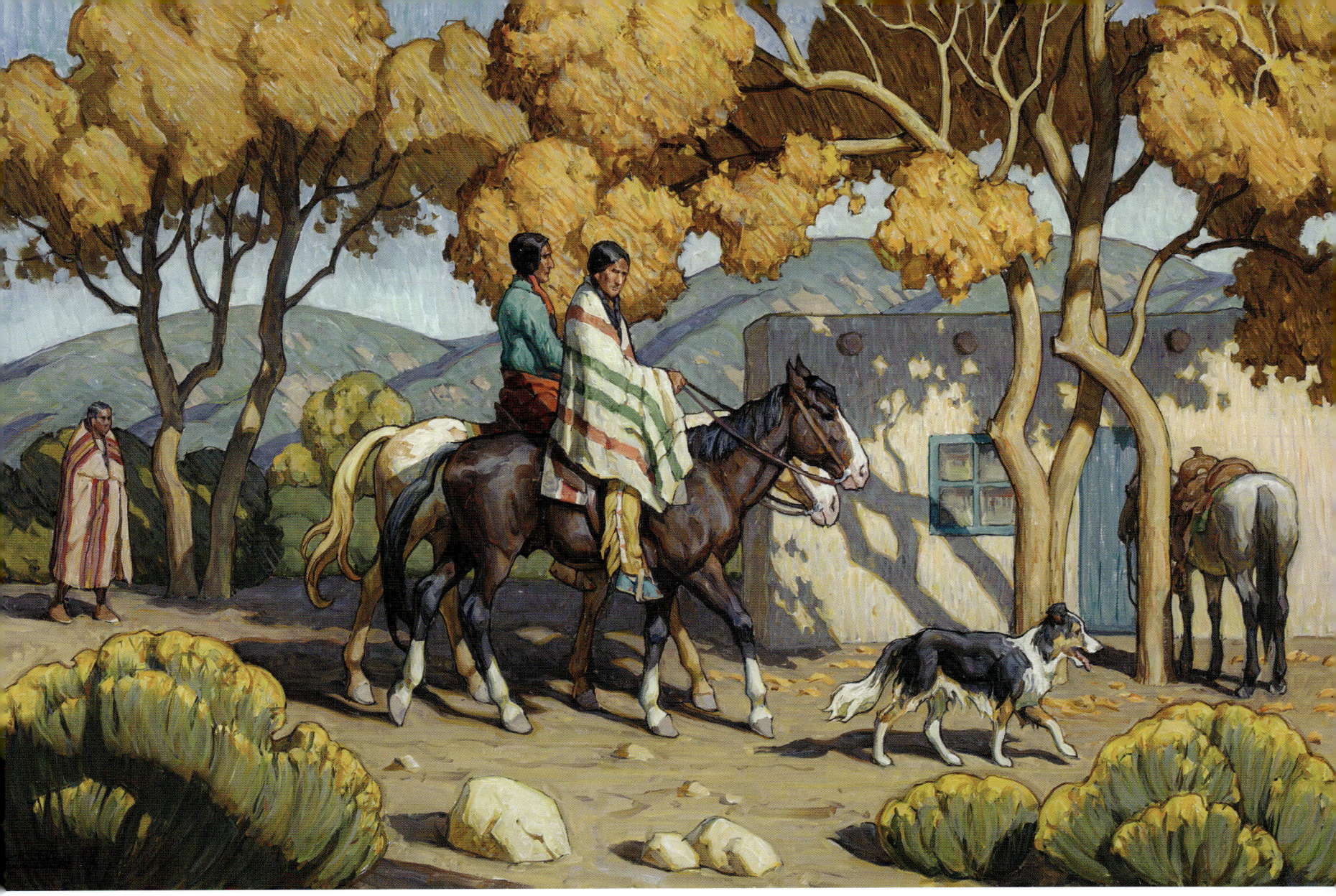

Taos Colors

(Oil on linen, 30" × 46", 2014)

"The colors of the Taos area are what makes many artists want to paint it. This is a typical early twentieth-century Taos scene, and all the figures show a feeling of contentment in their surroundings which colors the whole image. The adobe hut reflects the blue of the sky, mixing in with the shadows."

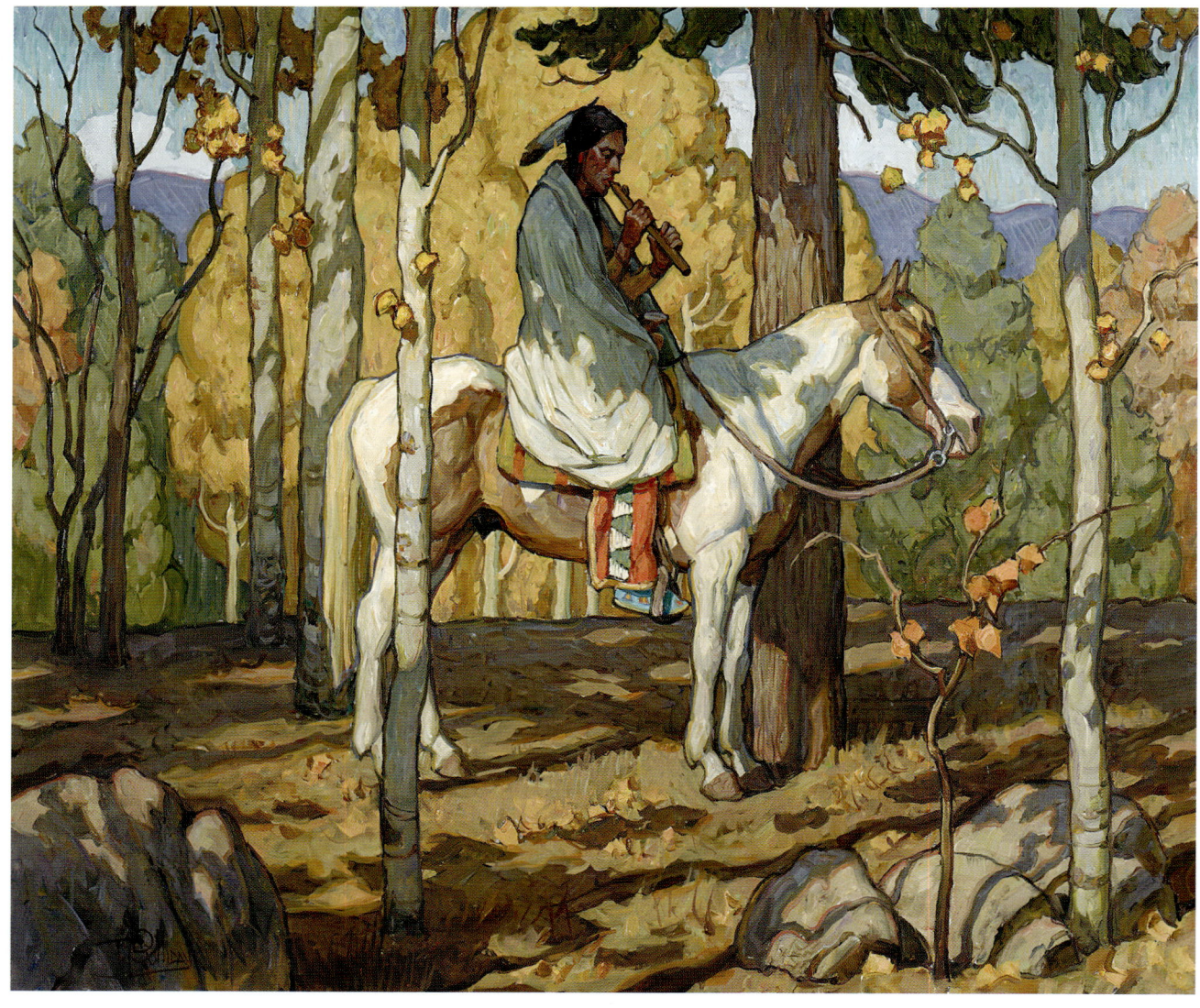

Woodland Song

(Oil on linen, 25" × 30", 2017)

"When people ask me why I paint Indians, this type of scene is one of the reasons. This shows a poetic spirit between man and nature. The Indians I paint tend to exist in this kind of state. I like Cowboys, but the interaction between man and nature is more pronounced with Indians. One of the challenges with this painting involved the white of the robe and the white of the horse. This is another example of reflected sky colors in the shadows."

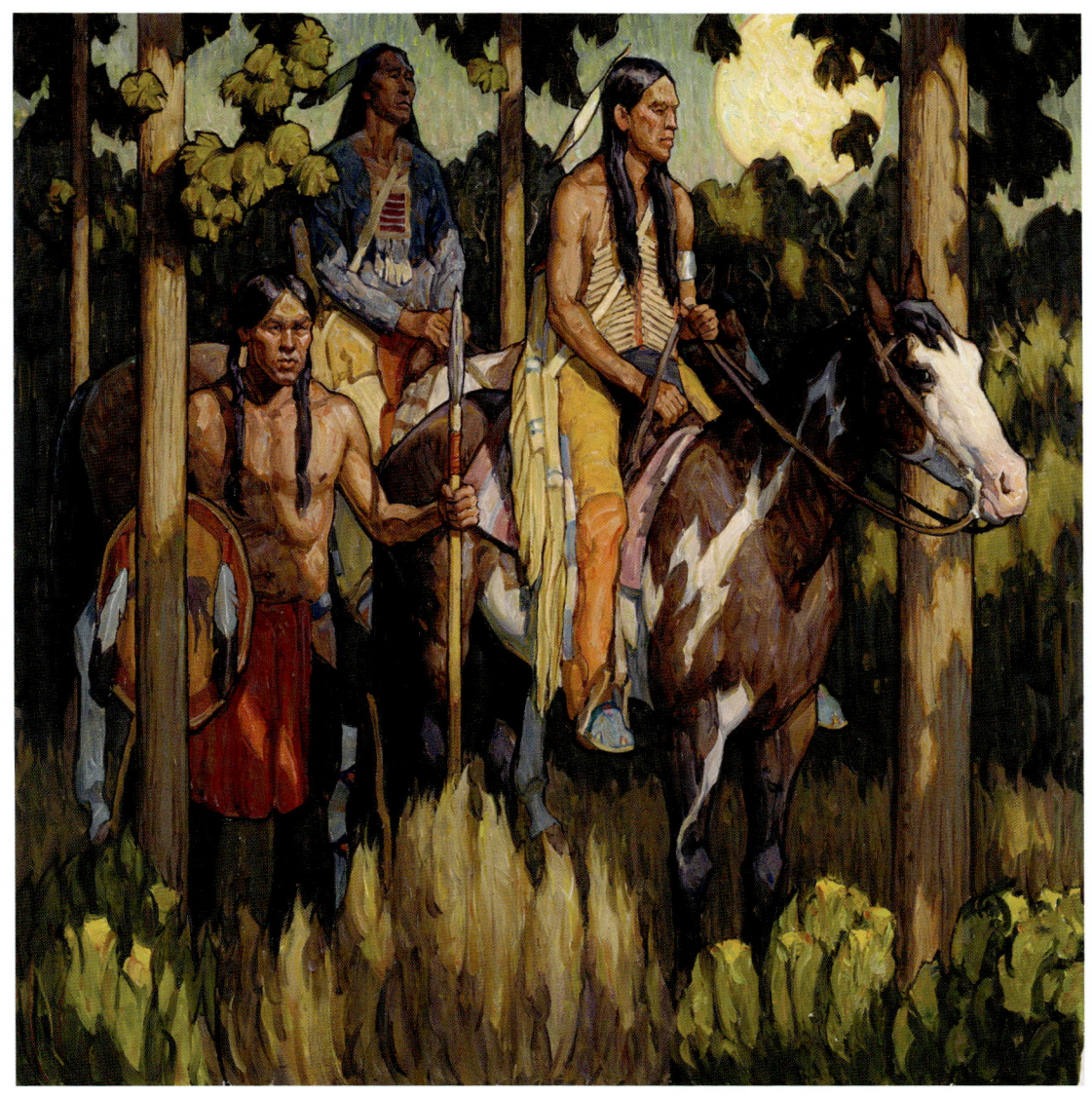

Colors of the West

(Oil on linen, 30″ × 20″, 2014)

"This picture is a good follow-up to *Woodland Song*. It shows the moon rise as the last rays of the sun light up the braves in the woods. This is a good example of costume research and color just before sunset. Whenever I can I like to use the moon—it has a poetic feel. Color and poetry combine to show the spirit that makes the West such a fascinating place."

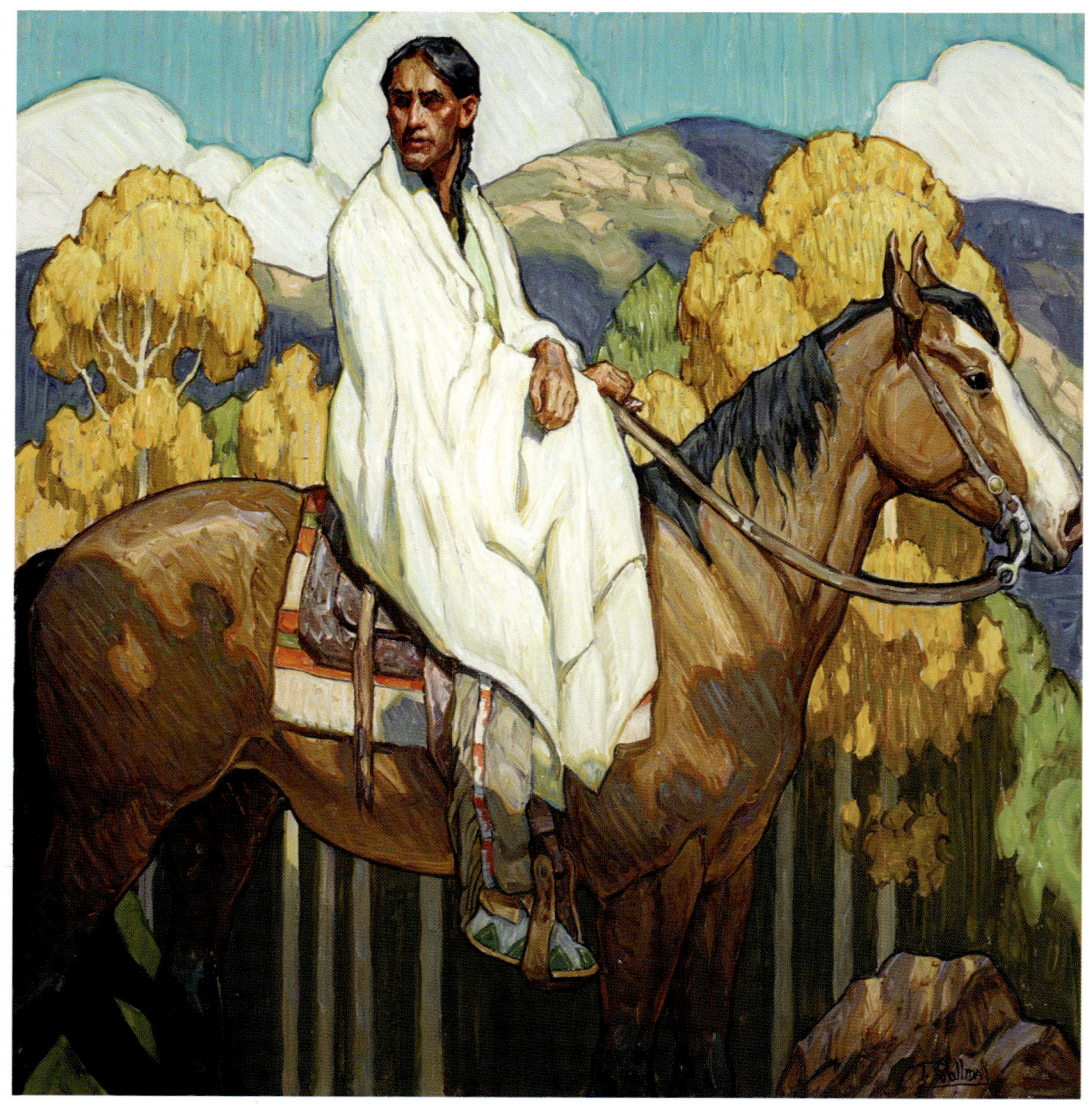

Majestic Hilltop

(Oil on linen, 30″ × 36″, 2016)

"This is another good depiction of a man and his surroundings sitting high on a hilltop. He feels the beauty of the land and looks at the panorama of hills, mountains, trees, and clouds. This shows outdoor light in a patchwork canvas. I wanted to keep your eye on shapes that are enhanced by color and light. All these elements work together to make the word 'majestic' have a significant meaning."

Packing In

(Oil on linen, 16″ × 24″, 2015)

"The old idea of partners was on my mind with this painting: the cowboy alone with his dog and his horse in a desert landscape with the bright sky and big clouds in the background, emphasizing the lonely life of a working ranch hand. I wanted a very intense blue sky against the clouds. I'm showing a remote point of view that you would get in a movie."

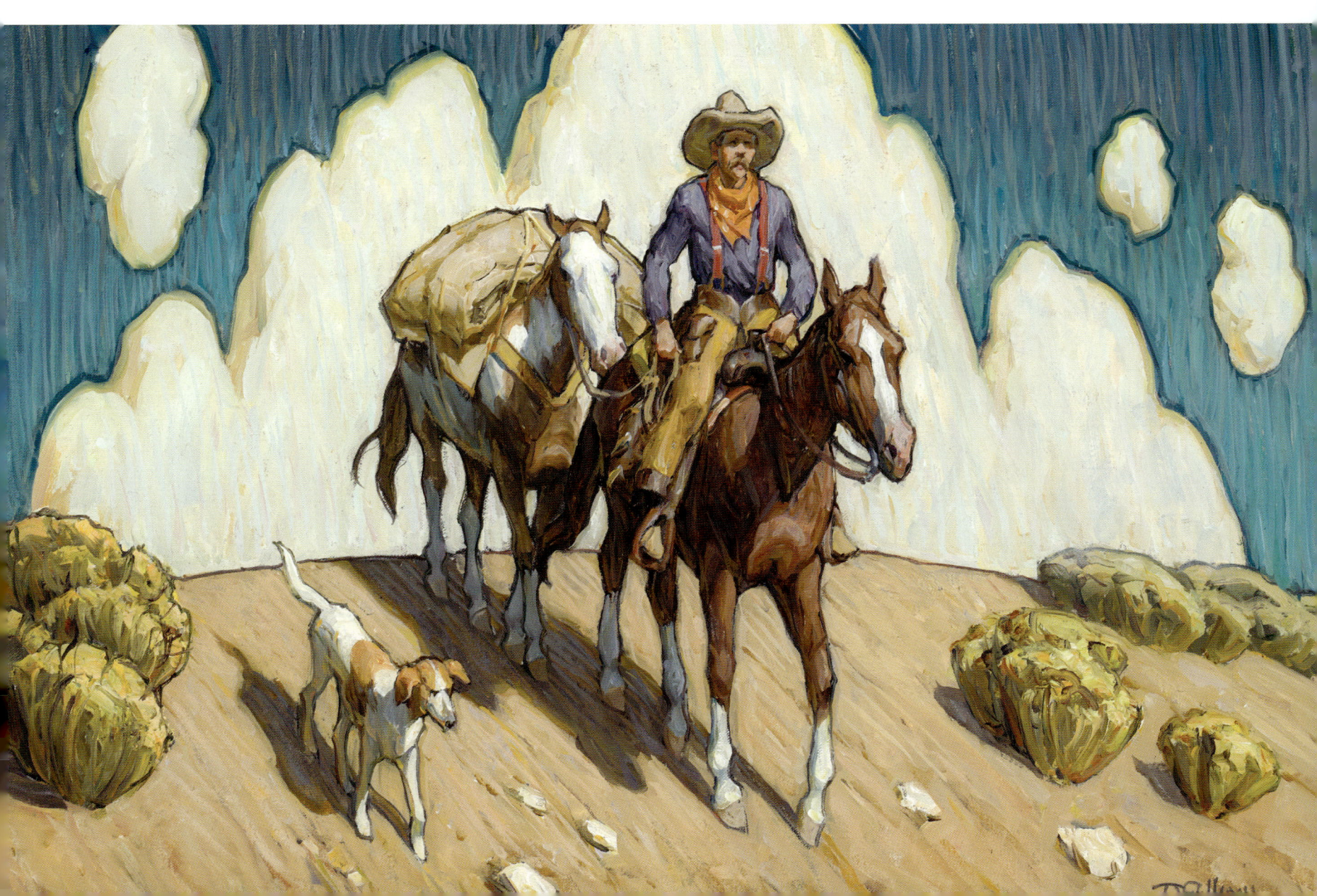

Billy
Schenck

CHAPTER 12

Billy Schenck

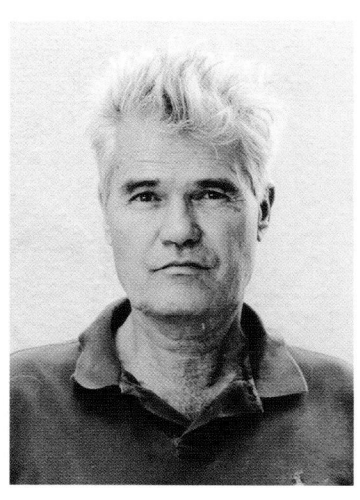

B illy Schenck is an Ohio native. He grew up north of Columbus in a rural area where there were five other houses belonging to uncles and aunts. The closest uncle raised Thoroughbred racehorses, and these were Schenck's introduction to horses. Schenck's preference for Western culture and images began in his childhood, springing not only from being around his uncle's horses but also from watching TV Western series characters like Hopalong Cassidy, Roy Rogers, and Gene Autry, just like so many others of his generation. In Central Ohio the Westerns were shown weekdays between 4 and 5 p.m. and hosted by "The

Wrangler" on local television. Schenck's father died early in his life and his mother married The Wrangler, who also had horses.

Schenck grew up with cattle, pigs, chickens, and horses all around him. He spent summers in Wyoming where he grew to love the high desert, local rodeos, and cowboy culture. From 1965 to 1967, Schenck studied at the Columbus College of Art & Design. While at the Columbus College, he saw an exhibition of the Andy Warhol Campbell's Soup Cans series and became inspired to see more of Warhol's work as soon as he could. Fortuitously, Schenck ran into a friend from back home in Columbus who told him he could get him a job with Warhol. When Schenck met Warhol, he was put to work help-ing with the lighting for the Velvet Underground, an acid rock band, which, coincidentally, was managed by Andy Warhol. This job allowed Schenck to become part of the New York art scene of the 1960s.

Schenck eventually returned to the Columbus College of Art & Design where his new ideas and styles were rejected by his college professors. He was dismissed from the college because of his attitude. His artistic style then was not Pop or Warhol-influenced but was, according to Schenck, raw and unsophisticated emulations of artist Francis Bacon. As a result, he transferred to the Kansas City Art Institute in 1967 and graduated with a BFA in 1969.

Post-graduation, Schenck moved back to New York City to pursue an art career. Thus began years of traveling back and forth between the Big Apple and Wyoming, where he loved the landscape and imagery. Schenck had been going to Wyoming every summer since he was a boy. He still likes to spend time there.

During the summer of 1970, Schenck began painting Western imagery from projected black and white movie stills. He drew his inspirations from watching Spaghetti Westerns made by Sergio Leone. Schenck thought these images to be light years beyond anything Hollywood had produced. He wanted to do to Western art what Leone had done with Western film, which was to give an entirely new look to an old genre. He was still going to Wyoming every summer and continued to do that while he lived in New York.

Schenck developed a new style of art that he referred to as photorealism married to Pop art. By turning projected black and white movie stills into a "paint-by-number system" (Schenck's description) he began to slowly realize he was producing a new generation of Pop art but with Western subject matter. This was happening during 1970–1971. He recalls, "I did quit painting emulations of Francis Bacon and began to appreciate both Warhol and [Roy] Lichtenstein to a much larger degree."

Schenck also took up residence in New York in a SoHo loft studio. His timing and luck were perfect to find himself there just in time to be part of the evolving Pop art movement. He was influenced by many of the artists he met there, though he continued to work with the black and white movie stills. In October 1972, when he was twenty-four years old, the Warren Benedek Gallery in SoHo gave Schenck his first solo show, which sold out before the show opened. After leaving New York, he moved to Wyoming. In time, Schenck decided he wanted a different landscape and moved on to Arizona, where he would become a winter resident for the next twenty-one years.

In Arizona, Schenck, Fritz Scholder, and Luis Jiménez broke out as the most prominent contemporary artists of the time who, using Western imagery, presented a counterpoint to traditional ideas of art imagery. Schenck was showcased in art shows in France, Italy, and Switzerland and in American museums, with his work going into the collections of major corporations including American Airlines, Sony, and Wells Fargo. His Western images gave Schenck a distinction as an artist separate from everyone else in a time when Pop art was setting the stage for contemporary Western art. He was still traveling back to Wyoming on a regular basis and shooting his own images at the rodeos there. Schenck eventually moved to Wyoming after 1974, where he expanded his imagery to match the landscape.

Painting color versions of movie stills in what he describes as a "paint-by-number process taken to the most extreme degree anybody ever bothered to try at all," Schenck developed a style relying on light and shadows to create a strong contrast in his works. He applies the same process when painting horses. He uses dark patterns to bring out the main focus of each work. However, it is the layering in his paintings that really stands out as his signature style.

Over the next five decades, Schenck perfected a hard-edge style and a compositional formula using multiple photographic images taken from a variety of sources, including movie stills, images appropriated from pulp fiction novels, popular culture magazines, and his own photographs. He combines photorealism and Pop art using Western landscapes, cowboys, cowgirls, and Native Americans as his subjects.

I was interested in showing a kind of system of patterns of shadows. I would drop shadows into straight black . . . and I would then separate the shadows with two or three colors and maybe one or two colors on the high contrast side. There might be four or five or six colors just in the shadow of a horse. So my palette will have maybe fifty, sixty, or seventy colors in a more complex pattern. I think my signature style is a marriage between photorealism and Pop within the paint-by-number process.

I try to capture emotion, period. I mean, that's my huge goal—to make these paintings compelling and not boring. I know it's going to have an emotional content.

Schenck began riding bareback and saddle broncs in rodeos during his summers in Wyoming: "I just completely got obsessed and hooked into the whole lifestyle. I never could get rodeo out of my blood." He keeps several horses on his property along with different saddles, blankets, and equipment just as if he were shooting a movie but without actually filming. He sometimes borrows horses of different colors than the ones he owns so that he can vary the images. For Schenck, the horse is part of the narrative of his paintings, not just part of the scenery. He says, "I tend to paint paints more often, but sometimes what I do is just turn a horse into a paint." In his works, shadows are very important.

Schenck uses imagery reminiscent of the old 1920s and 1930s Western magazine covers and transforms them into hard-edged, flat paintings. He demonstrates the influences of Lichtenstein, Warhol, and N. C. Wyeth in each painting. Maynard Dixon's painting showed him how to do stunning cloudscapes and mesas. Western movie stills are reflected in his images as something familiar, yet not.

Today, Schenck lives and works in Santa Fe, New Mexico. He has been featured in many prestigious solo and group exhibitions across the United States and in magazines such as *Southwest Art*, *Western Art Collector*, and *Fine Art Connoisseur*. His American West is what he's seen beginning with the classic Western films.

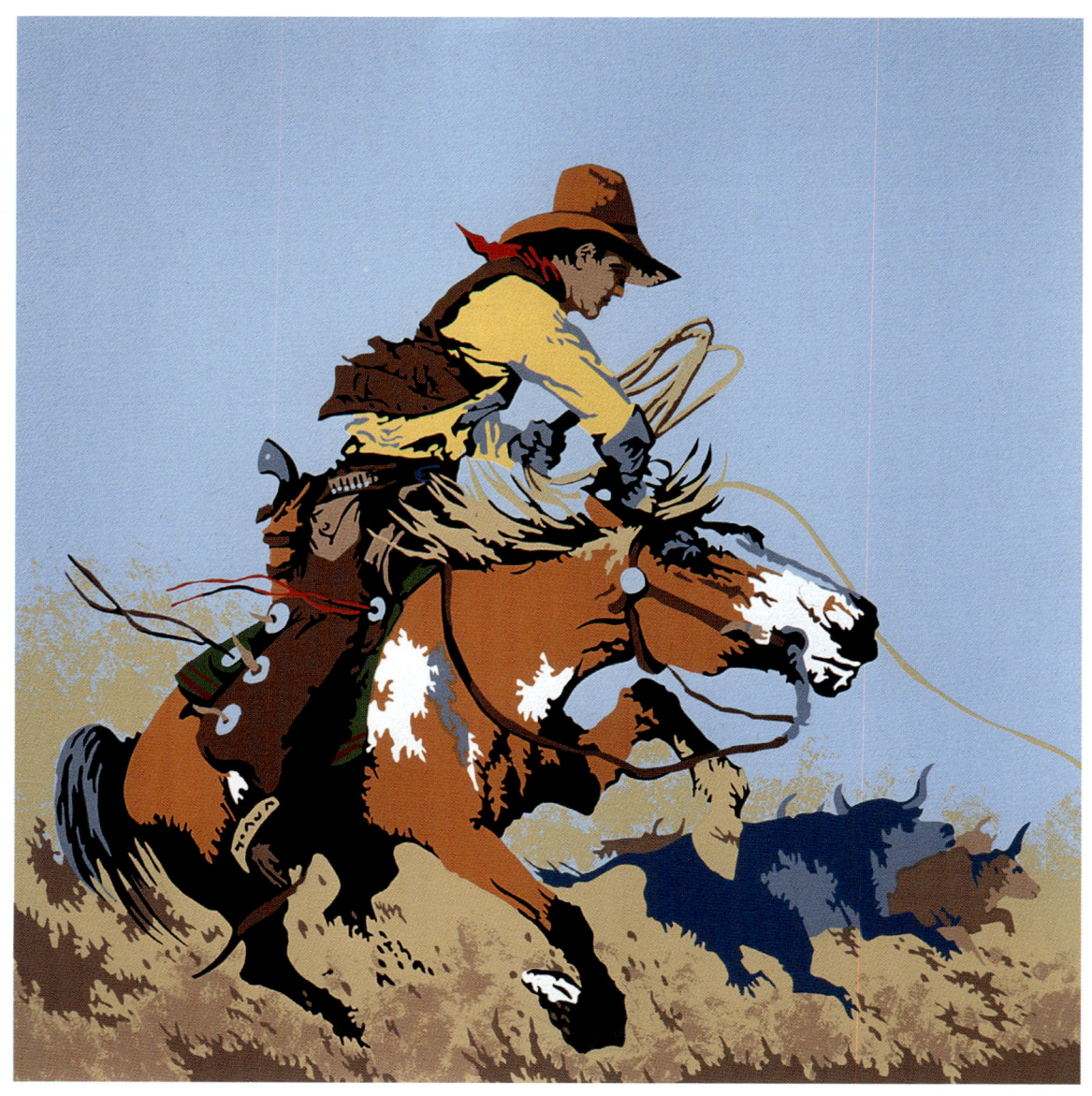

Waco

(Color serigraph,
53.34" × 53.98", 1981)

"This was the front cover illustration for *Ace High* magazine (1927). This was one of my first take-offs on the old pulp Western magazines that were really popular between the two world wars."

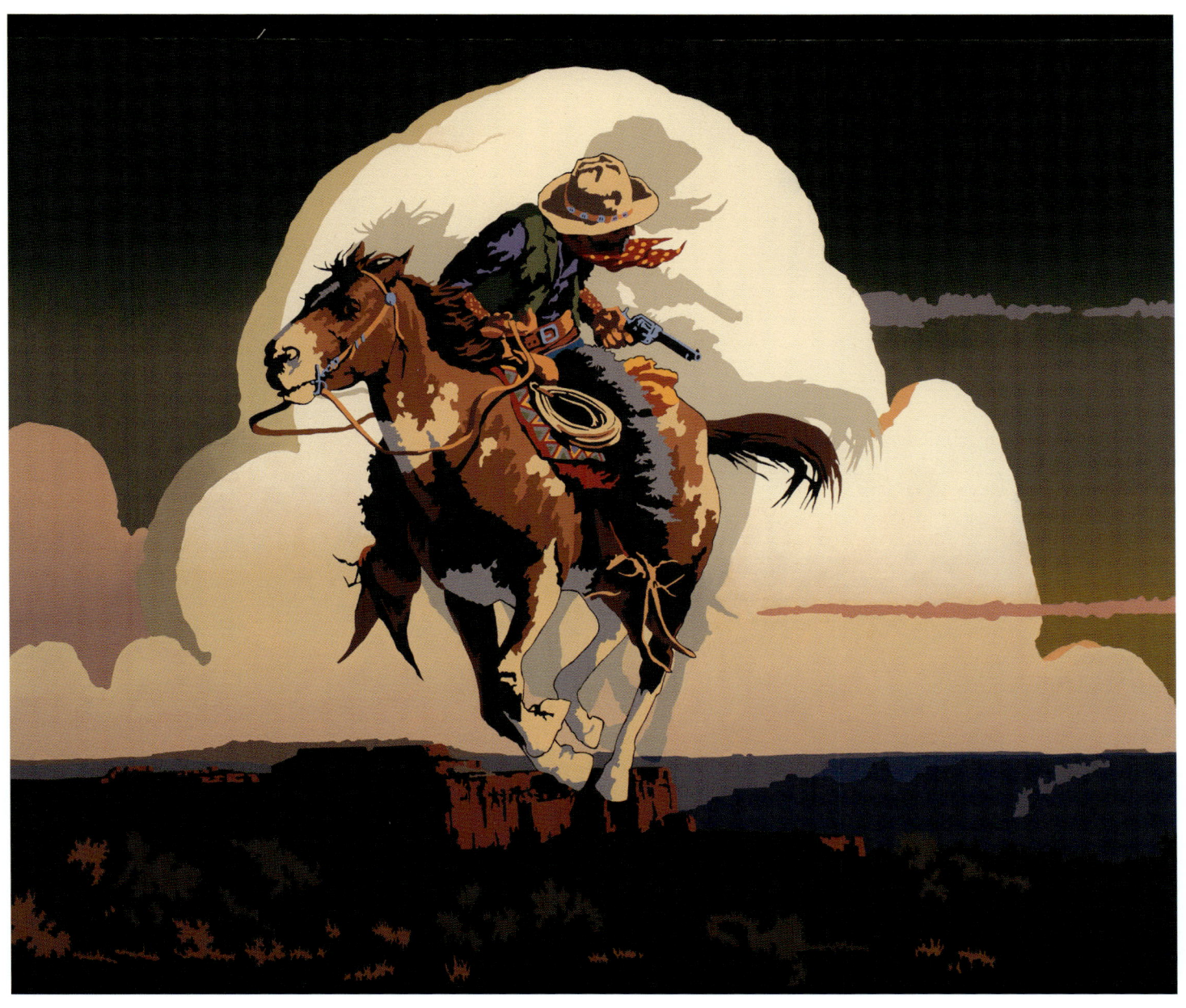

Blood on the Horizon

(Oil on canvas, 40" × 50", 2014)

"This painting was a takeoff on a 1919 painting by William R. Leigh. I put
the cowboy in the sky above Canyonlands, Utah."

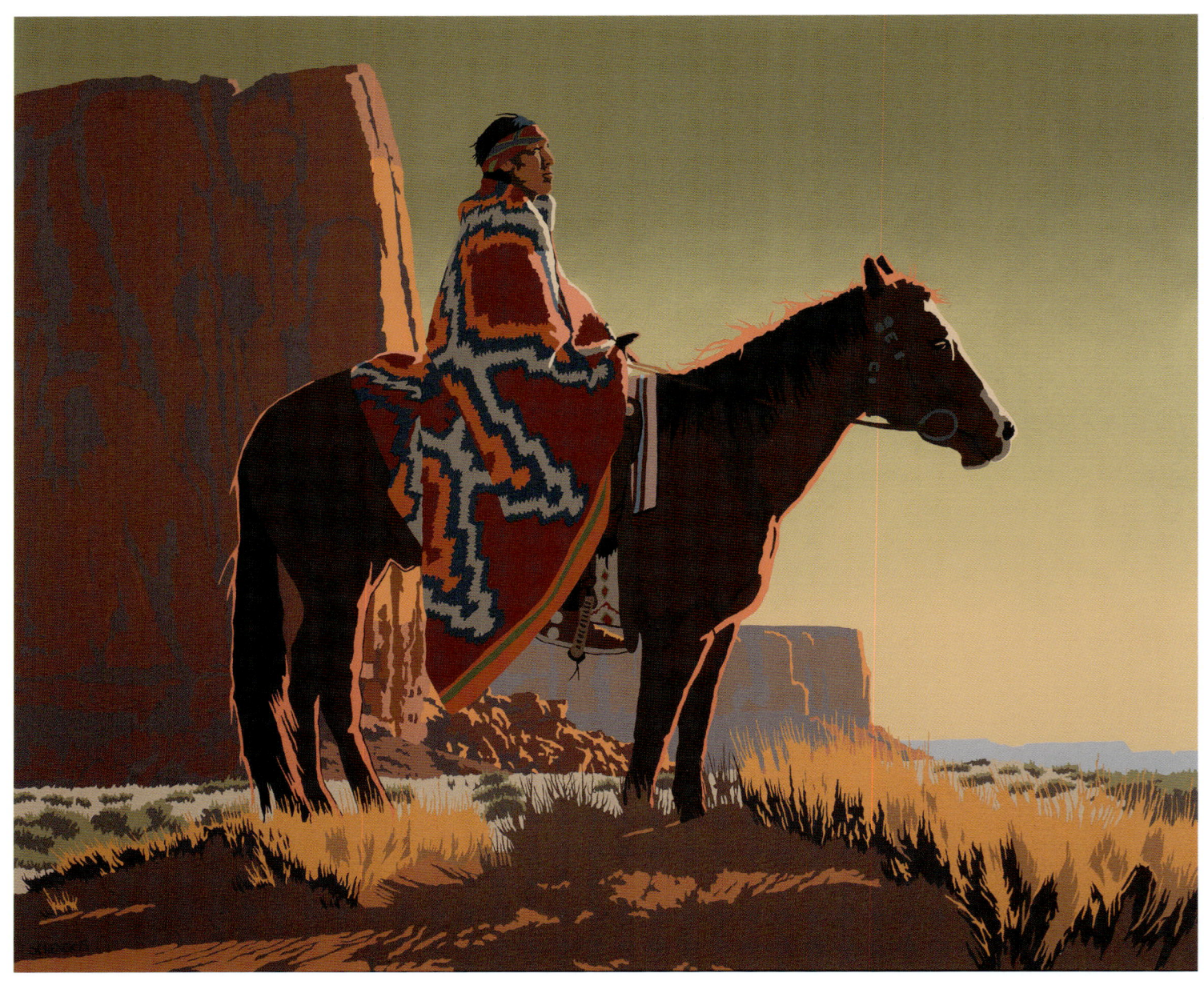

Respite in the Evening

(Oil on canvas, 40" × 50", 2015)

"This is a San Felipe Pueblo Indian who lives in Santa Fe. He has been in lots of my paintings for the past thirteen years. The horse was mine, an old Quarter Horse who had chased many cows over his career."

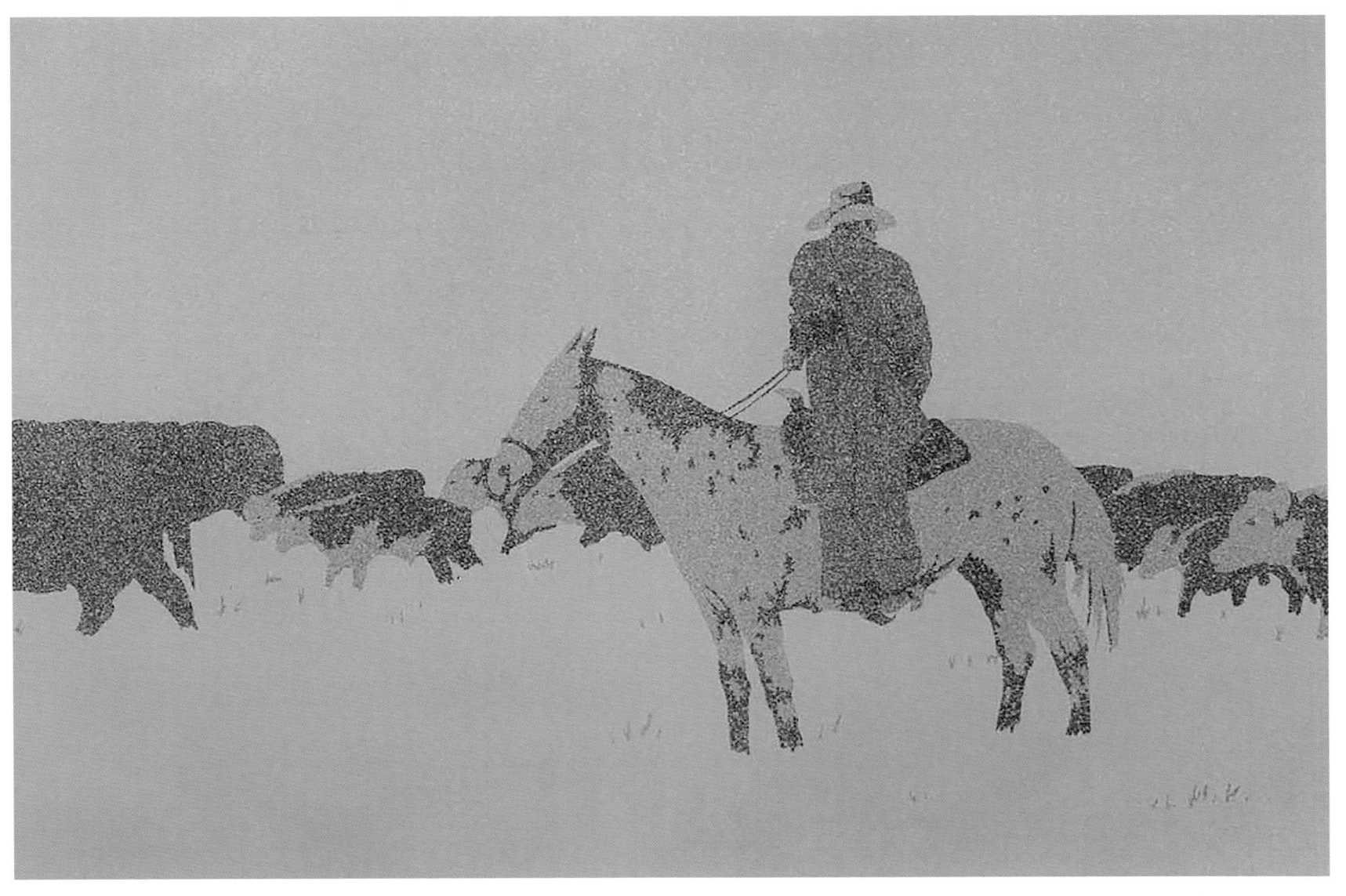

Spring Drive

(Serigraph, 24″ × 38″, 1980)

"This is me when I was thirty-one years old and I am riding
my knucklehead Appaloosa, Lyle."

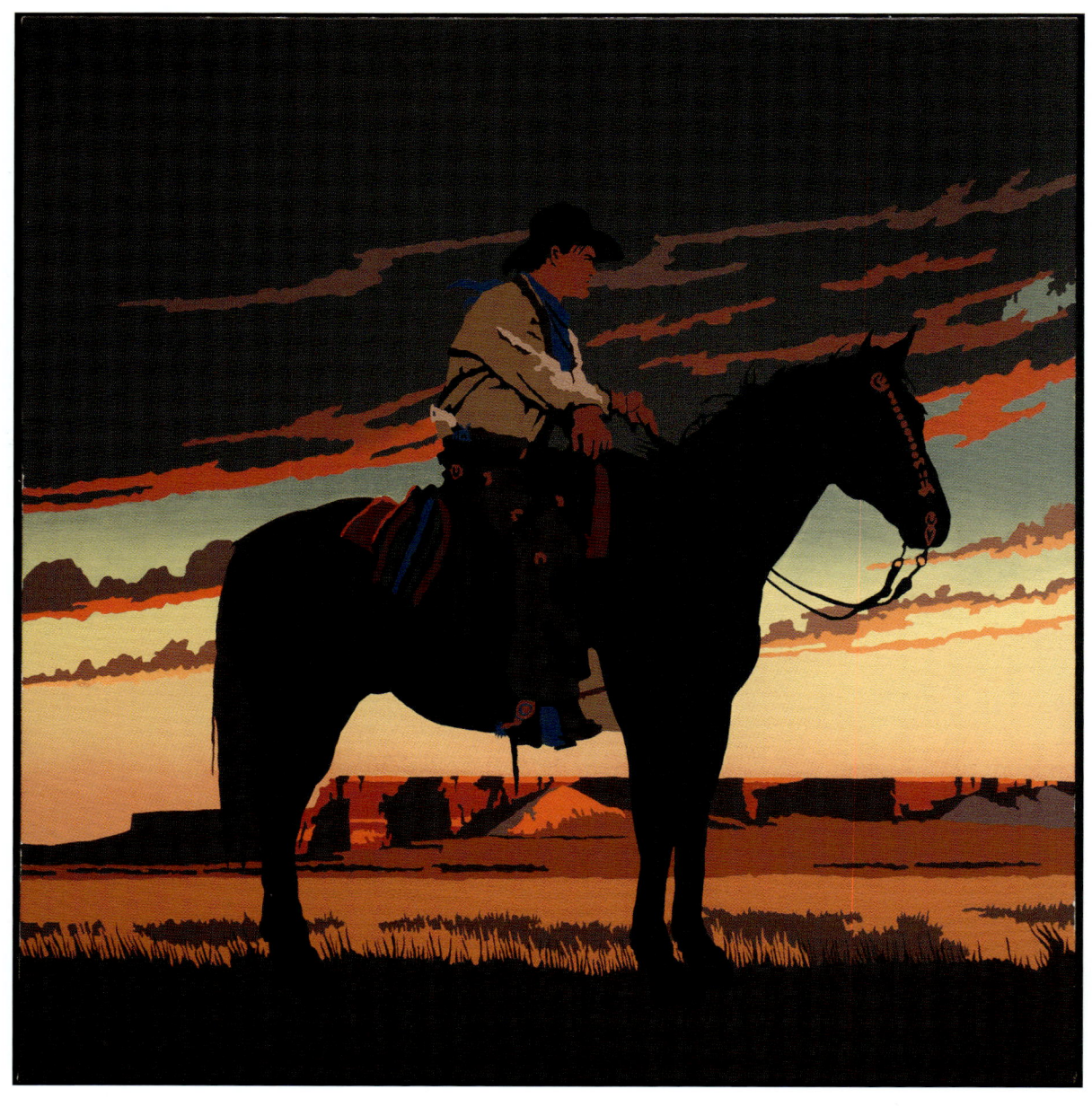

Where Have All the Cattle Gone

(Oil on canvas, 30″ × 30″, 2013)

"This is a self-portrait with one of my horses."

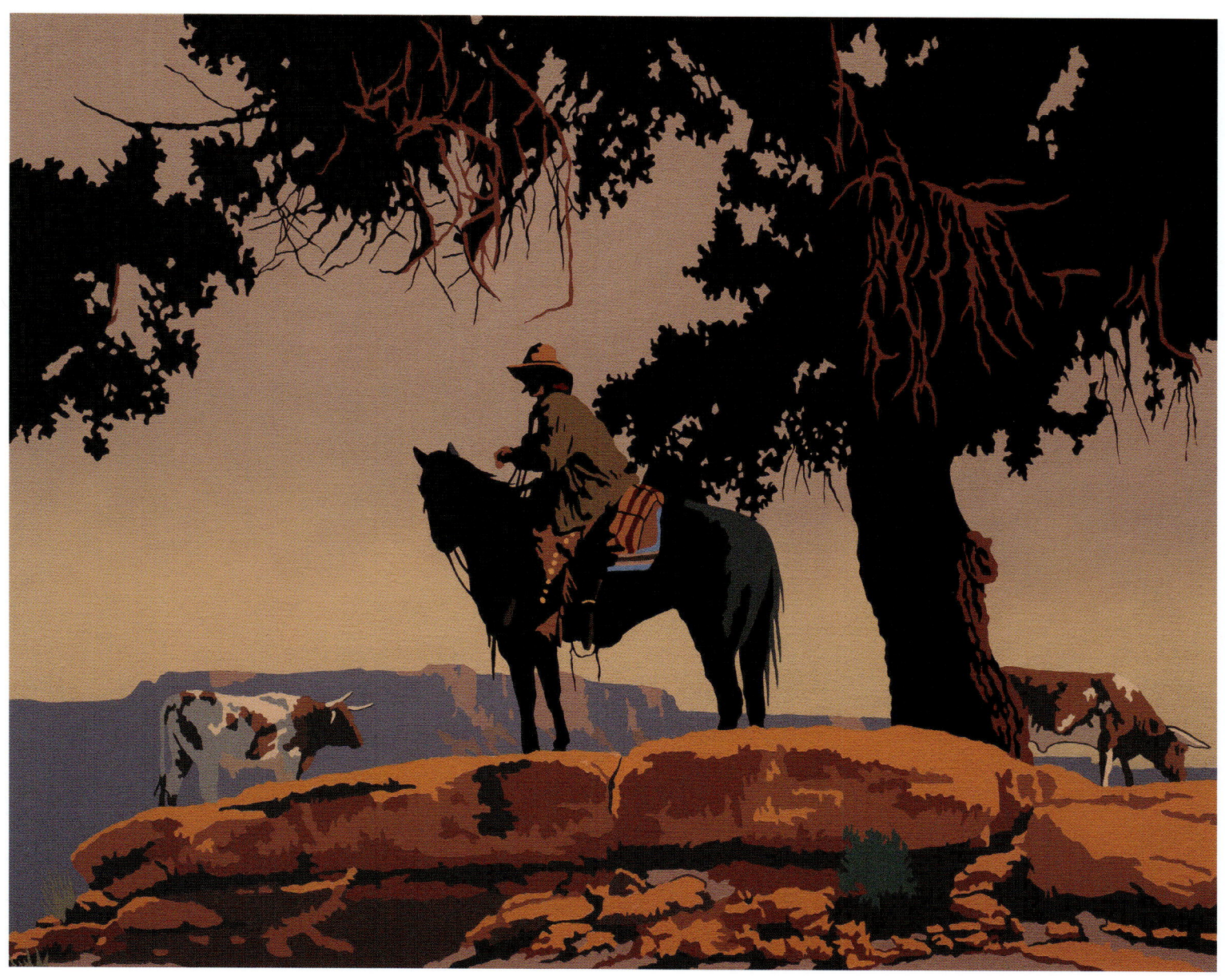

Winslow Ridge

(Oil on canvas, 22″ × 28″, 2015)

"I met this fellow in 1988 on a movie set starring Kris Kristofferson. The guy was a wrangler
for the movie *The Tracker*. I signed autographs on the set while driving my pink 1958 Cadillac."

PART 2

Photography

Barbara Van Cleve

CHAPTER 13

Barbara Van Cleve

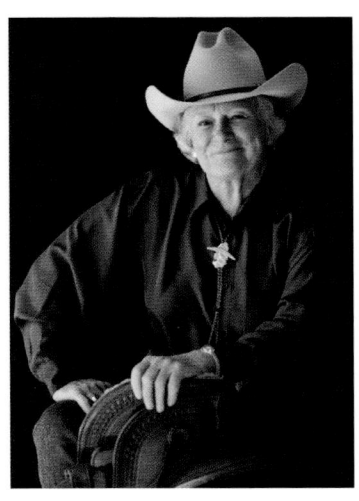

" I see in black and white ..."

The ranching roots of Barbara Van Cleve go back to the 1880s when her family founded and settled the Lazy K Bar Ranch near Melville, Montana. The ranch lies on the eastern slopes of the Crazy Mountains, where Van Cleve's grandparents raised cattle, sheep, and over 140 head of horses. Her granddad favored Thoroughbred horses and utilized Army Remount stallions in his breeding operation. Later, the ranch bred horses by crossing the Thoroughbreds with Quarter Horses, producing strong, athletic ranch horses whose offspring are still ranching in this tough country. The ranch made it through some hard times in the 1920s by diversifying into guest ranching while continuing traditional ranching.

Spike Van Cleve, her father, was educated at Harvard but returned to Montana to the ranch his grandfather and father built. He and his wife Barbara also built Otter Creek Ranch while ranching the Lazy K Bar. He authored two books including *Forty Years' Gatherin's*, a collection of true stories about this rugged country, and *A Day Late and a Dollar Short*. The couple had four children, including Barbara, born in 1935. The children were raised in this life that they loved, working long hours each day in the pens, corrals, and mountain pastures. Barbara loved riding the ranch horses and working with them in doing the jobs they were born and bred to do. She grew up with 140 head of horses that were mainly associated with the dude ranch portion of the property.

Barbara Van Cleve loved the ranching life so much that she was moved as a child to be able to share this love with others. She said:

I begged for a camera when I was eleven years old. I wanted so badly to be able to communicate to other people who didn't know about ranching how wonderful a life it was—I loved it. I just loved it. I couldn't draw and I couldn't paint, but Life *magazine and the* Saturday Evening Post *came into the house, and I saw the works of W. Eugene Smith who was a real documentary photographer.*

Van Cleve studied these photographs and others in the magazines and determined that she wanted to choose this way of representing the world around her and, most importantly, the horses in this world.

The best gift she received from her parents was a Brownie Junior box camera, which she joyfully carried with her everywhere on the ranch. At this time, she was restricted to being very selective of her shots and took only one photo at a time due to the costs of developing the film. To afford her photography, she negotiated with her parents to do odd jobs for money so she could go to the drugstore and print more pictures. A year later, her parents purchased a developing kit for her, which opened many new opportunities for creating images. In high school, she was selected for the yearbook staff because she had a passion for photography and access to a real darkroom.

Photography became her ardent avocation; however, she was fifty before she became a full-time photographer: "Like a lot of women of my generation, most were married and had families. But not for me; my passion was the ranch, and then photography."

Following in the footsteps of her father, Van Cleve pursued academics and enrolled at Northwestern University where she earned an MA in English literature, with an emphasis in Victorian poetry. Being a ranch girl on a limited budget, she made sure she earned her master's degree in nine months. She became the Dean of Women at DePaul University, taught classes for three years at Loyola University, and was then hired as an assistant professor at Mundelein College. At Mundelein, she built a darkroom and an enlarger in the basement of an old building and taught photography in addition to her other courses. Her classes were all held in the winter months so she could return to Montana in summer. As much as she loved the academic life, teaching could not keep her from her true love of working on the ranch and being with her horses. She said, "I spent every summer of my life on the ranch. Every summer. I always came back, and one of the beauties of being a teacher is that I had three to four months free."

In 1979, Van Cleve gave up her tenure-track position at Mundelein to move to Santa Fe, New Mexico, to see if she possessed the necessary talent to hold her own in the field of creative photography. She had enough funds for three years after selling the stock photo agency she built in Chicago. Santa Fe was a place where she could totally concentrate on photography. She was welcomed by the artistic groups and, after several group shows, she ventured into her first solo show.

Van Cleve became fascinated with making large prints, which became her specialty. This approach began to set her apart, and the size of the images was highly fitting for the expansive mountain ranching scenes she photographed. At her first show, Van Cleve sold all but one print, much to her amazement. She believes that this was the beginning of her photographic career.

I don't pose my photographs. My photographs are really trying to catch [horses] in their real life, what they're doing—working cattle or [when] a rider on them has roped a calf and is dragging it to the fire. . . . And, I just wanted to imbue those photographs with . . . my emotional feeling about the horse and the situation.

Although a self-taught photographer, Van Cleve credits her acute attention to composition and design in her photographs to a humanities professor at the University of Chicago who taught world art. This class discussed the classical composition of the great masters of art, the elements of which are strongly visible in her photographs. Van Cleve revealed that the biggest challenge in photographing horses specifically is that it lies within her to get into the right position for the shot, whether that be a close-up, medium, or distant position for each scene. She sees and captures diagonal lines that add to the composition in some of her work, such as *A Good Day under the Crazies*. She says, "That diagonal line of the hill . . . added even more composition and is so powerful. And, it has to be observed in my photographs."

Van Cleve has earned many honors for her photography. She was inducted into the Cowgirl Museum and Hall of Fame in Fort Worth, Texas, in 1995. She has been the subject of several television productions including "Barbara Van Cleve: Capturing Grace" and "Barbara Van Cleve: Tall in the Saddle," featured on *CBS Sunday Morning*. Her photography has been showcased in several books on life in the West. In December 2022, Van Cleve received the Governor of Montana's Award for Art and Photography. She has been especially passionate about making images of ranch women to ensure that their hard work in the West is recognized and preserved for the ages. Van Cleve has written two books, *Hard Twist: Western Ranch Women* and (with Susan Hallsten McGarry) *Pure Quill*, which earned the Western Heritage Wrangler Award for Best Photography Book in 2017.

Today, the ranch in Montana remains in the family and Van Cleve is always ready to lend a hand. She currently lives on the outside of Big Timber with a great view of the Crazy Mountains on one side and the Absaroka Beartooth Mountains from her back windows. She has plenty of room to hang all her bits and spurs. Currently, Van Cleve is exploring photography by moonlight.

Her true love for the ranch horse and life in the West comes through in her photographs. She appreciates the differences and characteristics of each horse and captures them on film to show their unique and personal beauty.

There are some photographs [of horses] with backlighting, for example, and you'll see the whiskers. You'll see big, long whiskers, or little, short whiskers, or long eyelashes, or short eyelashes. I mean, of course those are like people, you know, they've got all these differences. I try to make them look the way I feel about them—that they are beautiful, they're beautiful, strong, magnificent animals. They are great animals, and they teach you how to be a better human being too.

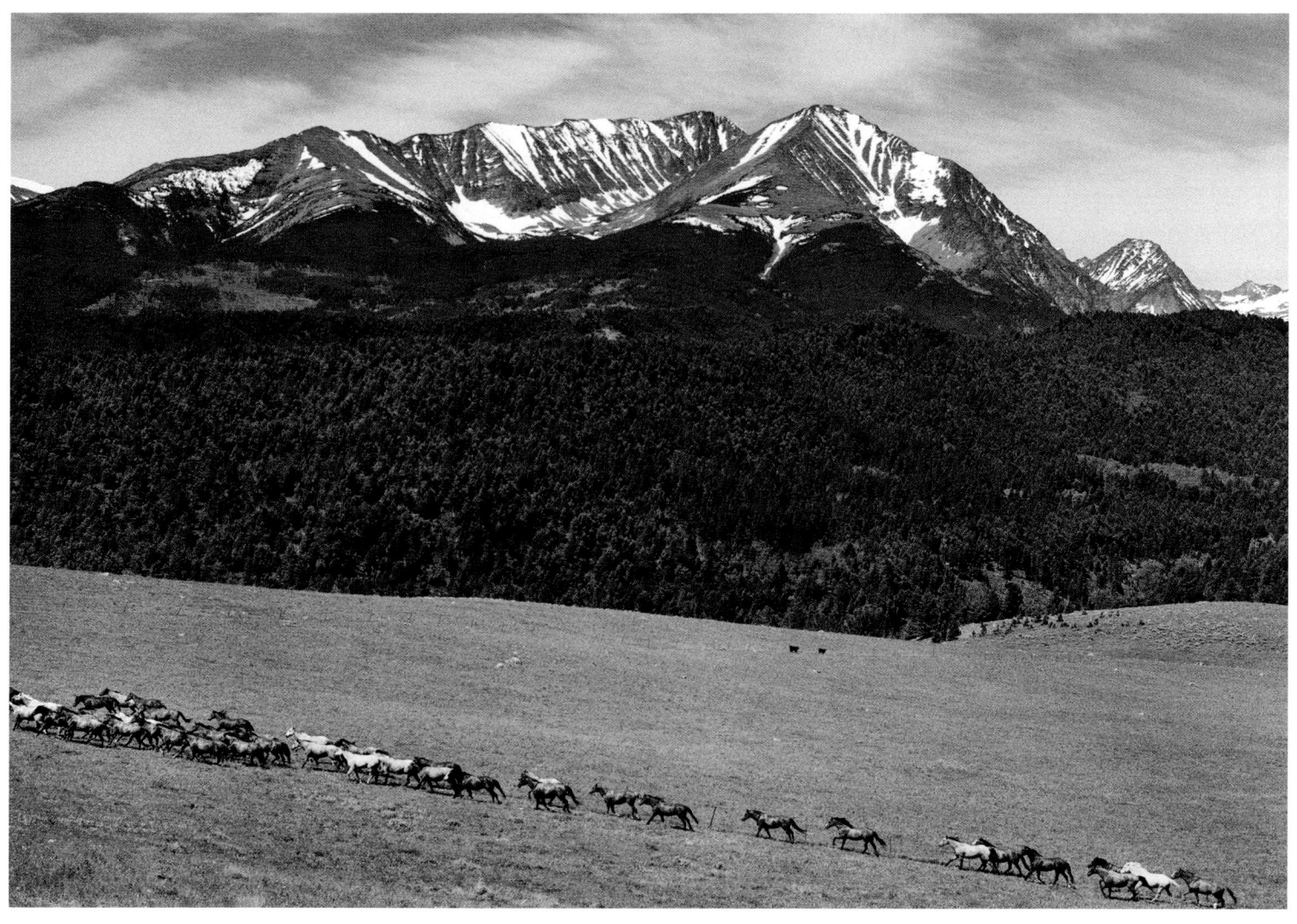

A Good Day under the Crazies

(2007)

"We were moving . . . about ninety-five head of horses up into the mountains to another part of our ranch. And as I got them headed up and I moved up to the side, up above them to make sure they went through the gate, all of them, why I looked back and I looked at the mountains with the snow and this was in June. Wow. I thought, oh my gosh, isn't that beautiful? I need to take a photograph. And I always had the camera with me. So, I made a shot. One shot. I'm kind of a one-shot girl. I learned to be a one-shot girl in order to save money, and that habit still goes on today."

Melody Feeding the Old Way

(2006)

"Melody Harding loved those teams. I grew up on a farm where we used horse teams
for everything. My mother loved driving the teams for my father in the winter."

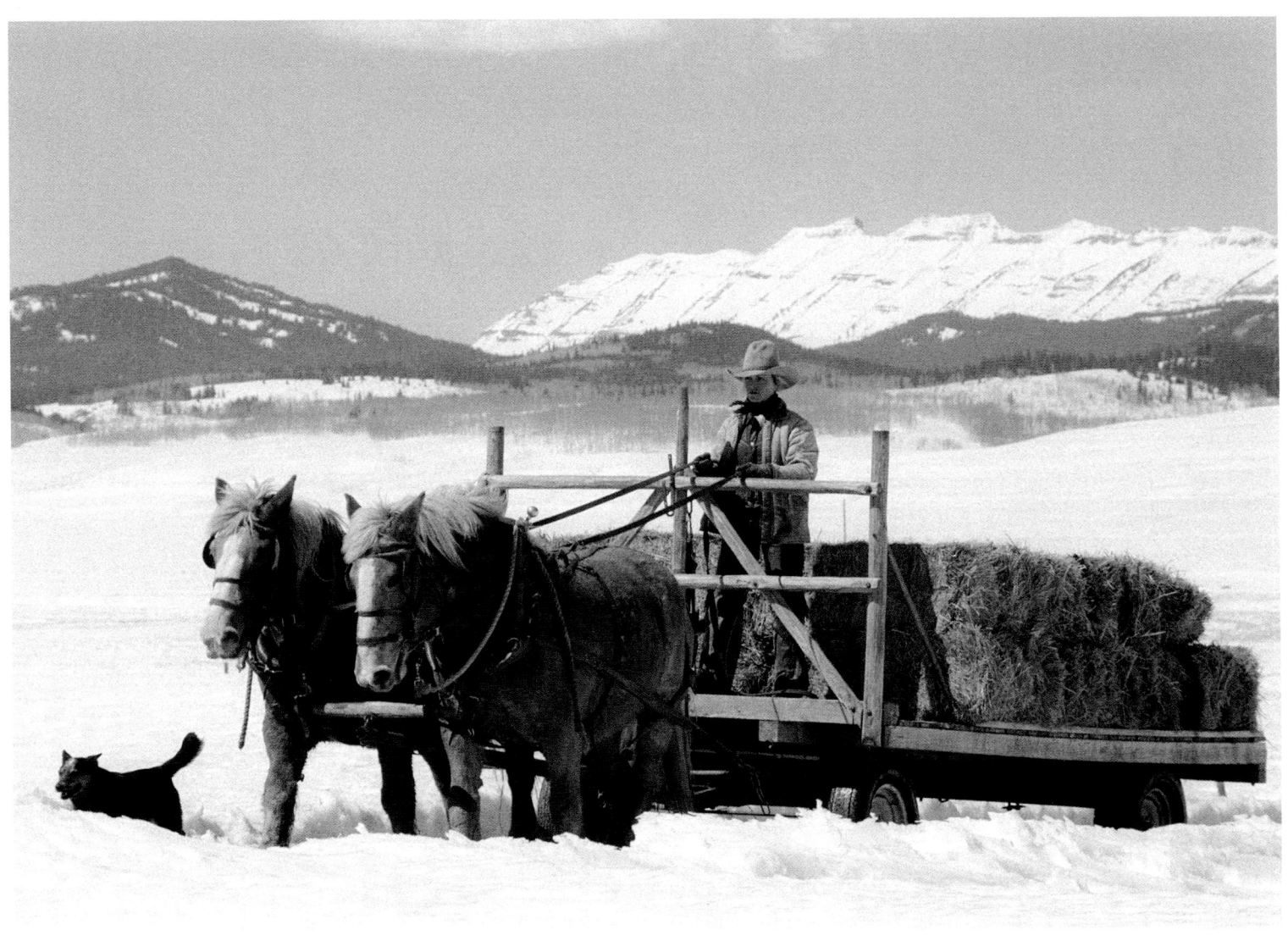

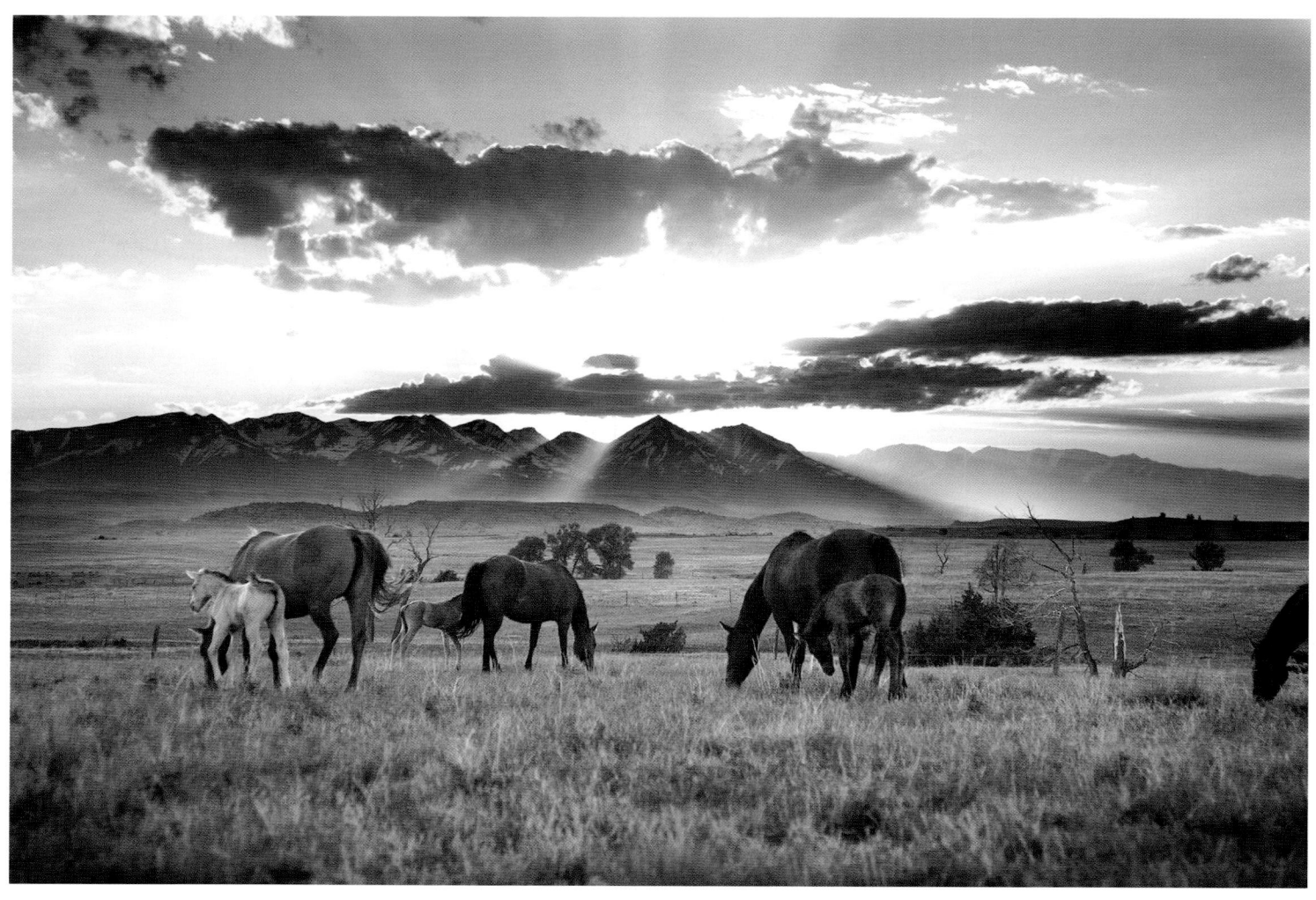

Early Summer Evening

(2009)

"I love that shot of sunset over my beloved Crazy Mountains. Those are horses and foals that belong to a friend of mine. You can see rim lighting on the foals' ears and shafts of light on the Crazy Mountains."

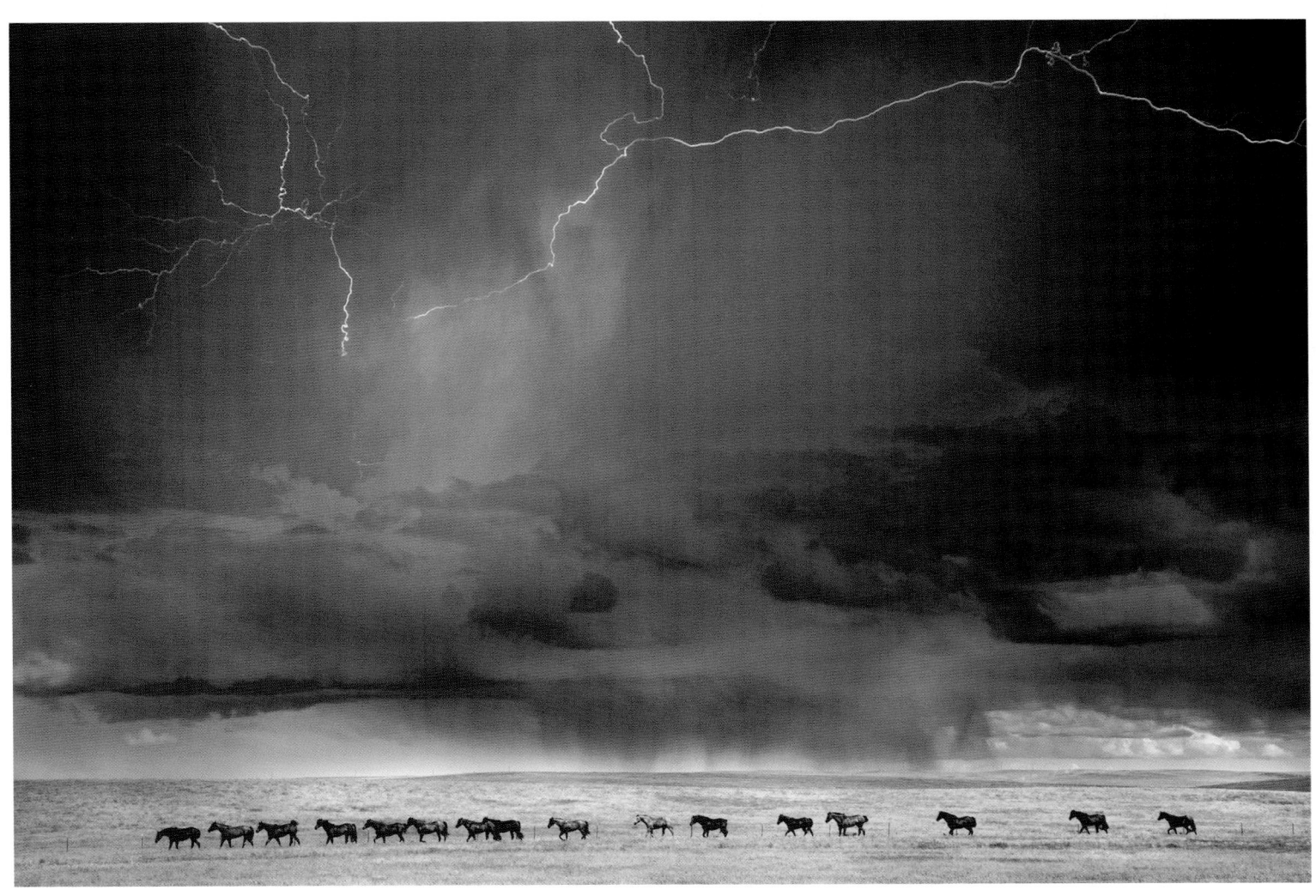

Movin' On

(2014)

"Let me tell you that this was sheer good luck to catch this lightning. You need to be pretty careful about lighting."

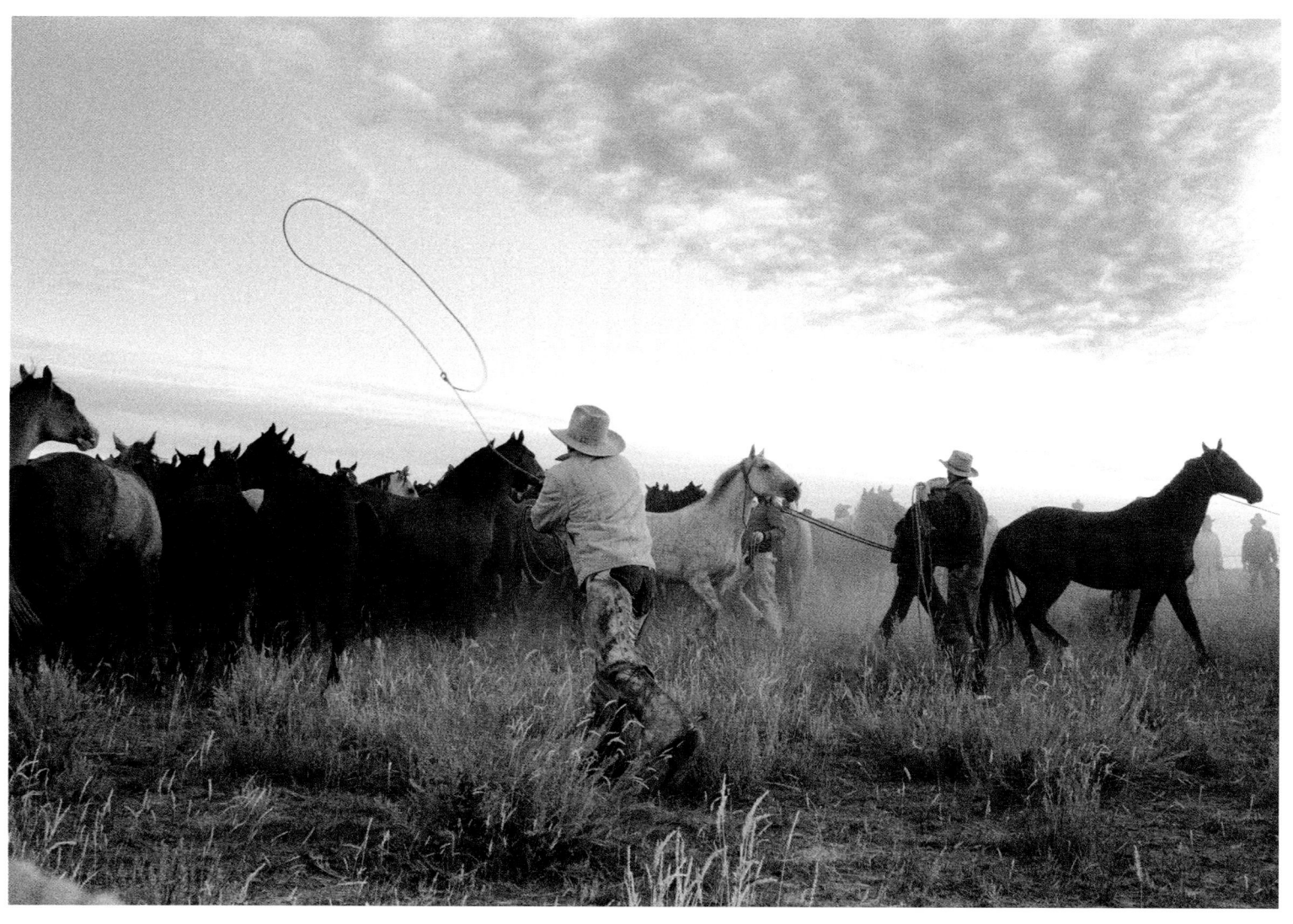

Dawn at the Rope Corral

(2001)

"That was taken during the great centennial cattle drive, driving 3,000 horses from Roundup to the stockyards in Billings. It was a huge undertaking, with two drovers from each of fifty counties."

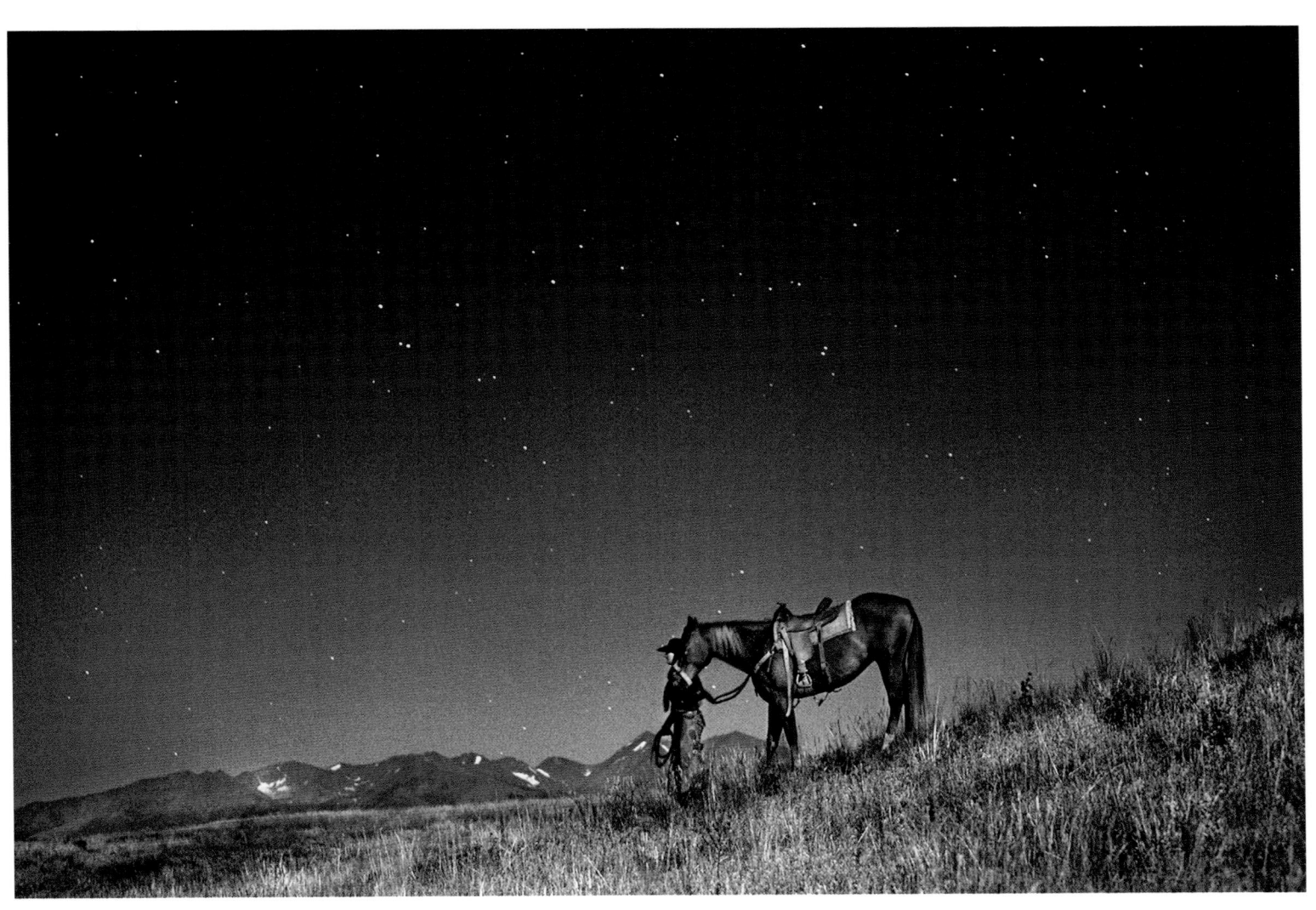

Starry Night

(2011)

"This is the first in a series I am working on by shooting only on the light of the moon. This longer exposure takes patience."

Emily McCartney

CHAPTER 14

Emily McCartney

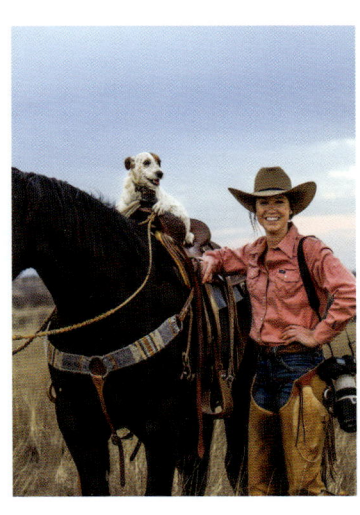

Capturing the spirit of the West in striking photographic images comes naturally to Texas native Emily McCartney. She is the sixth generation of the noted R. A. Brown Ranch, located in Throckmorton, Texas. The ranch was a recipient of the distinguished American Quarter Horse Association (AQHA) Best Remuda Award in 1997. McCartney's great-grandfather, R. A. Brown, was a founding member of the AQHA, and her grandfather, Rob Brown, served as AQHA president. The ranch's tradition of raising high quality Quarter Horses and top-producing cattle is deeply ingrained in all of the family members. Born in Weatherford, Texas, McCartney is the oldest of the five children of Todd and Marianne Brown McCartney, who also call Throckmorton their home.

My experiences on the ranch are an important aspect of who I am and who I've become. From a young age, I was enamored by the lifestyle that I got to live. As a kid, getting to ride horseback with my dad and the other cowboys was all I wanted to do. Horses are at the core of who I am.

McCartney's first exposure to photography came at age 11 when she borrowed her mother's point-and-shoot camera to take pictures of flowers and butterflies at the ranch for 4-H photography. Her parents were surprised at her eye for design and lighting in these early images and encouraged her to continue. McCartney credits 4-H with helping to cultivate the opportunity and mindset of producing images and preparing them for shows, including statewide competitions. At the age of 15 she received her first paying photography job taking senior photos for a friend. As these small jobs began to accumulate, McCartney invested her modest profits into more photography gear and self-education to improve her skills.

In 2013, McCartney became a third-generation Red Raider when she enrolled in Texas Tech University, where she majored in agricultural communications. This major suited her career goals well as it combined her love of ranching with photography and communications. During her time in Lubbock, McCartney earned her way through college by taking senior pictures and family portraits and with other photography work.

In May of 2017, when I graduated from Tech, I had to make a decision on whether I wanted to go full time [into] freelance photography and continue my career with the business I had built since I was fifteen years old, or if I wanted to have a safety net and choose a 9 to 5 job in the industry.

The decision was a difficult one, but she followed her heart and launched her career as a full-time freelance Western photographer. McCartney understands production agriculture and those that live it. Authenticity is a key focus in her photography. Small details such as spurs and bridles need to be correct for the job, and she appreciates what she is seeing on the ranches including the significance of the handmade spurs and boots. She believes, "It's in the details."

In only a few years, McCartney's portfolio grew quickly and now consists of ranch lifestyle, editorial, and commercial photography. She travels widely for photography shoots and her clients include YETI, Western Horseman, Resistol, and many other companies. Many of her clients are ranchers who want their ranches and history captured in photography.

For many of my shoots I keep the mindset that I am shooting for those cowboys and cowgirls I am photographing. I'm shooting for these people like me and my family that want to make sure our way of life is carried on and projected authentically.

McCartney has had very little formal education in photography. Other than the two general photography classes at Texas Tech, the majority of her photography education has been self-taught, through great mentors and workshops. One Christmas, her grandparents gave her the opportunity to attend a David Stoecklein workshop at the Saunders Ranch in Weatherford, Texas. The Browns had become very good friends with Stoecklein, and this experience had a large influence in McCartney's photographic development. Along with the late Stoecklein, McCartney considers Wyman Meinzer and Matt Cohen as invaluable mentors and inspirations.

In her ranch photography, McCartney chooses not to set up her shots but to instead allow them to happen. For her, the crucial thing is being in the moment at the correct time. She says, "I'm very much in tune with how things feel and what expression is given off. I consider myself a spiritual and religious person and I think that plays into it a lot."

McCartney's favorite times to shoot are morning and evening when the light is warmest and the sun is closest to the horizon. On many of her jobs, she is out on horseback with the ranchers, ready with her camera to catch the scenes in the light as the sun is just coming up on the horizon. In her travels to regions of Texas, Arizona, and the Northwest, she has seen a wide range of natural lighting. She states, "It has been a great experience to see the variation of natural light across the country." Her photography tends towards a warm palette, reflective of the West. She also uses black and white in certain images, creating a feeling of the Old West.

One design concept McCartney enjoys is layering and shooting "through" objects. She feels this approach prevents her images from being flat. She also loves to photograph the foothills and mesas in areas such as New Mexico and Oregon, where the horizontal mesas or foothills of the mountain create a layering effect to her images. She says that "depth is really important to me in a shot because I believe it allows the viewer to feel like he or she is there . . . having that experience."

McCartney also has a great eye for quality horses. She has grown up with them and has a natural knowledge of their behaviors and movements. This knowledge has greatly helped her in taking action shots and determining the ideal timing to get the horse's gait in each specific job on the ranch. She is an experienced rider, and while at Texas Tech she competed as part of the Texas Tech Ranch Horse Team, which won a National Championship. She has owned and ridden some very talented ranch horses at the home ranch and is often on horseback at the ranches she is photographing. She says, "The horse is everything to the cowboy, and I take it seriously to represent the horse in the very best light and form."

Her passion for horses and for all their contributions to the West is as strong as her passion for photography. She believes there are many reasons the horse is so universally significant.

The horse can be anything that we need it to be for anyone, of any walk of life, of any background, of any experience. For example, there are times that my horse is my best friend . . . getting me through a tough day. And then the next day that horse is my tool to get a tough job done on the ranch. That horse is my partner. I have to have 100 percent trust in that horse.

In 2023, McCartney married Oregon rancher Nick Eiguren. The two divide their time between Jordan Valley, Oregon and Throckmorton, Texas. The couple welcomed their daughter Blaze in 2024. McCartney Eiguren exhibits her work in the Summer Stampede Western Art & Gear Show at the National Ranching Heritage Center in Lubbock, Texas, and she is represented by the Davis & Blevins Gallery in Saint Jo, Texas.

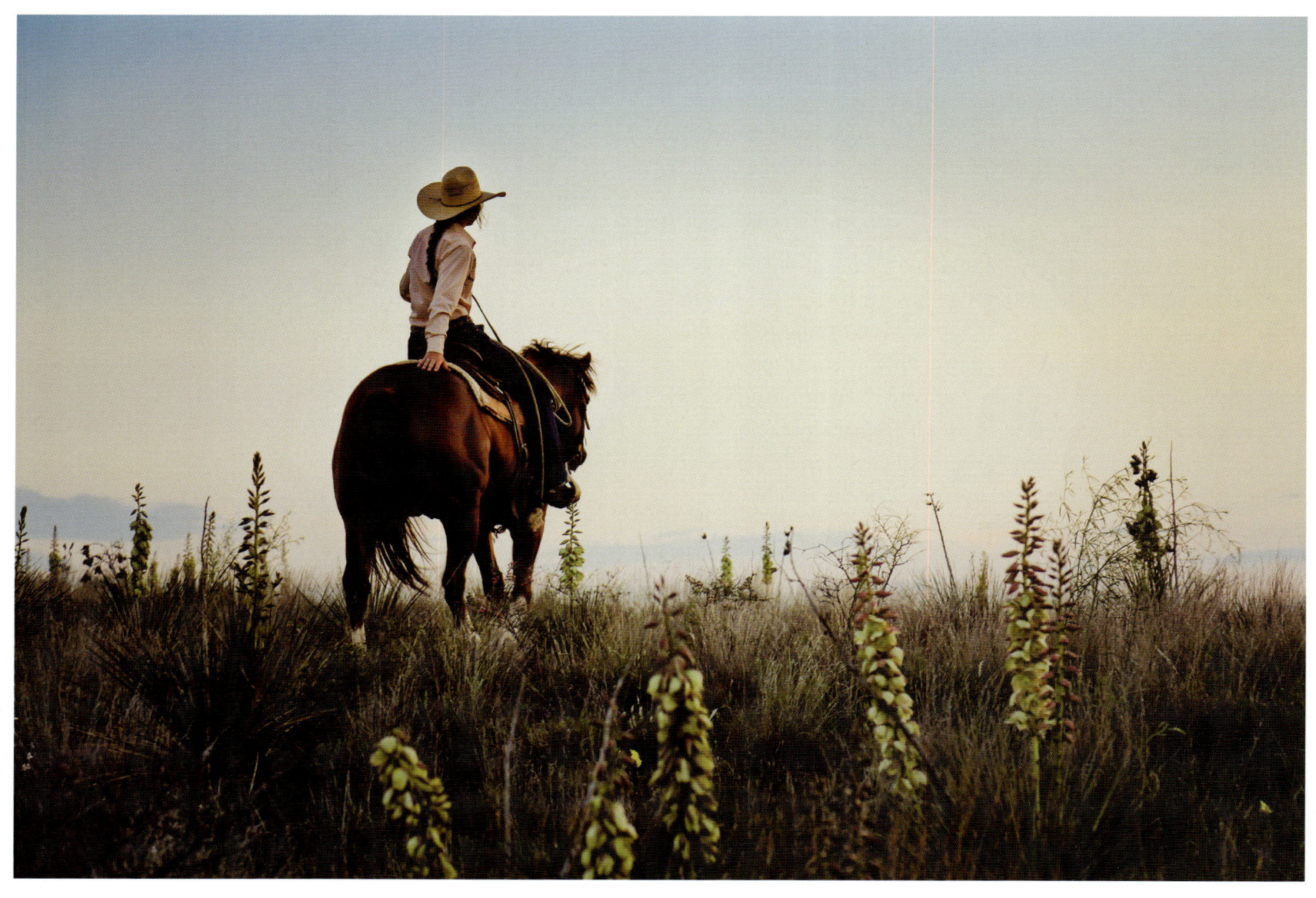

Partners

(2015)

"This image is of my cousin, Amanda Brown, on her parents' ranch in the Texas Panhandle. The yucca was blooming, and it was a gorgeous evening. I caught this moment of Amanda patting her horse on the hip as she rode away from me, completely unaware I was taking her photo. I call this photo *Partners*. The candid moments people don't know I'm capturing are my favorites."

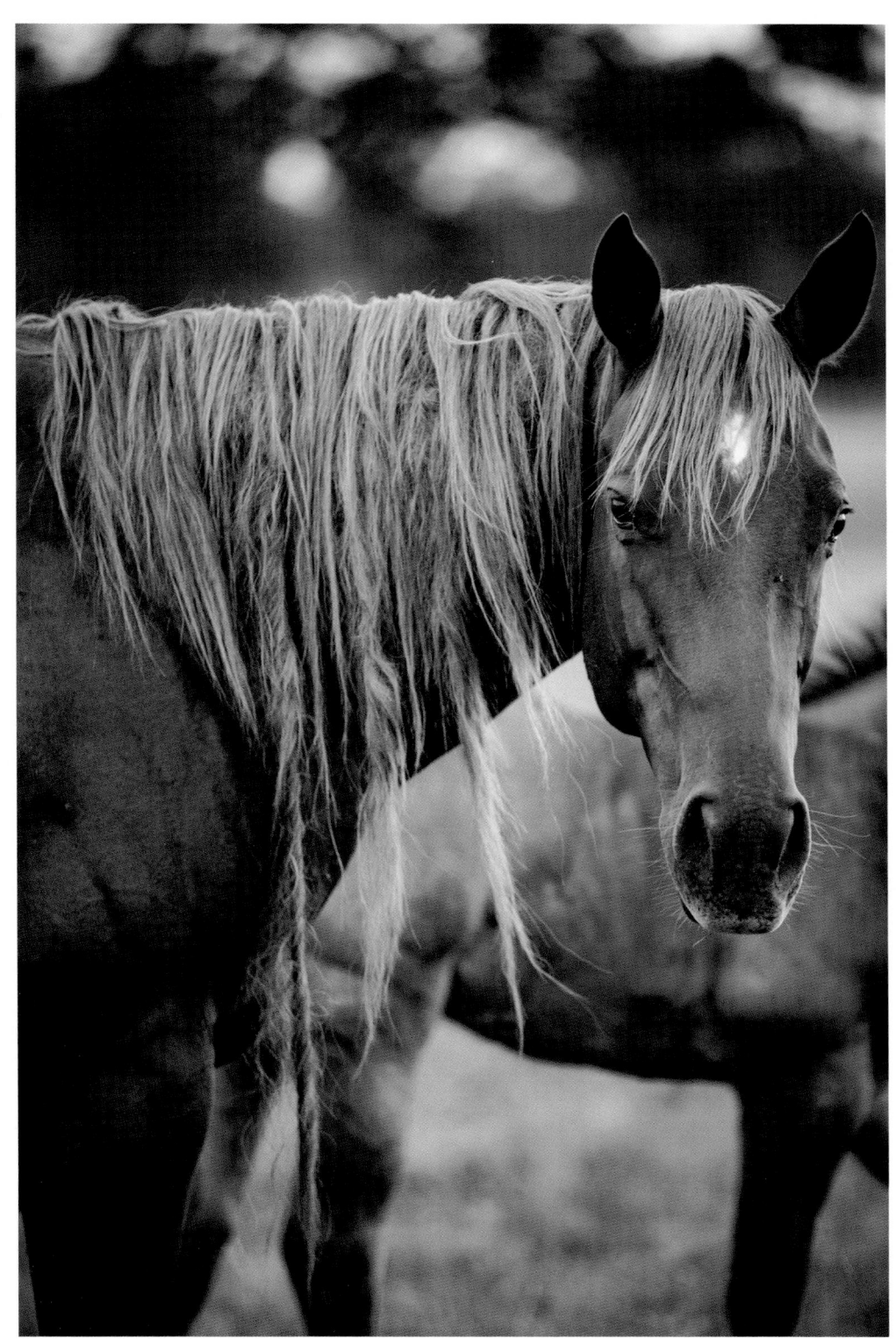

Hippie Mare

(2020)

"*Hippie Mare* was a photo I made at the A Bar Ranch in Claremore, Oklahoma. She was a broodmare that was in a large band of other mares with their foals at side. This specific mare drew my attention immediately—her knotted, unbrushed mane felt a bit relatable, I think. She had character, and I like to document character."

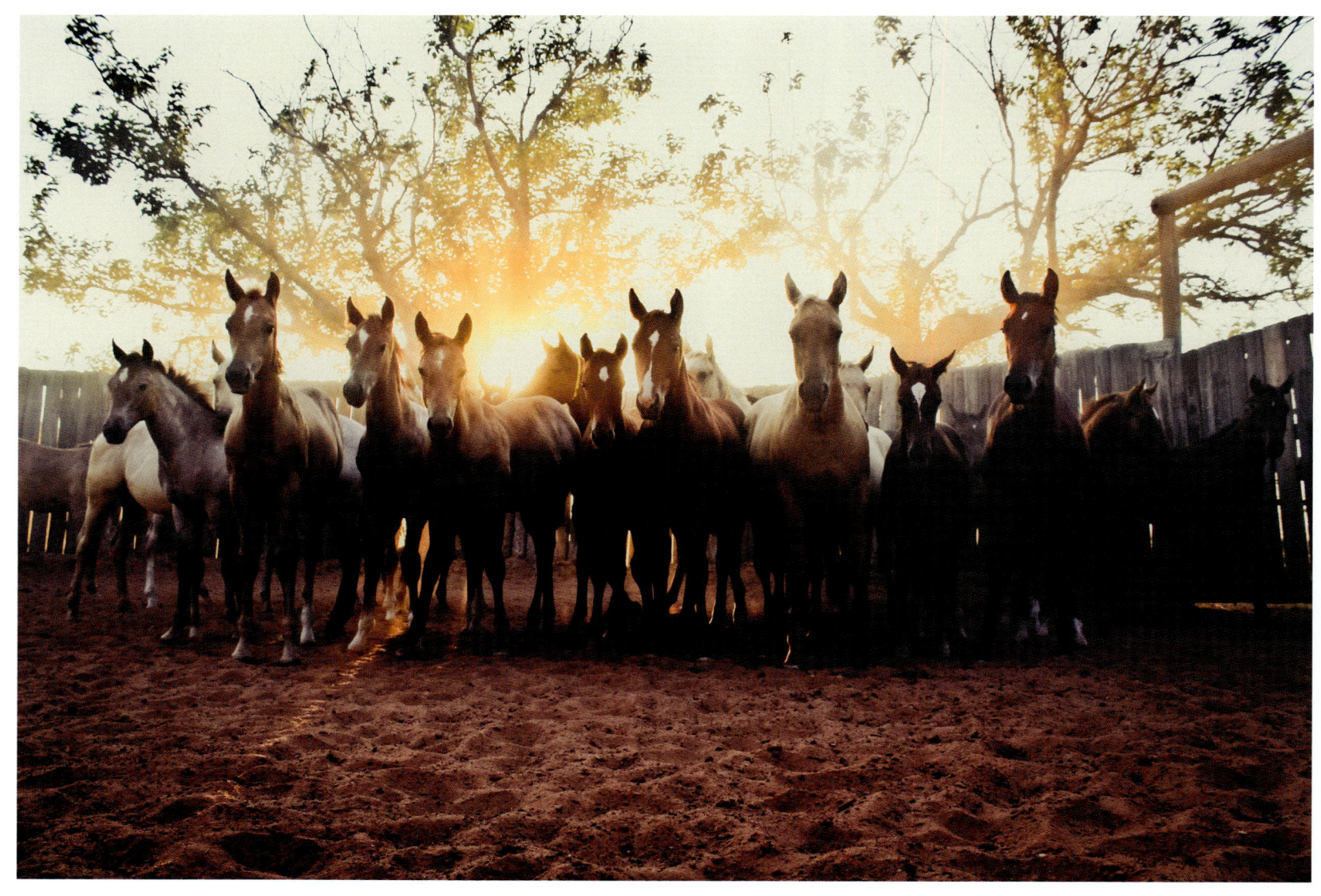

Brown Ranch Babies

(2013)

"I made this photograph in 2013, when I was 18. My dad was weaning foals and using the old round pen at headquarters. The evening light coming through the slats of the railroad ties and the mulberry trees caught my eye initially. The young foals were curious and posed up great around me with their ears perked; I couldn't have posed them better myself. That round pen is pretty special—it was built during my great-grandfather's era on the ranch and a lot of good hands and horses have been started in that round pen. *Brown Ranch Babies* was a clear title when I was choosing what to name this image."

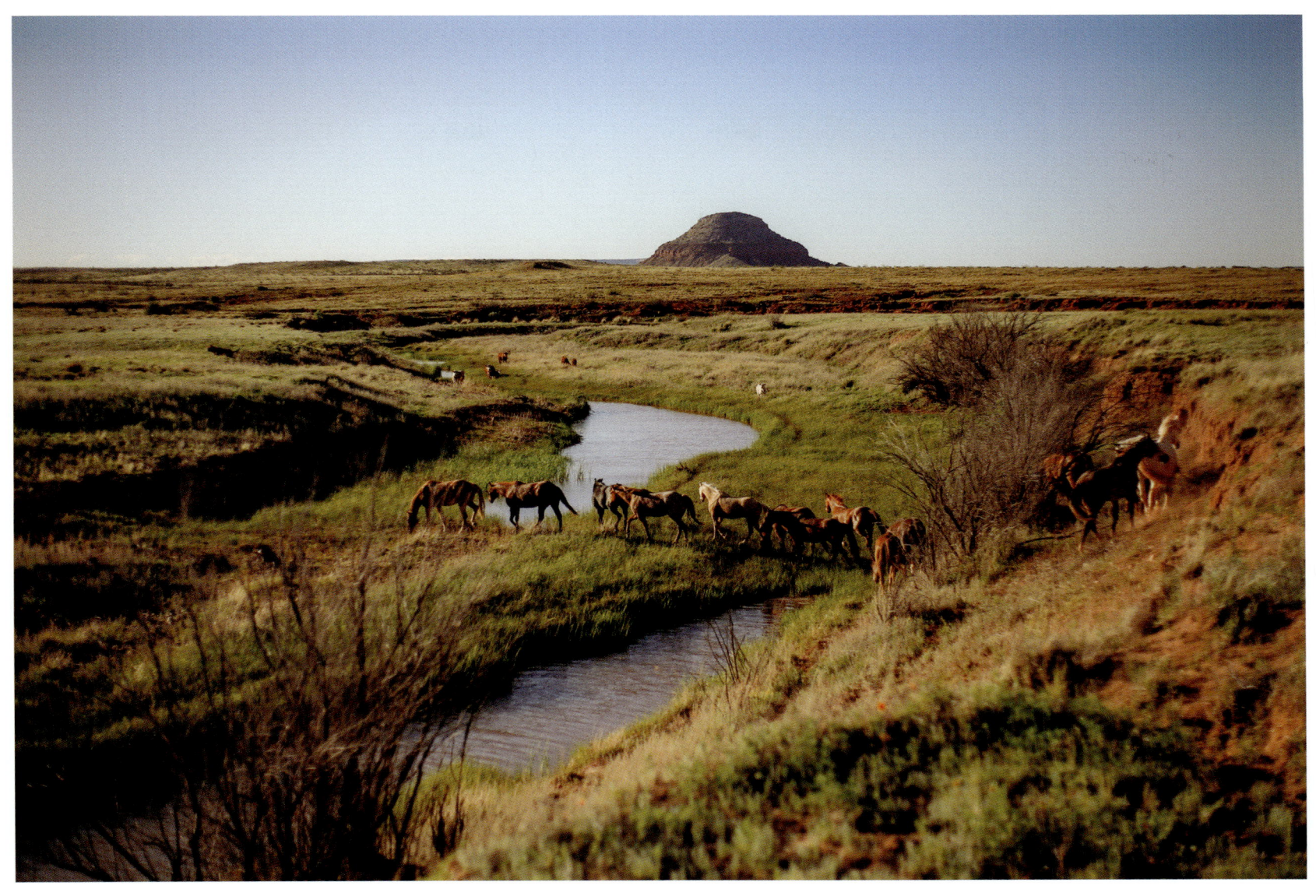

God's Country

(2017)

"This photo was taken from the back of a running-off horse. Lining up this shot was a true miracle but I'm so glad it turned out. This was at the Bell Ranch near Mosquero, New Mexico. We were taking saddle horses out to the wagon during spring works. The pasture we went through at one point had cattle in it that you can see in the distance. The mesa you see there is called Bell Mountain, that the ranch is named after. The scene of blue skies, green grass, water, horses, and cattle looks like paradise to me, so I titled it *God's Country*."

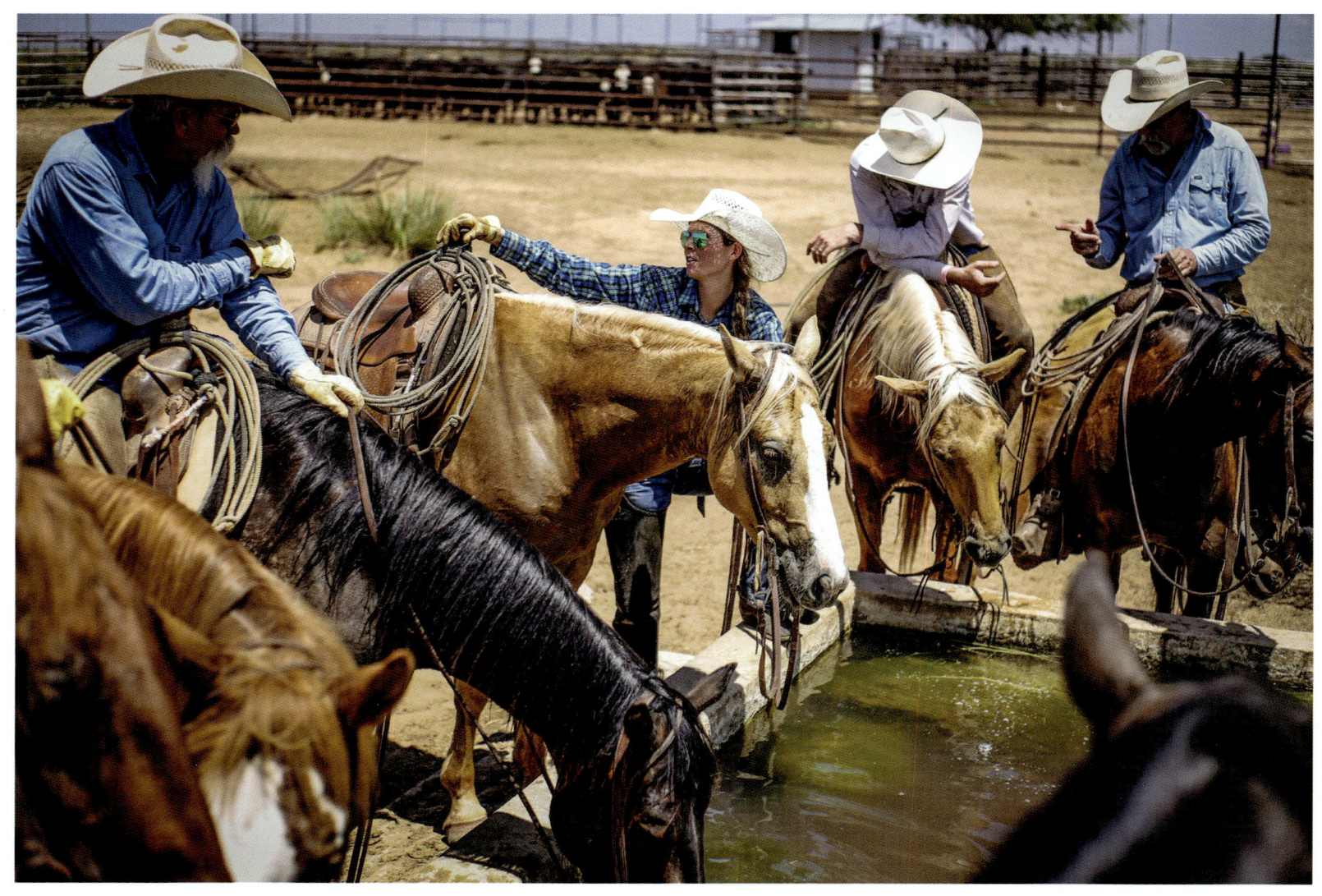

Untitled

(2017)

"This was taken at the Muleshoe Ranch, owned and operated by good friends of mine, the Anderson family. We had come in from the gather; it was a real hot morning so once the cattle were penned, we took our horses to water to let them drink. Everyone was relaxed and started talking and it created a cool scene. I stayed on my horse and kept a corner of his head in the frame to make the viewer feel like they are experiencing the moment."

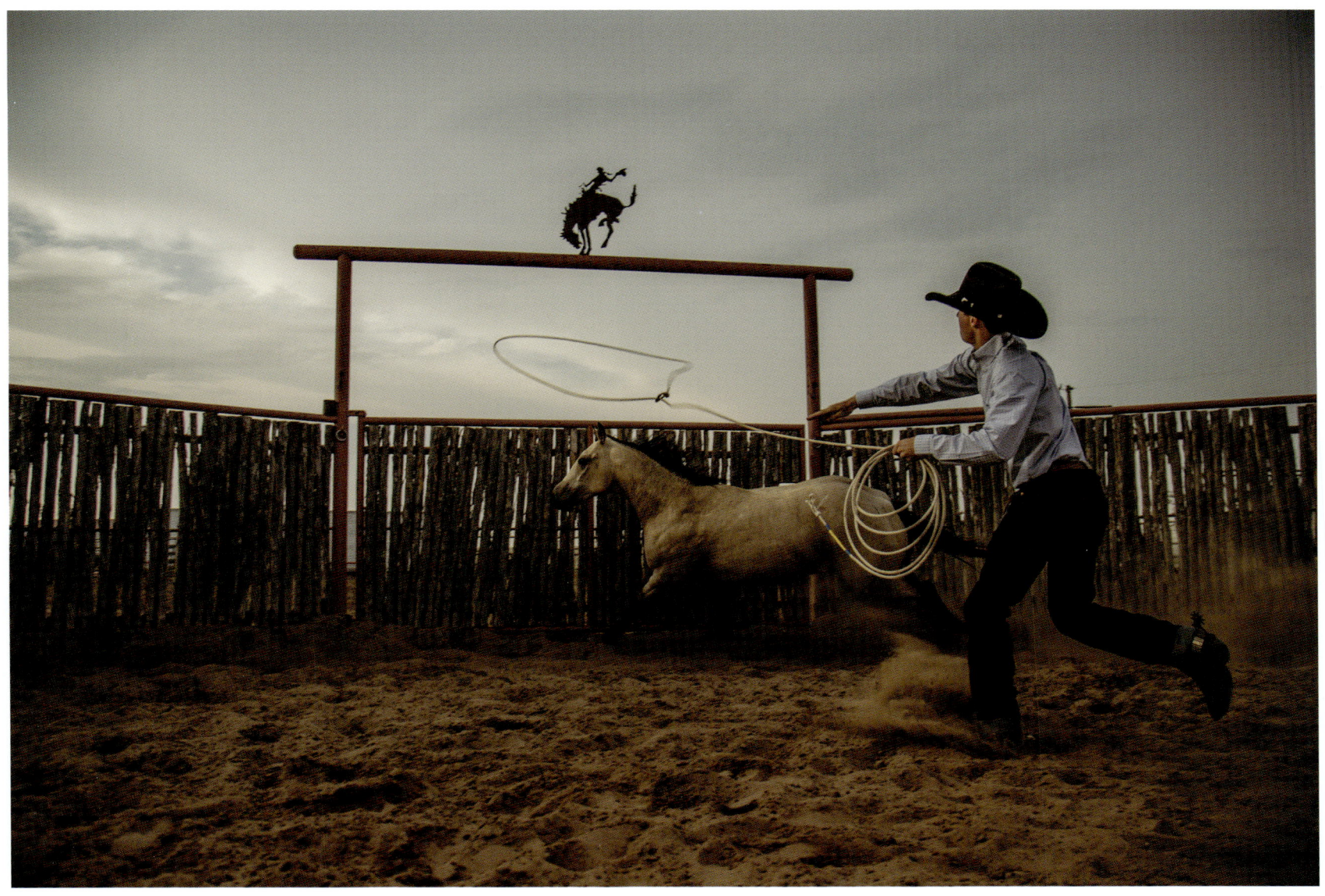

Formal Introductions

(2018)

"This is of Utah Eicke, in Happy, Texas, and I call it *Formal Introductions*. The photograph features a young horse that Utah was training. He was tough to catch . . . so he roped him in the round pen to get him saddled. I made this photo from inside of the round pen. You can do that if you stay in the middle, out of the way, and shoot with a wider lens."

Bev
Pettit

CHAPTER 15

Bev Pettit

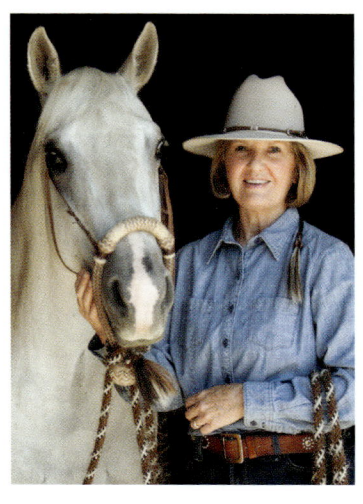

Bev Pettit was raised in a small town in Minnesota and comes from an agricultural family. Her grandparents and parents grew up on farms and ranches in Wisconsin and South Dakota. Her father started a business selling work boots to farmers and ranchers and then decided to partner with some of his brothers and began selling ranch and farm footwear in the city. They opened a store in La Crosse, Wisconsin, and soon after expanded to Dubuque, Iowa; Sparta, Wisconsin; and Winona, Minnesota. Pettit grew up spending a lot of time with her grandparents on their ranch in Geddes, South Dakota, where she developed her love of horses.

Pettit's mother, Frances, was raised on that ranch around cows and horses. Among her mother's chores was taking care of the cattle during the days when she was not in school. Her childhood days spanned throughout the long, hot Dust Bowl summers during which some local people left South Dakota for California and other places after the Great Depression. These families would just get up and leave their homes to head further west. They simply drove away, pulling wagons behind their trucks, leaving most possessions behind. Most of them planned to come back one day, but many never returned; their homes just sat empty. Pettit would go into these houses as a child, simply walking in because doors were left open. In some of the houses she would find household things that had been sitting in the same place for years, newspapers and dishes still on the table, covered with dust and dirt.

Pettit studied at the University of Minnesota and University of South Dakota, earning a BA degree in fine art and a BS in art education. Composition and design elements of art come naturally for her. After graduating, she moved to Phoenix where she worked in the design department for an engineering firm and in the Engineering College at Arizona State University. She then took an opportunity to work overseas for the publishing department of an American investment bank in Hong Kong and London for nine years. It was in Hong Kong that Pettit first took up photography. In her spare time, she would travel the backroads and back alleys of the cities and countryside of Asia and Europe to photograph life as it was. But after about a decade of living and working overseas, she and her husband returned and bought property in Northern Arizona where they could raise their family, be closer to nature, and have a home for their horses. She had grown up around Quarter Horses, and having her own again was a welcome addition to her new life.

Pettit was now able to concentrate on photography full time. She taught some photography classes and began to focus on equine photography, starting with her own horses. People began to get interested in her work, and Pettit began selling prints.

Most of the people that have horses love horses, love looking at horses, or just being around these beautiful animals. But I wanted to go one step further with my images: instead of just showing the beauty of horses, I wanted people to feel the emotions that horses convey in their expressions and body language.

One of Pettit's first photography shows was the Trappings of the American West event in Flagstaff, Arizona. She also regularly shows at the Phippen Museum in Prescott, Arizona, and was invited to show her work at the National Ranching Heritage Association annual Summer Stampede in Lubbock, Texas.

I think it's fantastic to be in shows that aren't necessarily just show-casing equine art. And I've been fortunate to have been invited to

a number of shows that exhibit sculptures, paintings, and exquisite hand-crafted Western gear in addition to fine art photography.

Pettit is friends with the owners of the 7 Up Ranch, north of Prescott, Arizona, and has had the opportunity to spend time with them riding and photographing during roundups. She was also recently invited to spend some time photographing on the historic O RO Ranch in Prescott, Arizona. Quarter Horses are bred, born, and raised on these big ranches so that they are able to meet the high demands of the rough country, consisting of hills and valleys loaded with volcanic rock. During the summer, when ranch work slows down, many Arizona working ranches enjoy a few days of family fun at the Cowpunchers annual reunion rodeo in Williams, Arizona. Pettit began attending in 2007, when the event was held during the wet and muddy monsoon seasons. They have now moved the date to drier weeks, but she's kept photographing the ranch cowboys and their horses in action during the three-day event for years after. Pettit likes to catch the intensity and action of the events of the rodeo in a way that lets the viewer see, feel, and taste the dirt and dust during these celebrations for skilled cowboys and good horses.

Pettit began focusing on photographing wild horses after she visited a wild horse sanctuary in Lompoc, California, at Return to Freedom. She spent a few days photographing the hundreds of horses at the sanctuary. While there, Pettit met the founder of the sanctuary, Neda DeMayo, who introduced her to different herds of wild horses that live on public lands. Pettit also began making trips to the Onaqui Range in Utah and the Sand Wash Basin range in Colorado to photograph wild horses.

We looked down and there were at least 300 horses grazing below us. So we spent the next week just following the herds over thousands of acres. They travel approximately 26 miles a day grazing on cheat grass and going from waterhole to waterhole.

Pettit says she doesn't like to follow specific plans when photographing horses, domestic or wild; you need to spend a lot of time with horses to see how they will react to circumstances and allow them to get comfortable with you. They usually dictate how a shoot will go, and she feels it is necessary to be prepared for anything and be able to adapt. Of perhaps hundreds of shots taken in a day, only a few may be ones that really connect with her. Communicating the moment in the image, the emotion and action of the horses to the viewer, is a primary concern to Pettit.

Pettit fears that the wild horse herds may disappear from our public lands one day due to the many current government removals and that they may not be around for future generations of horse lovers to enjoy.

I can't just go out and grab a picture of the wild horses. I sit with them and watch for hours on. I like to be there with them from sun-up to sunrise and have time in between to really "see" them in their natural states. I want to be with them all the time because that's when you can catch the moments that are so unexpected. You can't "set it up," you can't get a horse to pose for you there. Two or three stallions can be resting quietly together for an hour and then in a split second they start squealing and snorting, pawing the ground until they are consumed inside a cloud of dust before they get up on their back legs and start sparring. It is really quite exhilarating to watch!

Pettit's photography has earned awards internationally. Her photographs garnered recognition at the Siena International Photo Awards (Italy), the Moscow International Foto Awards, the Tokyo International Foto Awards, and Le Prix de la Photographie de Paris (PX3) Awards. In 2021, she was named the #1 Black and White Photographer in the United States. Her images are in private collections worldwide. Pettit currently lives on a small ranch in Northern Arizona surrounded by a national forest with her family and their horses where they can enjoy the peace and serenity of nature.

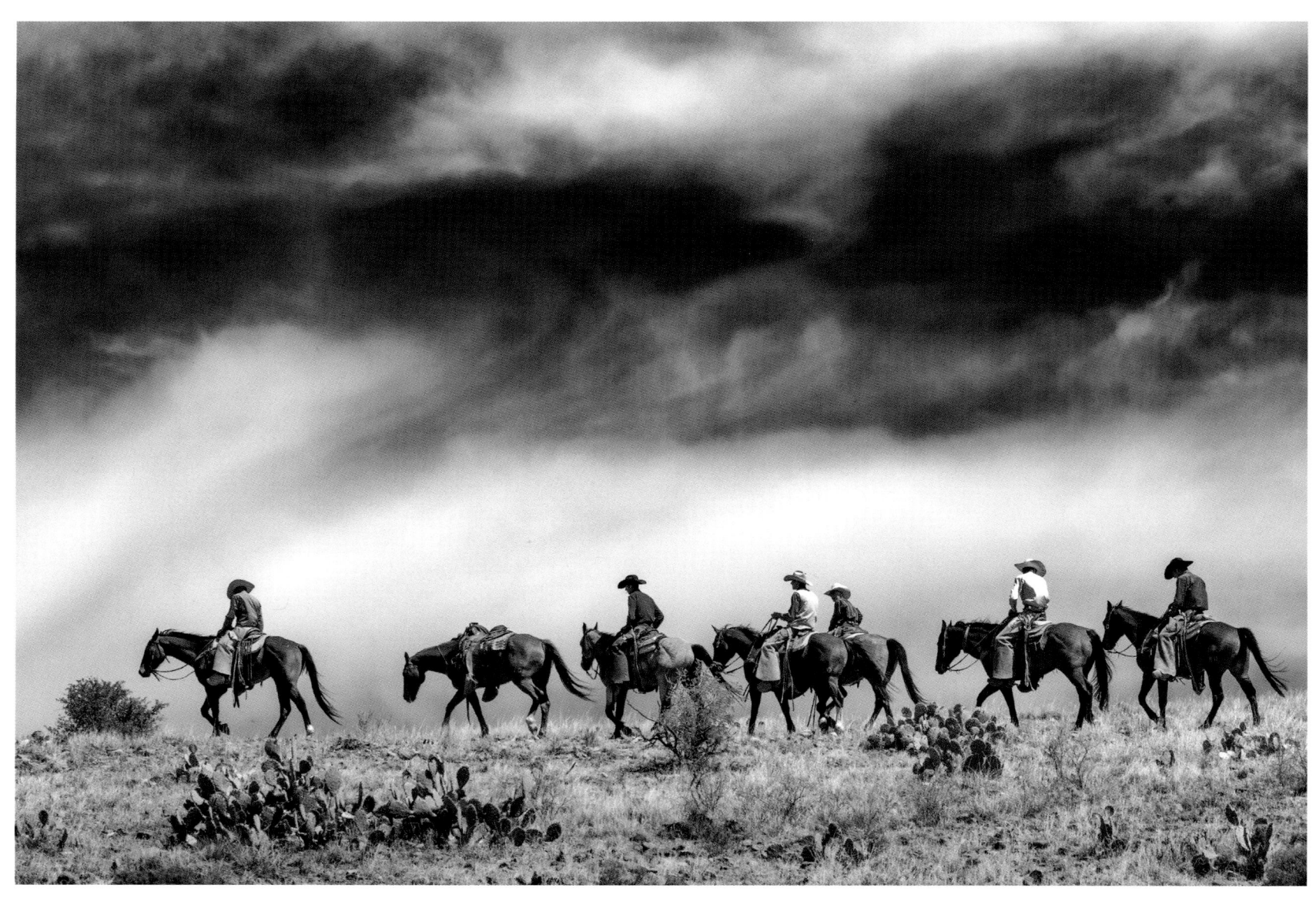

The RO's

(2022)

"After a long day's ride. A line of cowboys ride single file back to headquarters after saddling up before dawn heading out into the vast country on the O RO Ranch in Prescott, Arizona, to gather cattle for spring branding."

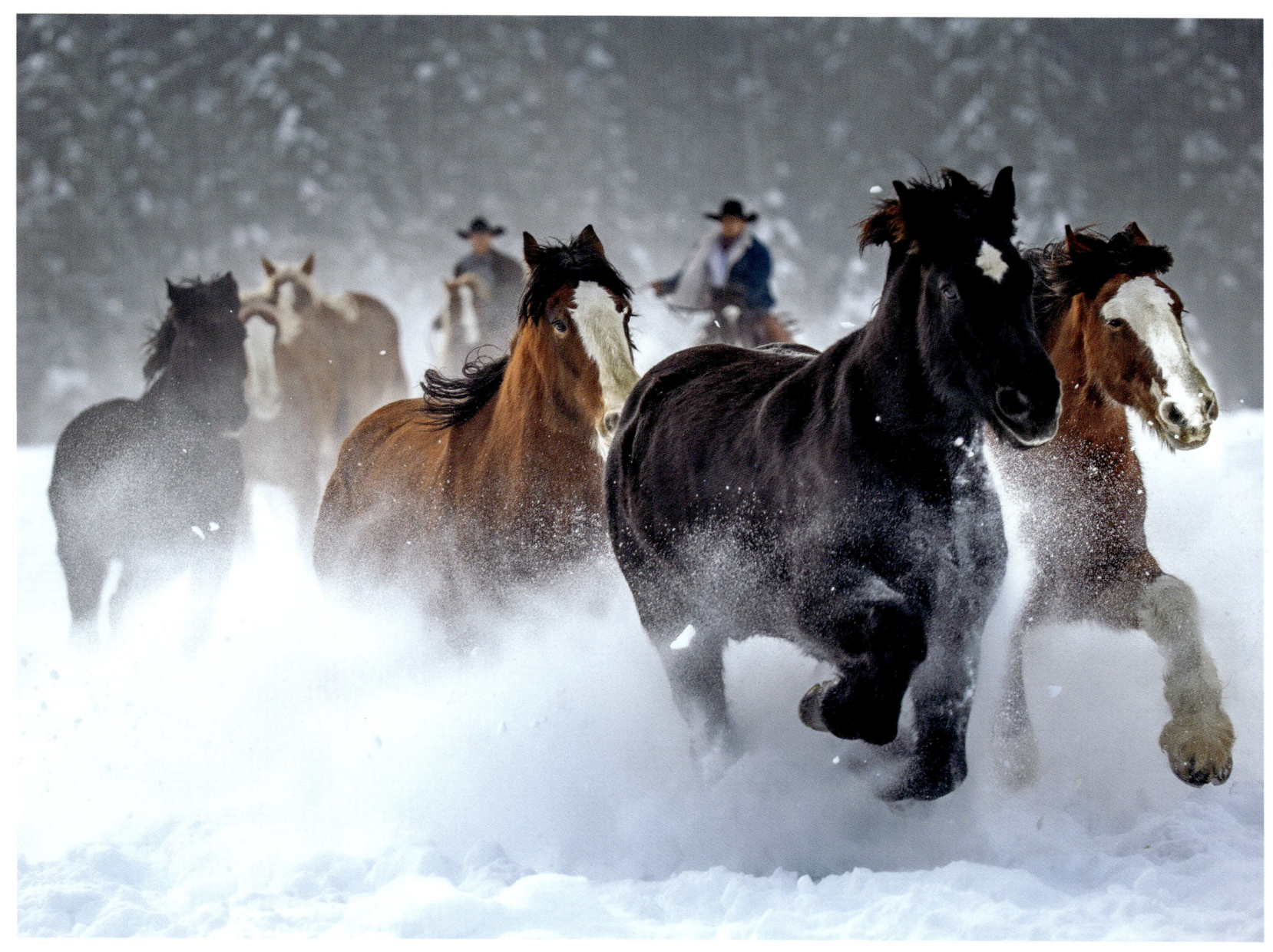

Drafts in the Snow

(2017)

"Bar W Guest Ranch, Whitefish, Montana. Two cowboys from the Bar W have fun bringing in the ranch's draft horses on a cold winter day. The sound of their thundering hooves in the snow at full speed is a thrilling experience."

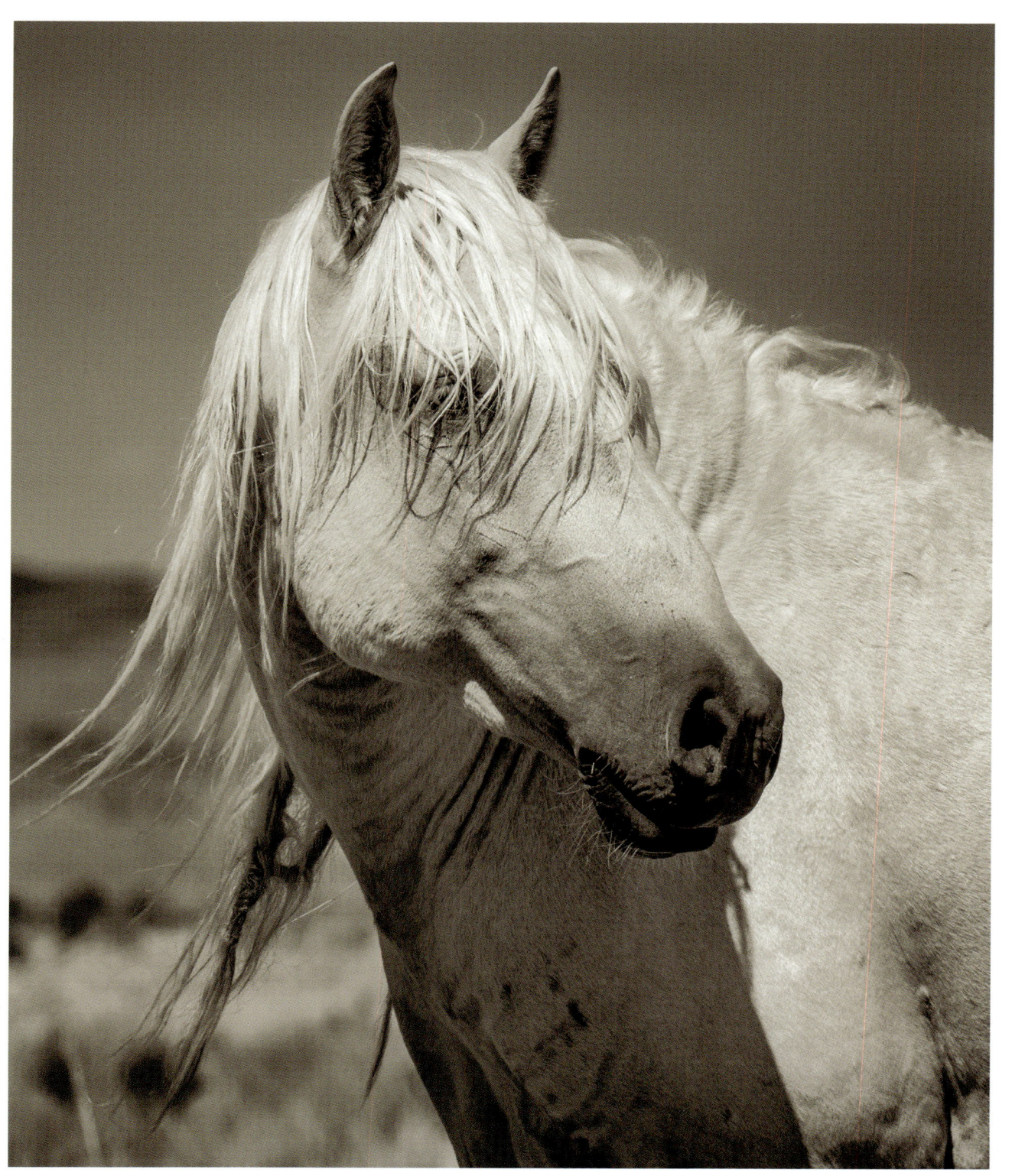

Sand Wash
Basin Stallion

(2016)

"Sand Wash Basin in Northwest Colorado includes 155,000 acres of public land. The few hundred wild horses that roam this vast country of sagebrush and piñon-juniper woodlands are mostly of Iberian Spanish descent."

Stormy Skies

(2014)

"The ranch horses at the historic Rancho de los Caballeros in Wickenburg, Arizona, are sent back out to their desert range as an evening monsoon sky threatens storms."

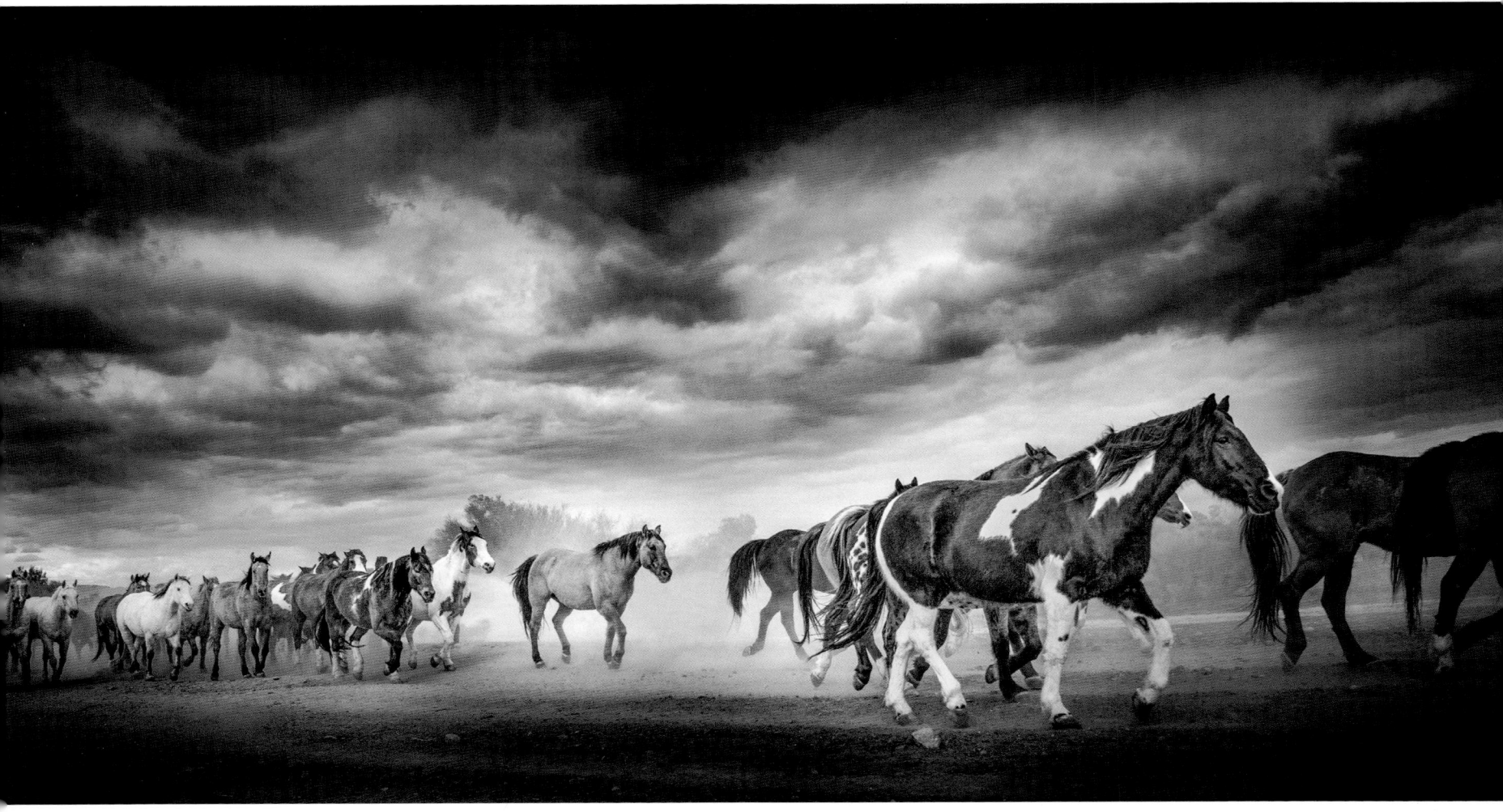

Ghost Horses of the Onaqui Range

(2017)

"Hundreds of wild Onaqui horses were gathered and auctioned out by the Bureau of Land Management (BLM) in Utah in July 2021. I call this photo *Ghost Horses* because I feel that the ghosts of the horses that were removed from their birthplace still roam freely there in spirit."

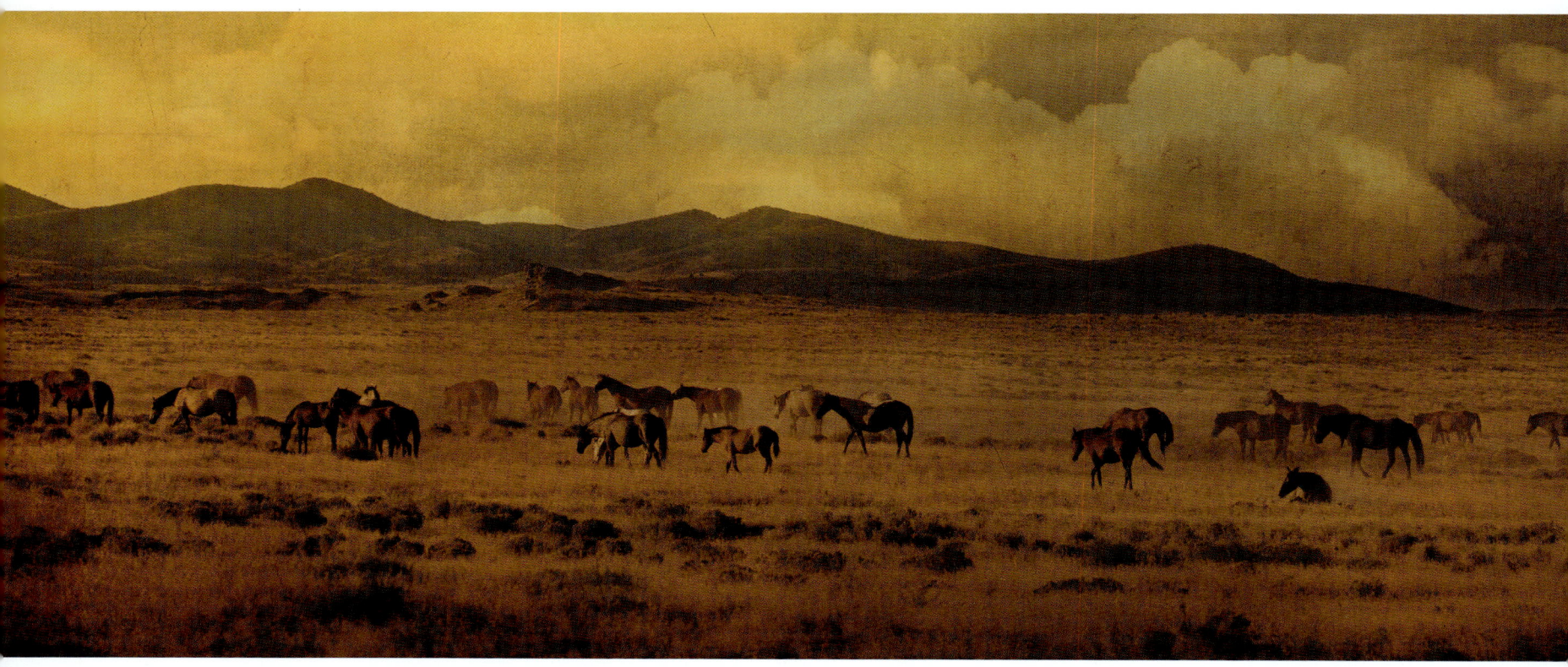

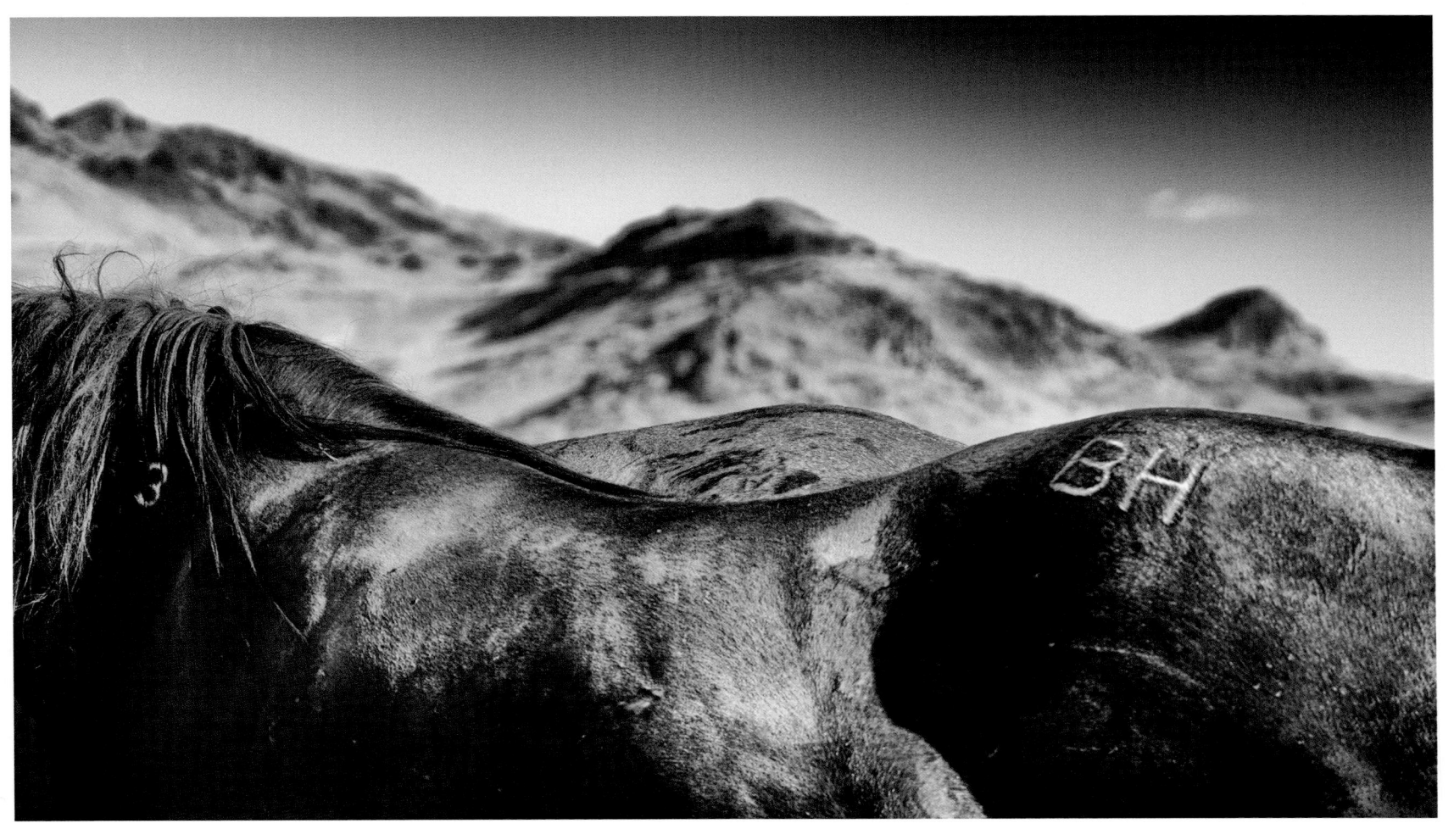

Wild Mountains

(2017)

"This is the Onaqui Range in Utah. Wild mares are treated with PZP, a time-release contraception. The horses are 'darted' by trained professionals using dart guns that are safe for the horses. When the darted mares are gathered, they are branded on their hips with the letters BZ or BH and on their necks with '1' or '3' so that when they are released back into the wild the treated mares can be identified."

PART 3

Sculpture

_____

Herb Mignery

CHAPTER 16

Herb Mignery

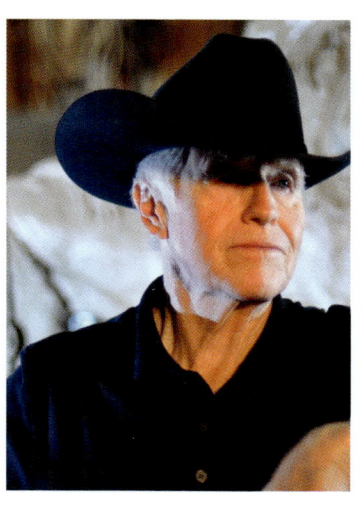

Herb Mignery was raised on the family ranch near Bartlett, Nebraska, which is in the central part of the state towards the eastern edge of the Sandhills. He recalled that the Sandhills stopped at the east end of their ranch. Bartlett was a small town of only 120 people at the time.

Mignery taught himself to draw based on life around him. His mother taught dancing and ballet and started a little string orchestra in the little hometown. While she embraced a more artistic lifestyle, his father, who showed scant interest in art, was, at various times, a cowboy, a rancher, and a law officer. As a result,

Mignery never felt that he learned much about drawing from them directly; however, his mother and father openly encouraged him as he developed his skills. People began to notice Mignery's attempts, and he got his first public art job when he was hired by his coach to paint the high school mascot, a bronco, in the middle of the gym floor. He was paid four dollars for it and still considers it his first commissioned piece.

Mignery spent four years at Wayne State College before serving two years in the Army. He returned to work on the ranch and later found employment as an illustrator for a large wholesale company in Hastings, Nebraska. Only then, in the early 1970s, did Mignery venture out on his own as a sculptor. He cast his first sculpture in 1973 and found his artistic voice.

And I had my idols, of course. Charles Russell. I always considered him to be the epitome of the cowboy art artist because . . . he

portrayed the horse exactly . . . the way I remember working horses on the ranch. He just had all of the nuances and movement of the ranch horse down.

Mignery considered growing up working with horses to be his training for understanding the movements, textures, and anatomy of the animals. And while drawing was easy for him, painting was more difficult. He said the colors did not come naturally for him. It was not until the illustrator who employed Mignery suggested he try sculpting that he found a natural medium for his talent. In sculpture, he could work out and explore the two-dimensional concepts used in drawing and painting. His first finished piece was titled *Veteran* and was a small work of an old cowboy. Mignery felt like he was finally walking on the right path.

Much of Mignery's work began as small sculptures about 8 to 10 inches tall before he moved into bigger art pieces. Early on he created a piece called *The Encounter* which was a pack horse and rider trying to avoid a bear. The sculptures kept getting bigger, and he created his first monument in 1982 for the ConAgra Company in Omaha, Nebraska. Since that time, he has made almost sixty monumental installations around the country and in Hawaii.

Mignery spends a considerable amount of time on design, although he never believed himself to be a "refiner" of his works. His artworks are not slick but contain what he calls "pockmarks," along with rough textures and flaws. The sculptures do not reflect the hours and days spent getting an arm or leg positioned just right, or a turn or lift to fit the action just so. He tries to portray his theory of movement in each creation.

The horse has always been a source of inspiration for Mignery. He remembered being six or seven years old and trying to imitate the movements of a horse. He and a cousin would run around running, jumping, and galloping, pretending they were the horses on the ranch. Mignery says he was always enamored by the movement, the flow and grace of the horse. The horse, to him, was and

is a symbol of something free. He developed an affinity for the movement of a horse when he was riding. He tried to develop a riding style moving closely with the horse and, in doing that, he realized that the rider can be an asset or a detriment to movement for the horse. He discovered that when he moved with the horse, adjusted his weight, and coordinated his motions with those of the horse, he could see and feel how much easier the horse could move. In his work, Mignery sometimes uses cattle in what he refers to as "a supporting role," but it is usually just an excuse to do another horse.

Later on in life, I started dwelling a little bit more on people. I was raised with the cowboys and, of course, the farmers, where the sand hills ended and the clay country kind of started, and it was just the humility and the quiet heroism of those people that fascinated me. But the first part of my career with the Cowboy Artists of America just basically dwelled on the horse.

Mignery rode his first horse when he was about 10 months old. It was a Shetland pony, but it sparked a relationship with horses that has never ebbed. His father raised some horses but bought most, preferring the Hancock bloodline because of their temperament. Mignery said those horses had a little more intensity and a little more anger, which made them good working stock. He believes this exposure to these animals, the ranch horses and cattle, shaped his idea of the images he created. His creative process always relied on his memory, which he believes gives his work more spontaneity and emotion. This spontaneity makes his pieces instantly recognizable.

I would rather see a little bit of variation . . . in anatomy, and maybe it might be a little bit wrong if you take the calipers. I don't use calibration measurements. Because to me, the eye is my caliper. And it matters not to me whether a piece is exact dimensionally, you know, perfect, as long as it appears to my eye to be correct. As long as the anatomy appears to be correct in my eye.

Mignery prefers to focus on the movement and action of the horse in his works. For him, the only theory he keeps about creating horse art is "if it looks right, leave it, and if I don't like it, then tear it down."

Another feature of Mignery's artwork is that it is all based on diagonal lines. He does not like to use vertical presentations because he feels a vertical line will stop the action whereas a diagonal line creates movement. When he began sculpting in the early 1970s, he noticed that most artists at the time used flat ground underneath their action pieces, which really did not present the right movement of a horse, rider, or anything else in the art piece. Mignery had experience in drawing cartoons, and he realized that he could take that style and apply it to his sculpture bases. He would draw "swish lines" to indicate movement by roughing up the base and creating lines that move up around the feet and legs to duplicate the swish line. His horses are also portrayed lean and tough.

I prefer lean horses. Some of these Quarter breeds are so heavily muscled. They are beautiful horses, you know, I mean, a guy should love to have one like that. But, as far as movement and design, they're a little obstructive for me because it's kind of like . . . trying to get a lot of visual movement out of tennis balls in your basket.

Eventually, Mignery moved away from monument-sized sculptures, moving his studio into his house and selling the monument studio. He wanted to concentrate on doing more sculptures with the time he had left. Monuments take up to six months to complete, and he had so many concepts he wanted to create that he decided to do smaller pieces.

Mignery has won several important awards for his sculpture and other artwork. In 1996 he was elected as a member of the National Sculpture Society. He is a member and past president of the Cowboy Artists of America and has won the Western Art Associates' Kieckhefer Award and the Best of Show Awards at the Cowboy Artists of America Show in Phoenix, Arizona.

Well, I guess it depends on the extent of your knowledge of these things, you know, just having some knowledge of cattle drives and things . . . like the gear. I tailor-make the gear for an era, and the clothes for the cowboy to wear in those days. They didn't always dress like Roy Rogers, you know.

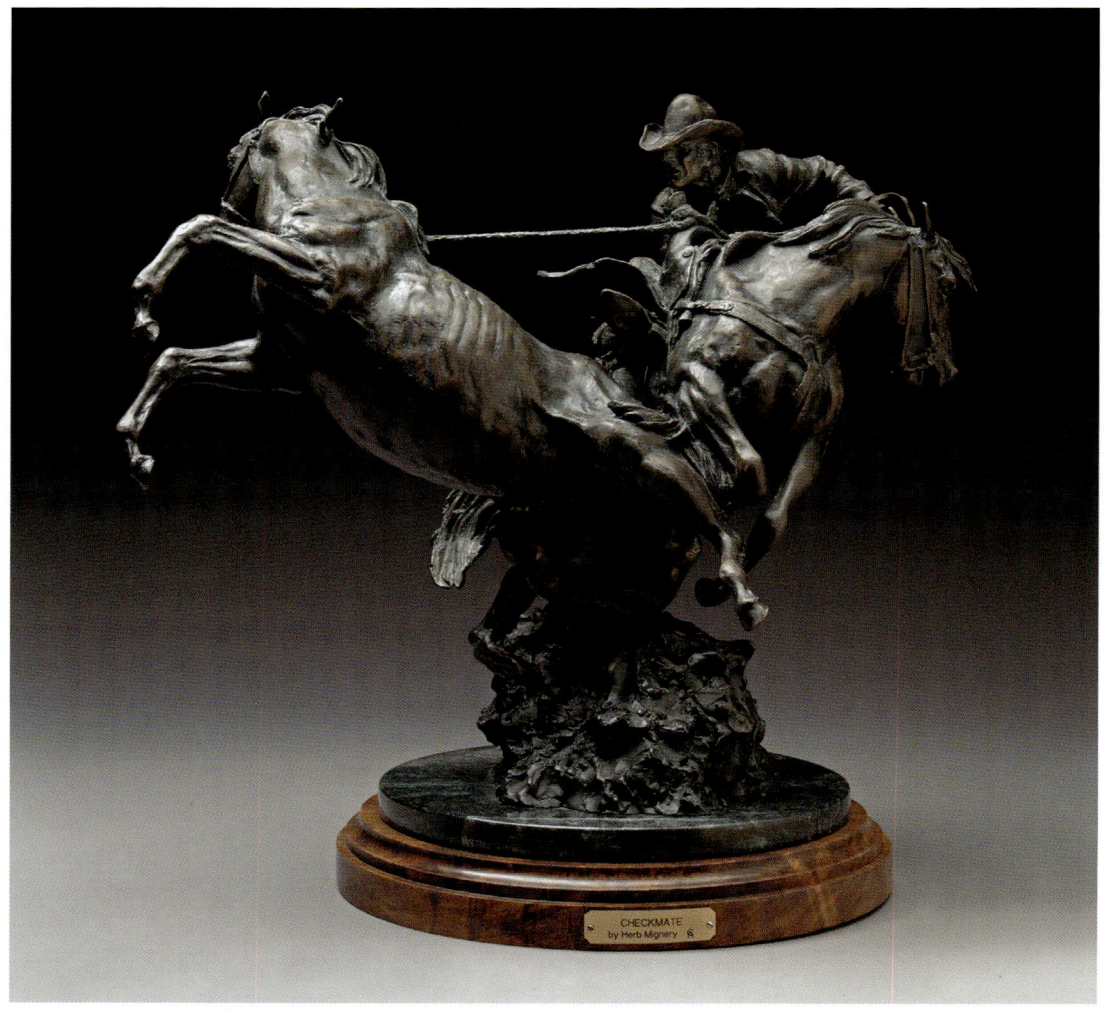

Checkmate

(Bronze, 20.5" × 14" × 12", 1985)

"An old method of breaking horses was to snub a young horse up to an older solid horse. Then a second rider would saddle and get on the horse. And that way you have some control over him. You know, lead him around. Here they have a halter on that horse that's starting to rear apart. The rider had him snubbed up and then let the dally slip away and the young horse almost got away from him. It's almost a toss-up which one's going to win."

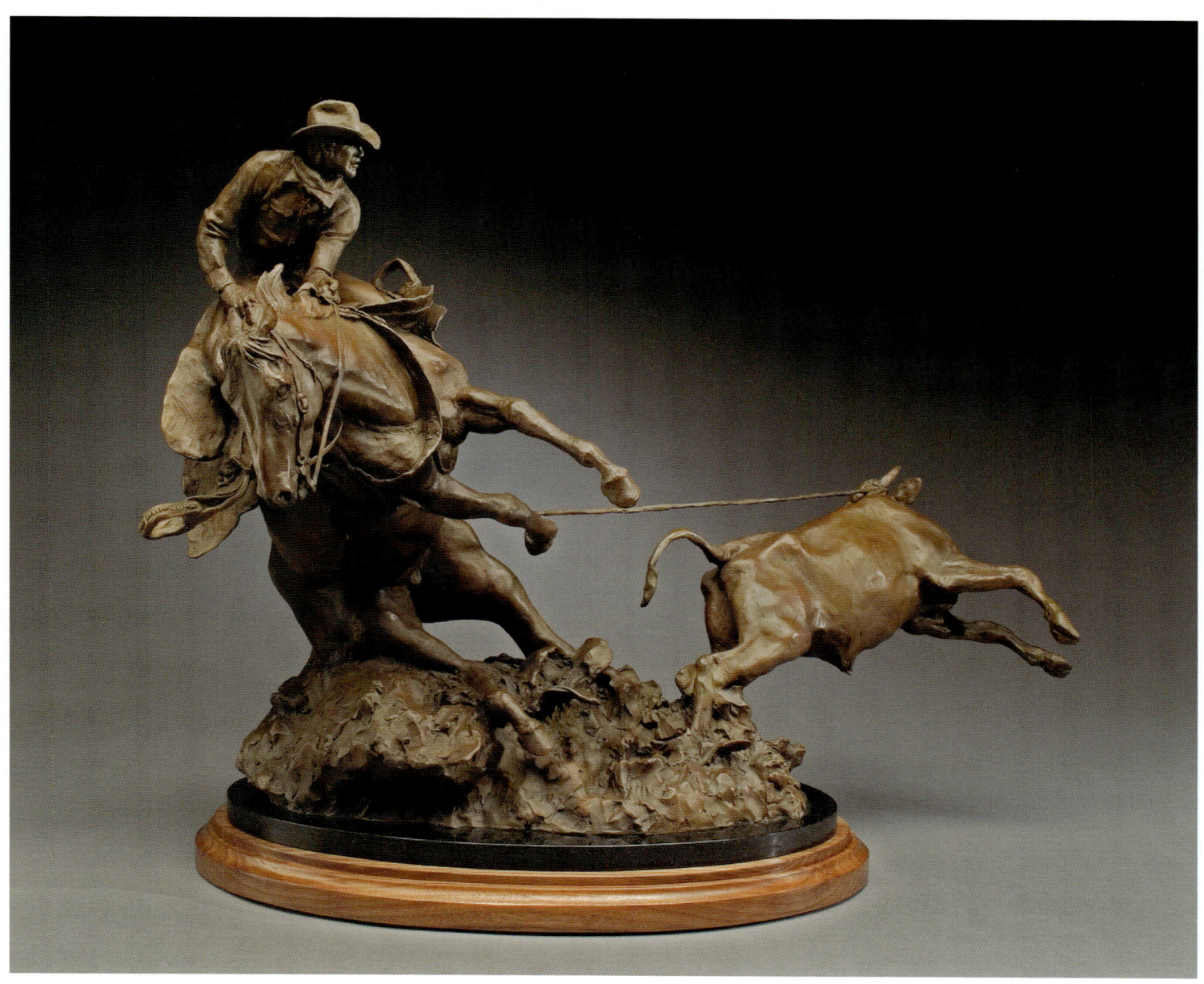

It's a Cinch. It's Trouble

(Bronze, 21.5" × 30" × 17.5", 2008)

"What's happened is the rider's back cinch has snapped and the steer has pulled the rider up over the withers of the horse. The front cinch is the only thing connecting. Obviously, the guy's in trouble."

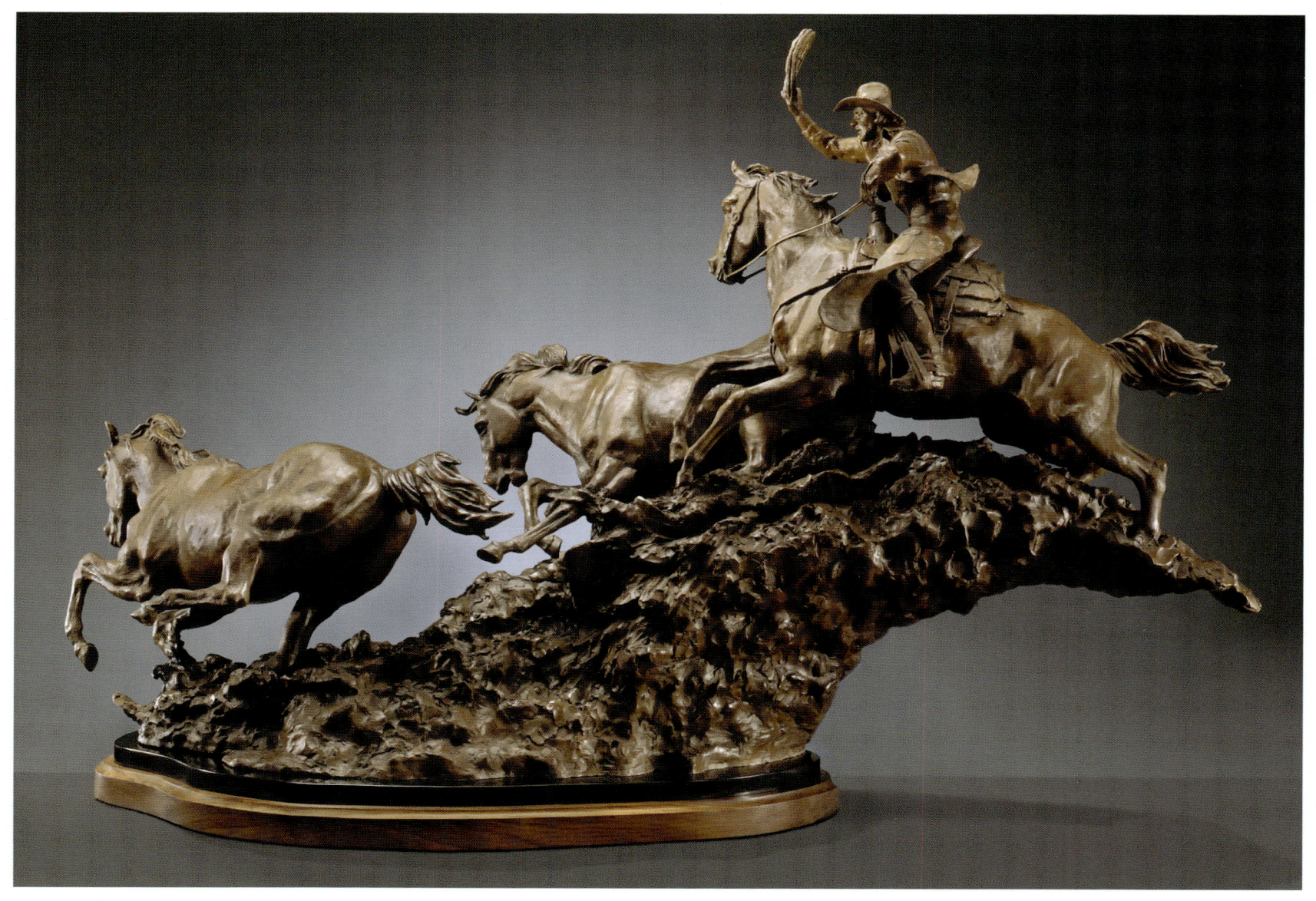

Return of the Remuda

(Bronze, 31" × 15" × 51", 2000)

"They are bringing the remuda back from pasture. Kind of an exercise in movement and design and motion. I tried to keep the movement so it's pleasing to the eye and a little variation. Rather than a bunch of straight lines. I like to disturb the ground a little bit around pieces. I've found that it creates movement."

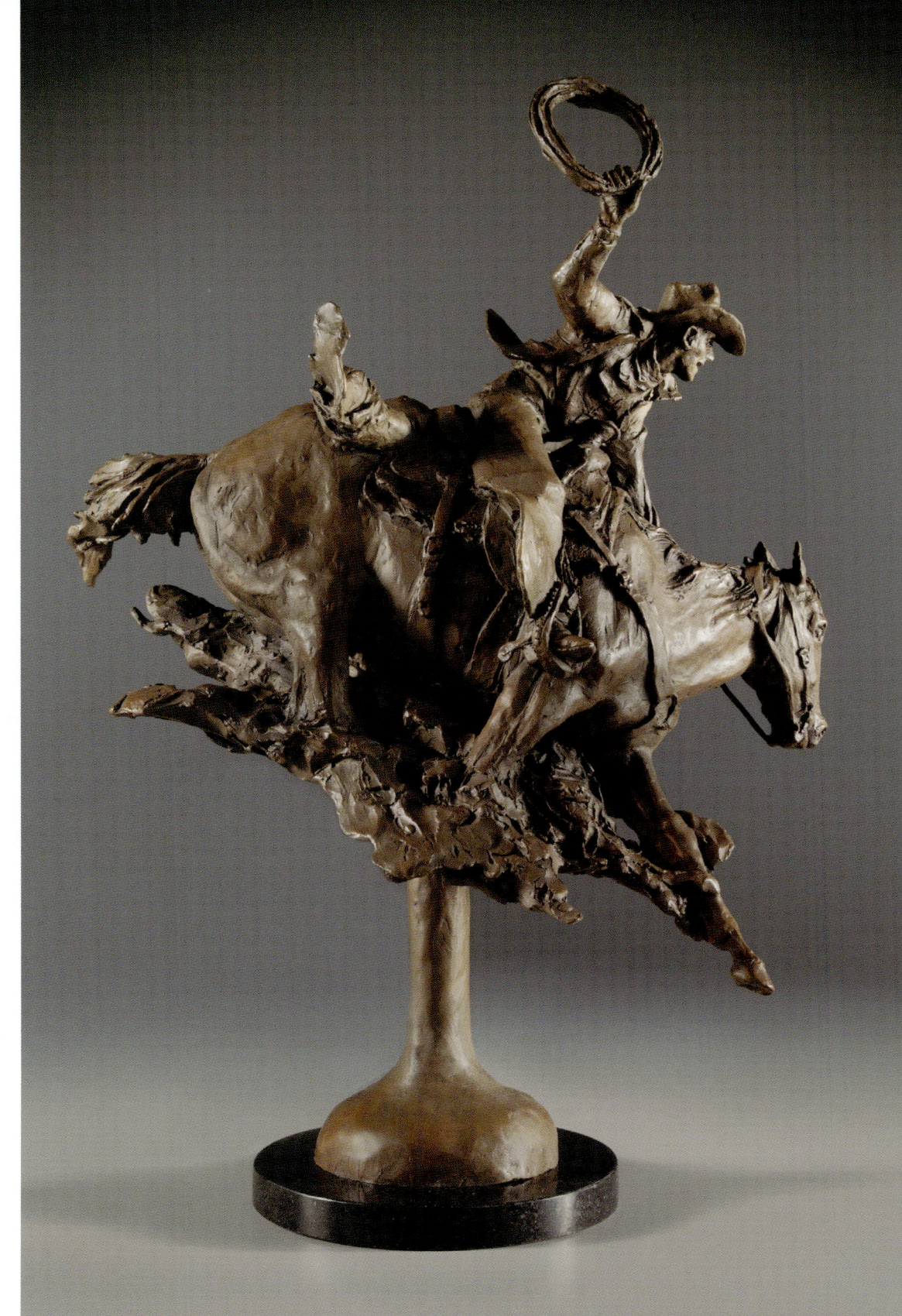

Ridge Rider

(Bronze, 20″ × 8″ × 15″, 2015)

"This is a cowboy coming down off a ridge. He's trying to head off some cattle from getting into a difficulty. There is not really a story behind it, it's just a study in movement. I'm not a real refiner, I don't believe in slick finishes. That doesn't match the subject."

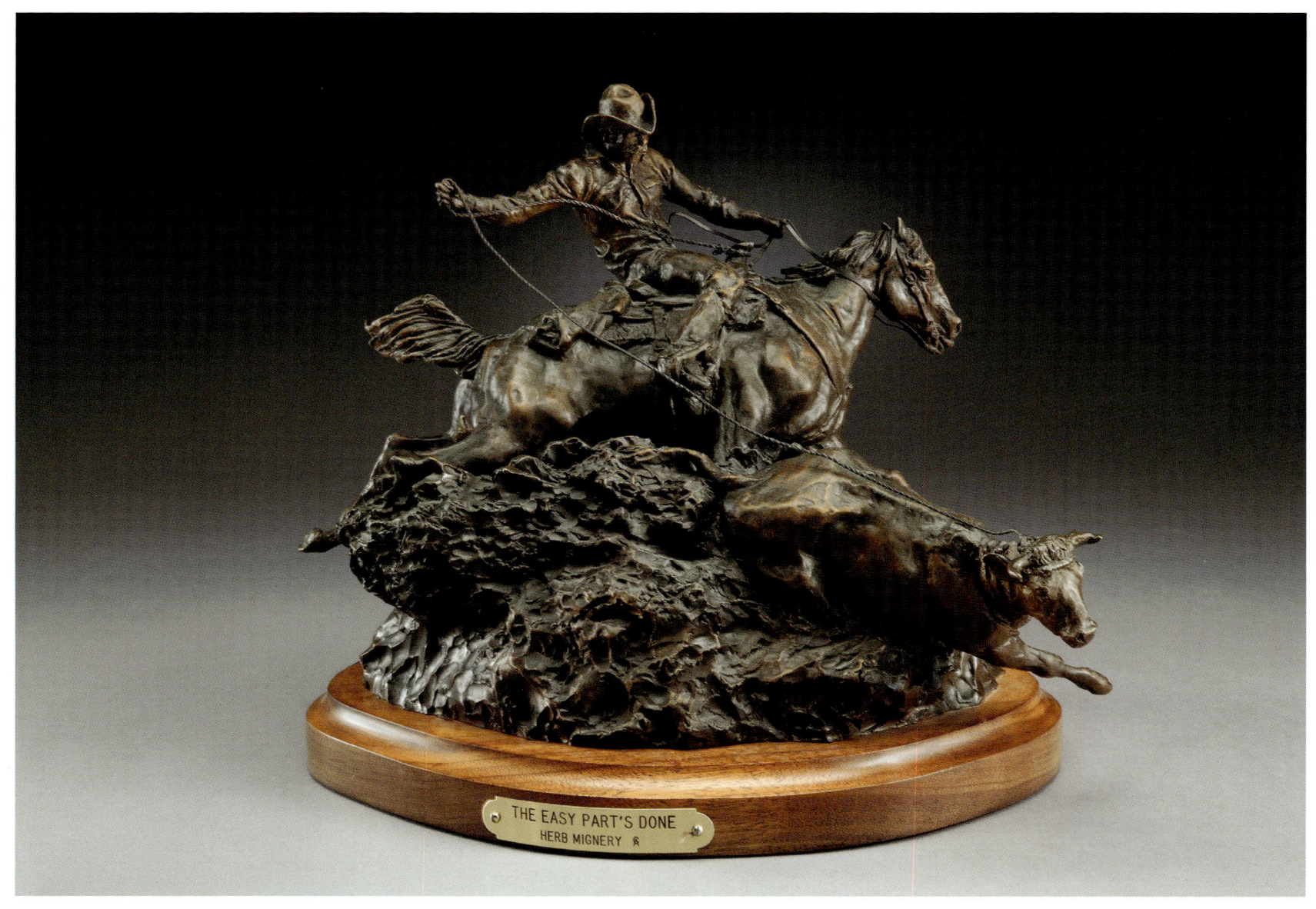

THE EASY PART'S DONE
HERB MIGNERY

The Easy Part's Done

(Bronze, 10" × 9" × 12", 1985)

"The guy has roped a steer and he's tied hard and fast. He's done the easy part. He's out there alone. He's still got to bust the steer to get him down so he can handle him. It's showing the old steer roping style so he can bring him down and try to get to him before he gets up. That was my first piece in my first CA show."

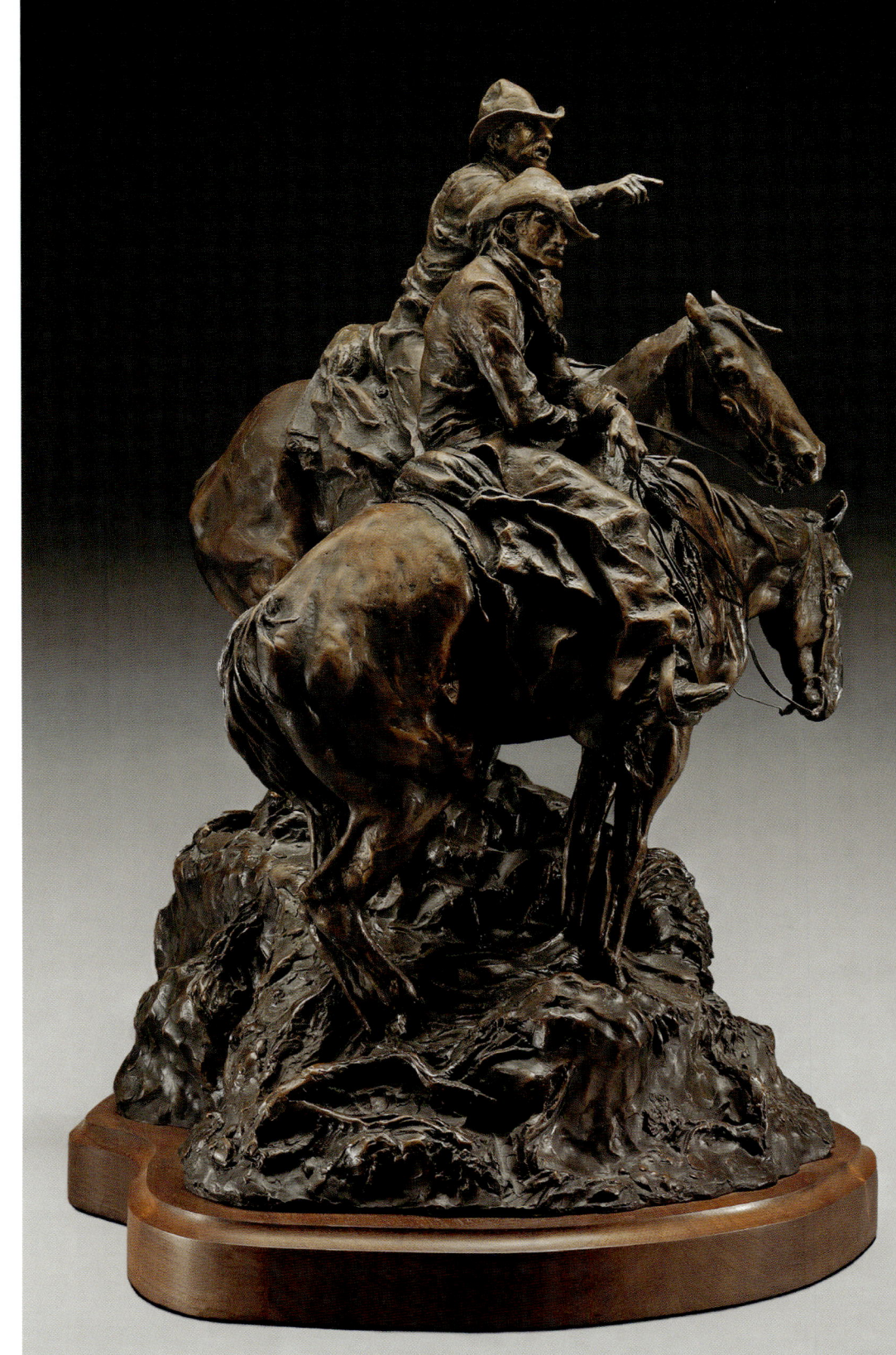

The Steering Committee

(Bronze, 24.5 × 16.5 × 18, 1989)

"This is the scouts on a cattle drive. The horses are lean and look rough. They were out there all the time, being ridden, and really got exercised. On these cattle drives, they didn't have a lot of time to stop and let the horses eat and get fat. They had a job to do. I have developed an affinity for that particular look."

Bill Nebeker

CHAPTER 17

Bill Nebeker

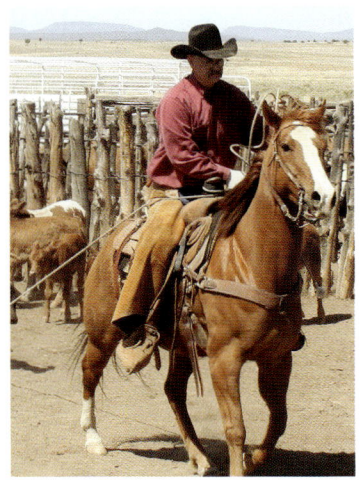

Bill Nebeker was born just outside of Twin Falls, Idaho. His parents farmed and ranched there and kept a dozen or so horses. When Nebeker was about five years old, he developed asthma. His father then moved the family to Prescott, Arizona, after reading that it had the cleanest air in the country. They found some-one to run their farms and moved to the mountains where Nebeker's father found work at the Long Meadow Ranch. This ranch had a reputation for raising excellent cattle. When Nebeker recovered from his asthma, the family moved back to Idaho for another five years until the symptoms of his asthma returned. At this point, the family sold all their Idaho property and moved back to Prescott, where Nebeker completed school. He attended college in Flagstaff, where he got involved with the rodeo club. Nebeker was only there a year before he went home, but he had the rodeo bug by then.

During his early years in Prescott, twenty-two-year-old Nebeker was introduced to Western art when he attended an art show at a local bank featuring George Phippen's work. He was mesmerized with the bronze pieces and decided to teach himself how to create artwork like those. He bought some clay at a local store, which turned out not to be the right kind, and began trying to sculpt. Phippen opened a foundry at his studio in Skull Valley, Arizona, where Nebeker went to work to learn the business. He quit his two-dollar-an-hour job with the Forest Service, went to work for $1.50 an hour at the foundry, and set out to learn how to cast bronzes. He continued to pursue how to build figures with clay. He studied books on anatomy and would go out to his horses and measure them from head to toe. His first completed piece that was cast at the foundry was a horse with a cowboy standing beside it. He sold that one almost as soon as it was finished.

I didn't know anything about art. I mean, we didn't have museums to go to for art. We didn't have classes in high school for art. It was all crafts. But I spent my whole life making things, whittling horses, and making a little leather saddle for it and the bridles and reins.

A Scottsdale art gallery began showing Nebeker's work; he was with that gallery for about five years before moving over to the Trailside Art Gallery. He found that he could make a better living making artwork part time than working at the foundry. He followed the inspiration of George Phippen and continued to focus on Western art sculptures. He went full time as an artist in 1976.

Nebeker got to ride on a number of local Arizona ranches near him such as the O RO Ranch, the Perkins Ranch, and Cynthia Reagan's ranch, which was a four-generation ranching operation. They would call him and he would rope and drag calves at brandings for them. Some of his friends ran cattle on leased ranch land and he began roping with them, eventually starting team roping with the group. He roped at the Arizona Cowpunchers Rodeo for four years, even winning the team roping. He thought he was living the best of two worlds. He got to do a lot of day work on ranches then go home to create his artwork.

Nebeker carried a small camera with him when he worked on a ranch. He said he was so busy he didn't have time to take many photos, but he observed the men, horses, and cattle around him. He looked at what kind of leggings the cowboys were wearing, what kind of saddles they were riding, and what kind of headsets they used. These observations would give him ideas for his sculptures. He has also built artworks from the things he heard about in stories. He doesn't sketch out an idea but is able to see a finished image in his mind before he builds an armature and begins to sculpt the clay. He builds and adjusts the figure as he goes along.

Nebeker builds monuments using the same work pattern. For one of his most popular monuments, *If Horses Could Talk*, Nebeker had been developing the idea for the artwork for years. When he completed it, he sold out an edition in one evening. He created the work by combining several ideas about a mule deer and a horse. In this sculpture, the cowboy does not see or hear the beautiful deer standing just below him, but the horse is fully aware of it. It was a very popular piece, and it also showed some of the personality of the horse.

Nebeker does extensive research before beginning a piece. He searches for images of the landscapes and ranches of the time period he wants. He collects books of cowboy gear like ropes, hats, armbands, holsters, and bits. He studies the horses of different eras in books because the kind of horse he often has in mind may not exist anymore. For horses in his artwork, he studied the pictures of Texas Rangers and their horses. In his mind, a cowboy piece without the horse is only half a cowboy. The cowboy, the cattle, and the horse together form a complete picture. Some of the actions seen in his sculptures come from his knowledge of how a horse moves in rodeo events. He wants his riders to be in step with the horse's movements: "It's like dancing. If you are dancing with a girl, you don't want her to fall down with you. You better be in step on a bucking horse or you're not going to make it. You have to dance with the horse."

Sometimes Nebeker uses the scenery as support for his sculptures. In one of his sculptures, he suspended a horse blowing up over a big sotol bush. This is a common scene on some of the Arizona ranches where cowboys are trying to ride green-broke horses. When the young horse begins bucking, the cowboy tries to stay in the saddle, just like dancing.

Nebeker was invited to become a member of the Cowboy Artists of America (CAA) in 1978 and was elected president of the organization four times. He was commissioned to create several larger-than-life sculptures in Arizona including *Early Prescott Settlers* that depicted four people as early Arizona pioneers. He made *Territorial Sheriff* for the city of Glendale, Arizona, and *Memorial to Fallen Officers* for the Arizona Department of Public Safety headquarters. He created *Lest We Forget* for the Yavapai County Courthouse to honor fallen law enforcement officers. Nebeker has been featured in magazine articles in *Arizona Highways*, *Art of the West*, *Southwest Art*, *Cowboys and Indians*, *Western Horseman*, *Horse & Rider*, *Phoenix Home and Garden*, and *Persimmon Hill*. His sculptures can be found in both museum and private collections all over the world.

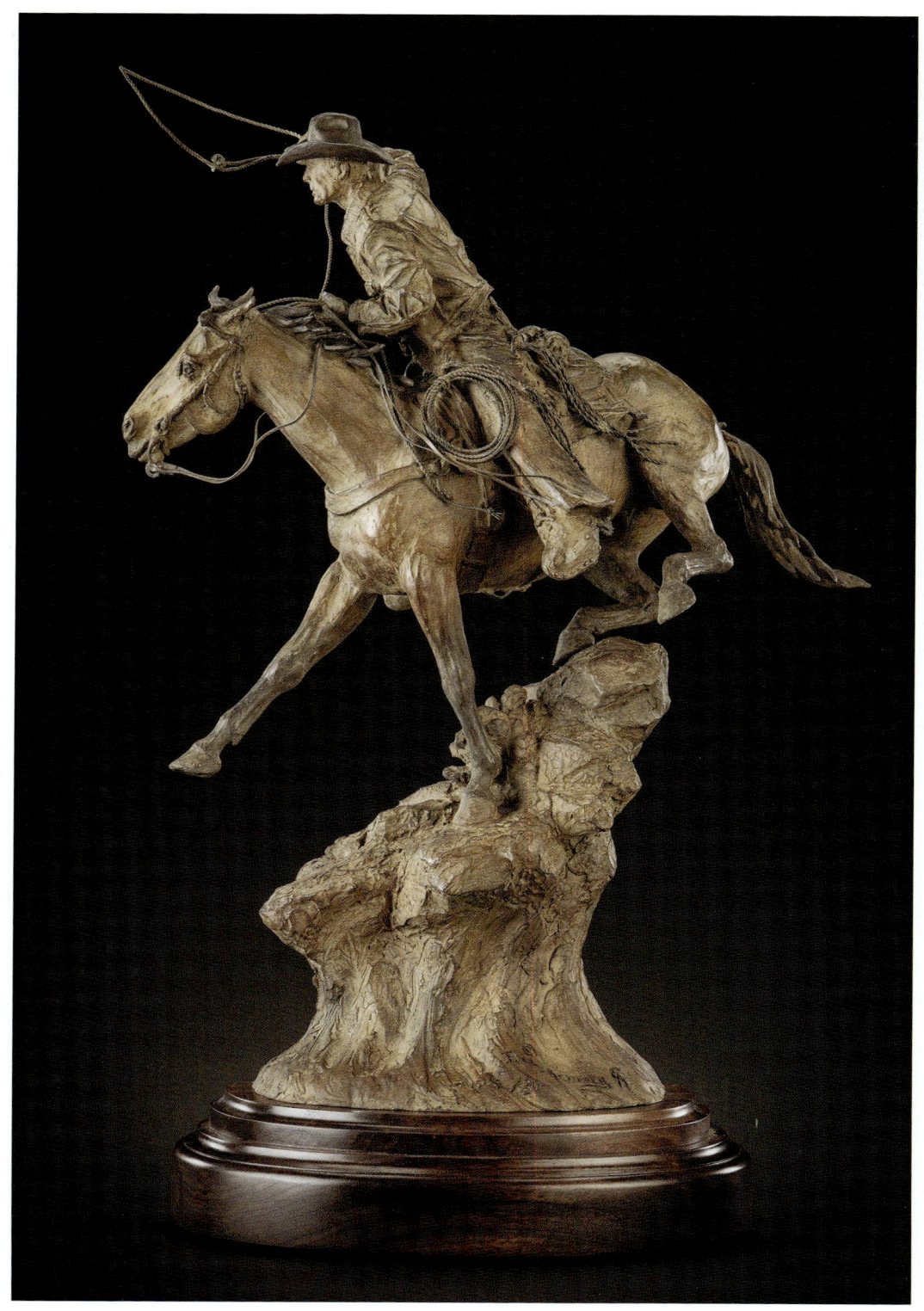

Chasin' Mavericks

(Bronze, 23" × 17" × 9", 2017)

"During roundups in rough country, some cattle get smart and hide out when they see or smell any riders. After a few years ranches may have five or six four-year-old bulls, big unbranded calves, wild cows, and steers who have learned to stay away from ranch hands. I guess a lot of people know that these unbranded and unearmarked cattle are called 'mavericks.' This cowpuncher has jumped a bunch of mavericks and is chasing them in hot pursuit."

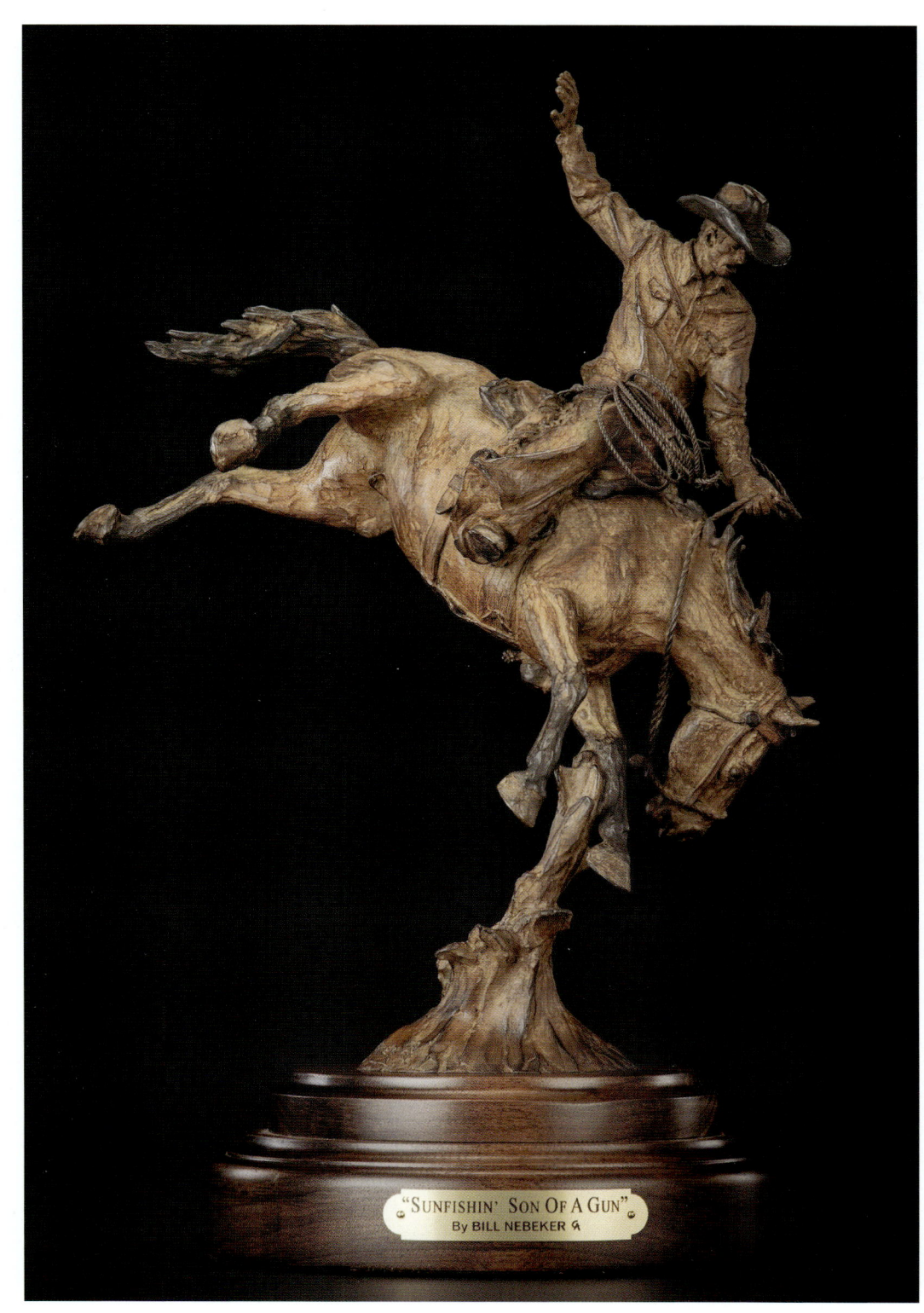

"SUNFISHIN' SON OF A GUN"
By BILL NEBEKER

Sun-Fishin' Son of a Gun

(Bronze, 16″ × 13″ × 7″, 2020)

"Nothing represents an image of the West like a cowboy on a bucking horse. There have been many poems and songs written about hard-to-ride horses referred to as sun-fishers. This refers to a horse whose front is going one direction, his hindquarters the opposite direction, and his belly up towards the sun."

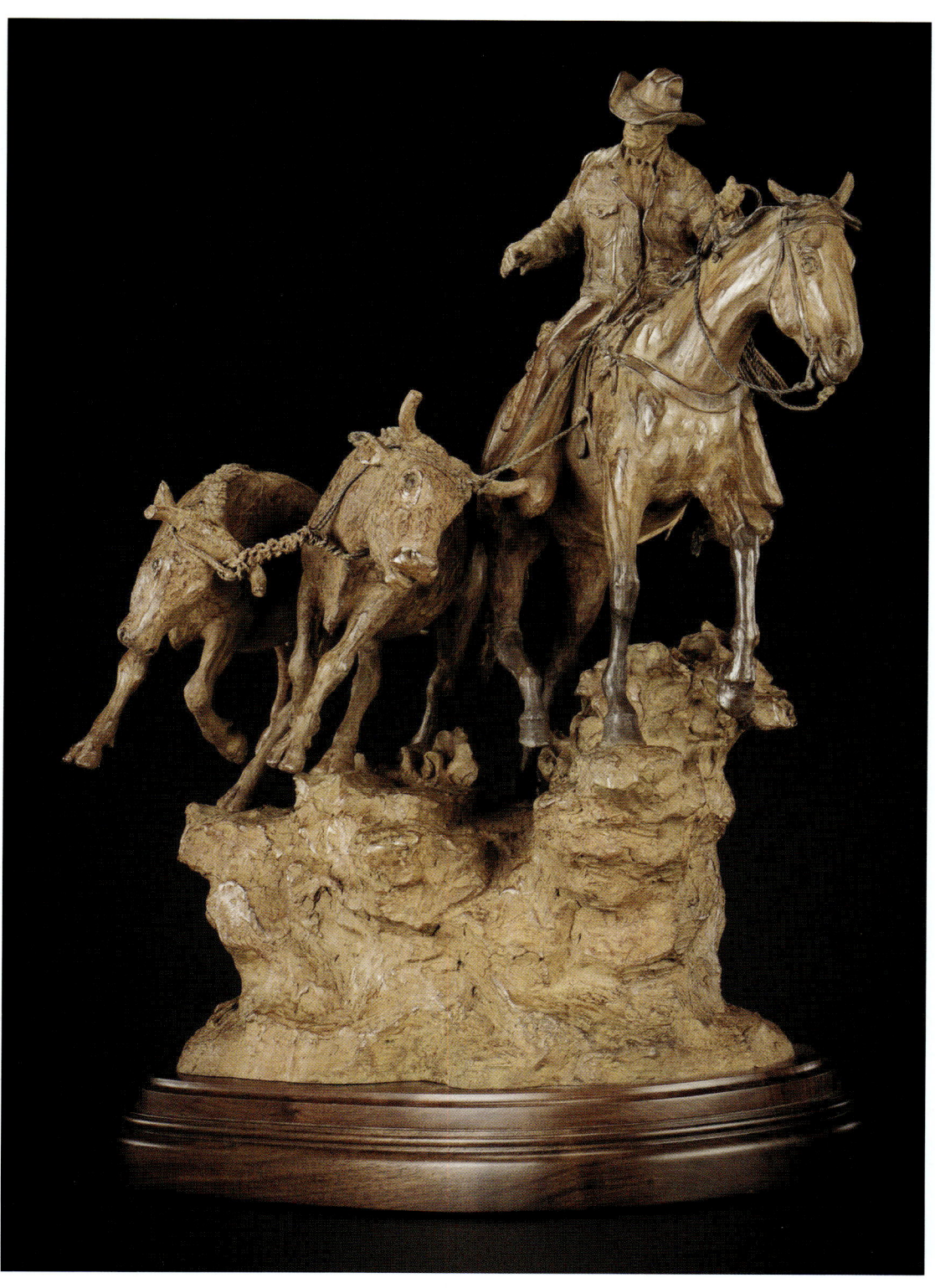

Double Trouble

(Bronze, 29" × 27" × 16", 2015)

"This piece shows a breed of cowboy I admire greatly. Their job is roping to lead in wild renegade steers or maverick cows. He has tied them to each other and to his saddle. Maverick cows haven't been caught or branded. Renegade steers are branded and ear-marked, meaning he was caught but escaped years ago, growing wild and very large. George Phippen, the first president of the CAA, inspired me to sculpt this piece."

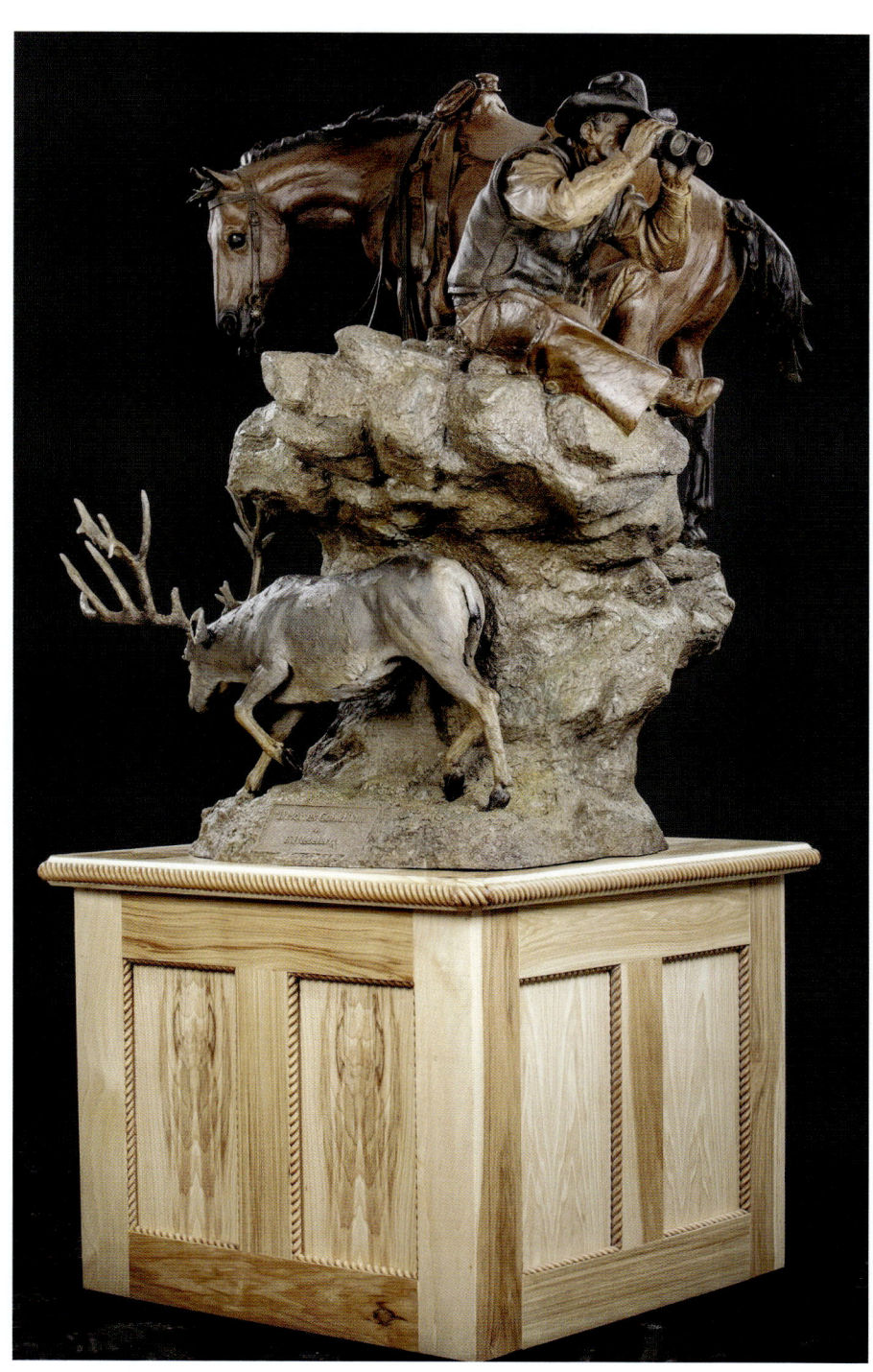

If Horses Could Talk

(Bronze, 48" × 47" × 36", 2020)

"My dad started a tradition of hunting, fishing, and camping, which now continues with the fourth Nebeker generation. This sculpture depicts a hunter unaware of the big mule deer buck below his rocky perch, sneaking away, as the horse sees the secret getaway. I've seen this scene several times. All my friends who hunt know it has happened to them, and the non-hunters are happy the deer gets away."

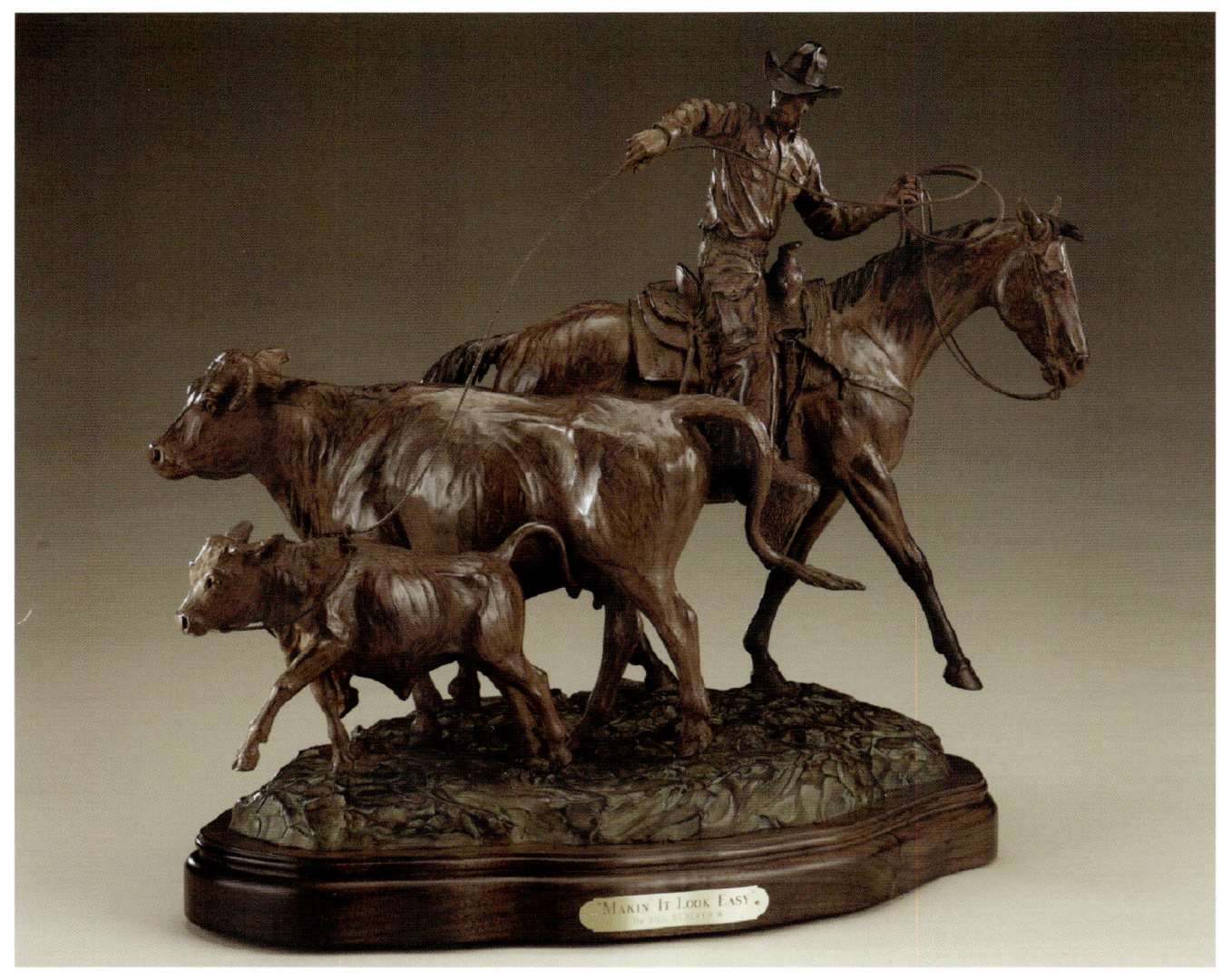

Making It Look Easy

(Bronze, 20" × 22" × 14", 2007)

"I always like to watch a cowboy who is a good hand with a rope. The cowboy in this sculpture has separated the cow and her long-eared bull calf from the rest of the herd. Somehow this calf was not found during the earlier spring gathering. I wanted this cowboy to ease in close, moving slightly past them in an easy way so he does not cause any excitement. This cowboy turns and is throwing this pretty little back hand, houlihan loop on the calf without Mama knowing."

Made Mama Mad

(Bronze, 24" × 23" × 16", 2021)

"Working cowboys gather cattle from sections of a ranch in the spring and fall, separating calves from their mamas to get them branded or doctored. It's not unusual to have one old mama cow who is really protective of her calf. I made this showing this cowboy who roped a calf just as mama tries to rescue her baby."

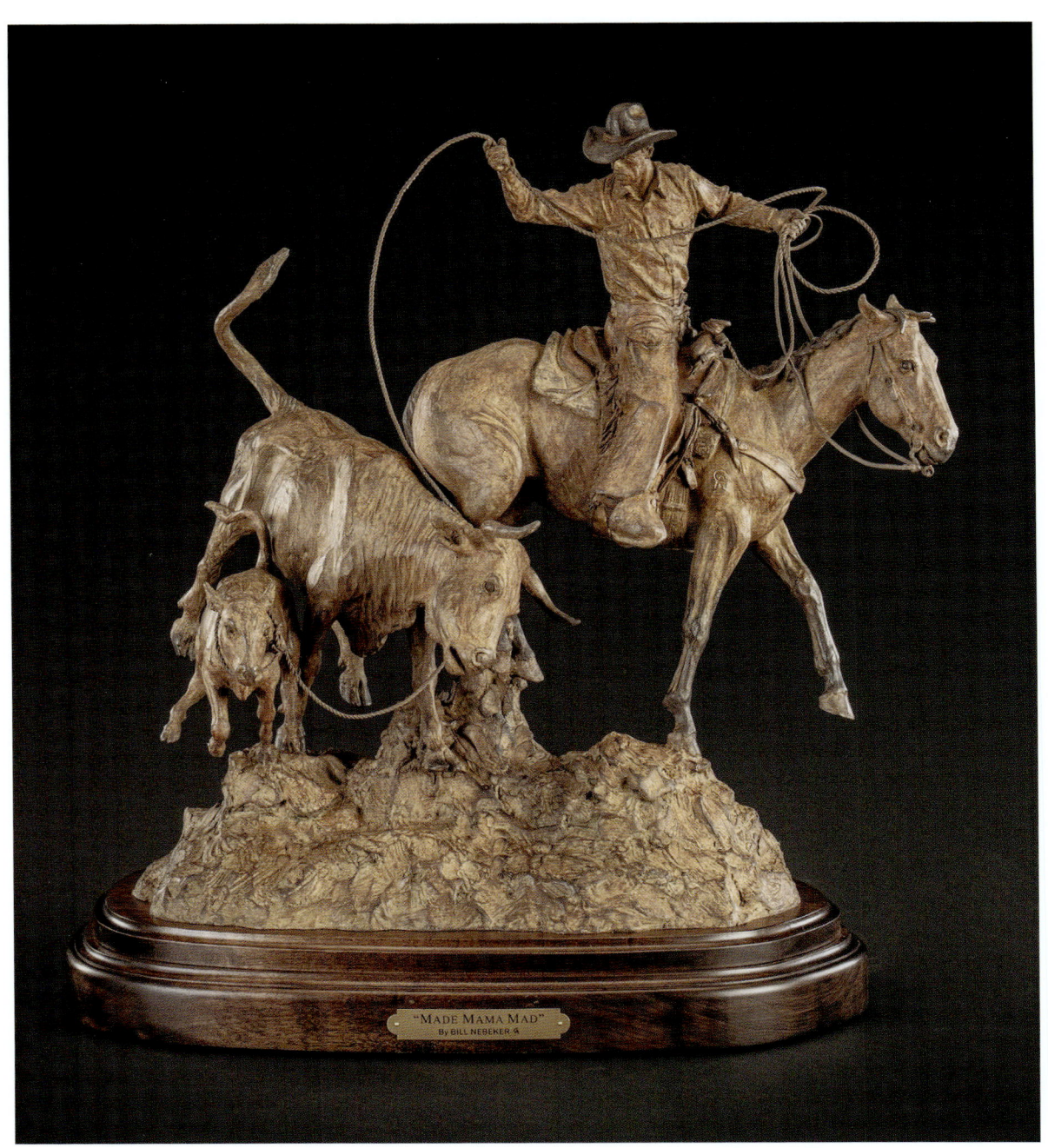

Dustin Payne

CHAPTER 18

Dustin Payne

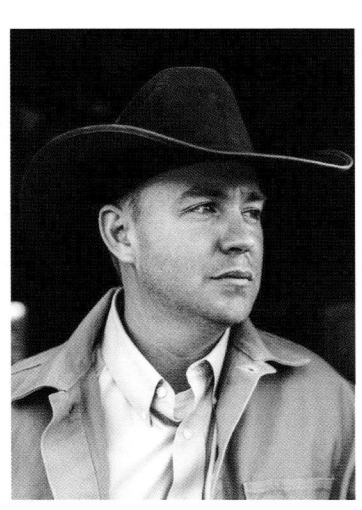

Sculptor Dustin Payne was born in Alamogordo, New Mexico. He grew up around ranching and rodeo and the Western way of life. Because his grandfather was a rancher in Piñon, New Mexico, Payne experienced the work of raising both cattle and horses. He is also a descendant of Hiram Daugherty and Mary Jane Goodnight, Charlie Goodnight's sister, linking Payne to one of the pioneers of Western ranching. Early in his youth, his family migrated north. He rodeoed at Odessa College in Texas for a short time before heading to Wyoming because of health issues. His father, with whom he stayed, was in Lander, Wyoming, working on some big monuments. Payne transferred to Central Wyoming College, made the rodeo team there, and met his future wife.

Payne is a third-generation sculptor and so grew up around art. He spent time at his father's, and grandfather's, sculpture studios. The family also had art galleries in Sedona, Arizona; Santa Fe, New Mexico; and Jackson Hole, Wyoming, where he was able to study the sculpture and paintings of other artists. He took art classes in each of the colleges he attended and, almost by default, began working in his father's studio. Payne was strongly influenced by books of Charlie Russell artworks and the drawings of Will James, just as his daily care and riding of horses gave him the intimate knowledge of the anatomy of those animals. The historical nature of the sculptures by his grandfather and father have also given him a perspective of Western American history.

Payne sculpted his first artwork when he was ten years old; he quickly discovered his skills as an artist and began selling his work alongside that of his father. His work around horses and cattle gave him the knowledge of what the ranching life looked like. The artworks at the Buffalo Bill Center of the West supplied him with ideas of how the Old West looked and influenced his own artwork.

Horses have always been a part of Payne's life, whether it was on a ranch, a rodeo, just for pleasure, or in his art creations. He thinks the horse shapes his style and creativity.

Well, I tell you the problem I run into. I often think that I have too many horses in my work. I have to struggle not to have too many because the horse is one of the passions I have. I bet if you talk to many Western artists, it would be the same.

One of the things he finds in most Western art is how the artist makes the horse look over certain periods. On a recent monument for the Former Texas Rangers Foundation, Payne created four riders on four horses, all from different time periods. The artwork is titled *The Legend, The Lore, The Law* and is in Fredericksburg, Texas. He used a modern Quarter Horse for one of the pieces and some older horse depictions for two of the others. But he had trouble finding a model for the oldest Rangers horse until he discovered one of his neighbors had an adopted wild Mustang. Payne was able to use the Mustang as a perfect model for the oldest horse. The tack, or what is on the horse, has to be correct also. Payne researched the gear, clothing, and weapons used by the Texas Rangers in the different generations of men who served. He believed that accuracy was the key to honoring this law enforcement agency. He wanted to show where the Rangers came from and where they are today. In most of his other artworks, that same drive to be accurate is mixed with creativity. Payne also considers the location and style of the locations for his monuments, so he is able to make them fit into the landscape more naturally.

Payne learned from his grandfather how to create but keep the natural aspect of his artworks. He is careful in shaping the head of a horse and the way a rider sits in the saddle. He begins with small clay studies or sketches in clay and works out his ideas that way before beginning a larger piece. He uses an iPad for photographs of his subject at the beginning and as the project continues. He takes measurements the same way. Payne follows the inspiration of the work of the nineteenth-century sculptors who he believes were the best in America: "You can see how all the horses are different and the emotion, just in their faces, is the most difficult thing in doing the horse in sculpture."

Payne uses his own horses for models for most of his artwork. He said that there are always a lot of different horses coming and going because his sister buys and sells horses.

If you look at the horses in some of these old photographs of the horses the guys were riding in the 1800s, you wouldn't be able to recognize them. If I made one look a lot like that, I would have a hard time selling it.

One of the most difficult parts of creating artwork for Payne is not overworking a piece. The strength and character he wants to instill in each piece comes from his intention to carry on the spirit and traditions of the old cowboys and ranchers. Payne has a great respect for the history of the American West and wants to pass that on to others through his sculptures. Payne seeks to make his work reflect the authenticity of older times. It is amazing to him what his ancestors went through and how much strength it must have taken for them to overcome adversities such as the Dust Bowl and the Depression. He thinks it is important to try to put that strength into his images.

Payne's sculptures can be seen in art galleries and private collections across the West. He's been featured in Western art magazines and has been the artist-in-residence at the Whitney Western

Art Museum in Cody. He was inducted into the Cowboy Artists of America in 2017. Payne won the Gold Medal for Sculpture and the Ray Swanson Memorial Award at the 2021 Cowboy Artists of America Show. Payne and his wife Tammy live in Cody, Wyoming.

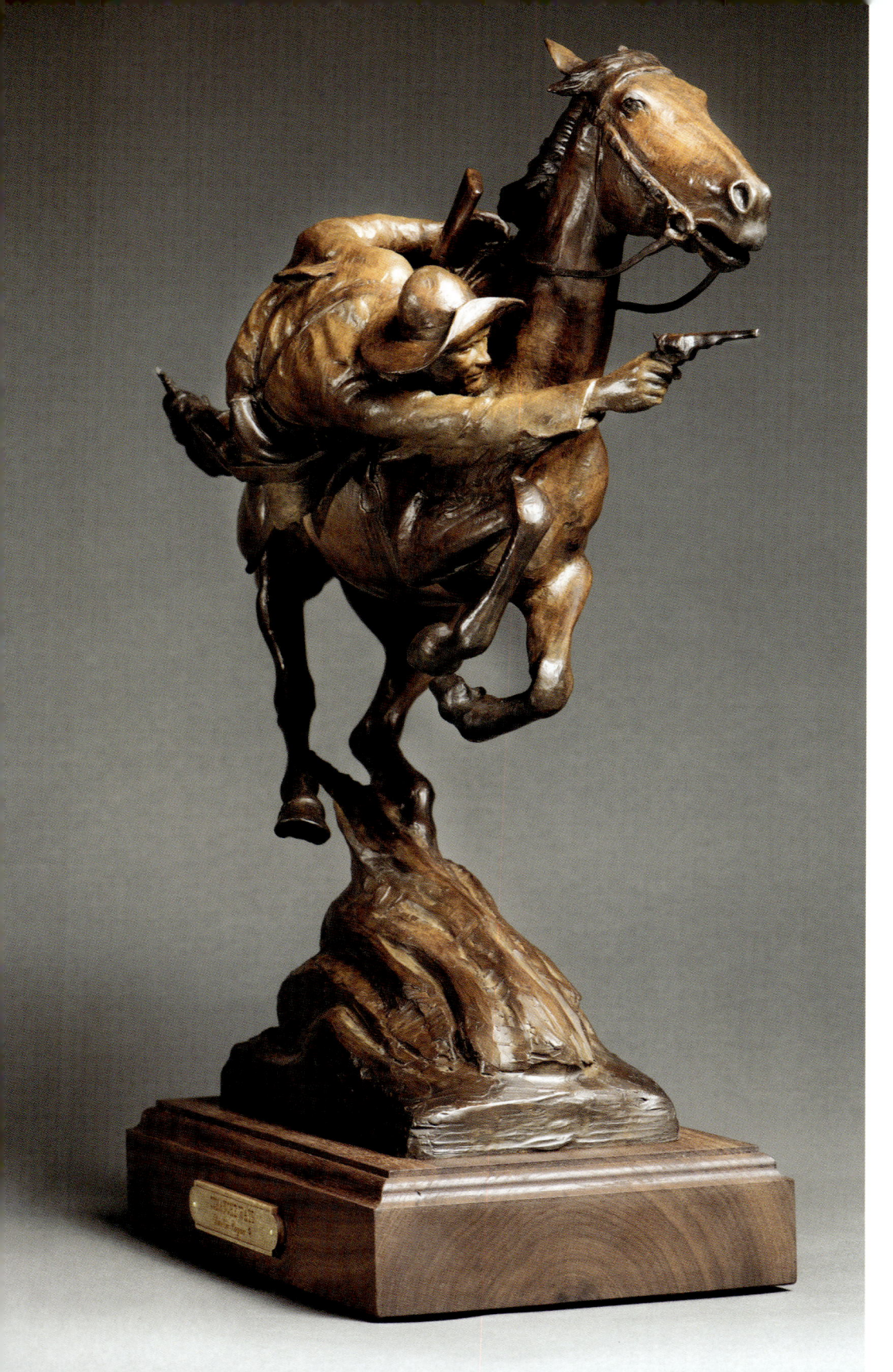

Comanche Ways

(Bronze, 16" × 18" × 7", 2020)

"You know, I don't want to be the guy that's just decorating somebody's corner of their house. I'd like to think that 100 years from now, or 200 years from now, the world still goes on and somebody will look at something I made because that's how they get it, that's how that worked. I still do a lot of my stuff kind of Old West themed and goes back to the Old West and that's because of my passion for history and the founding of the way our Western country was made."

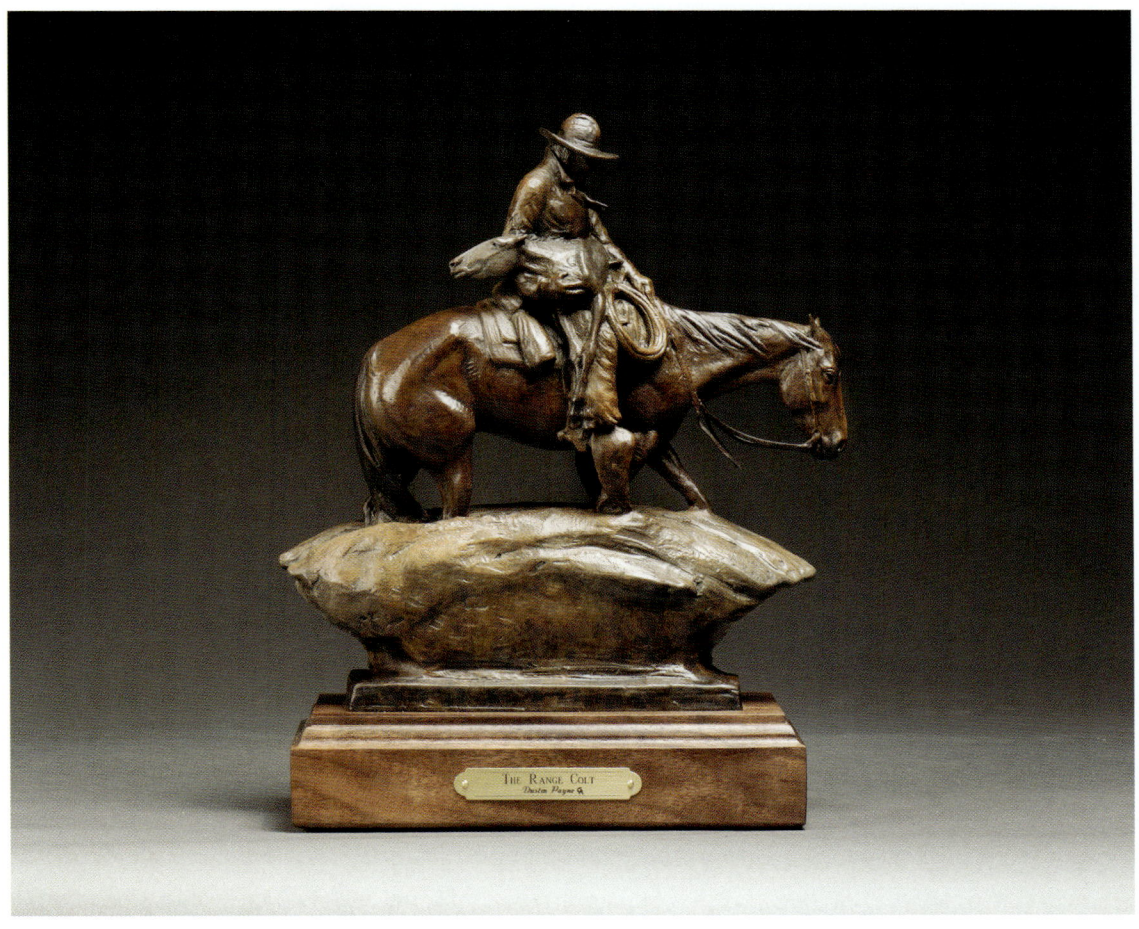

The Range Colt

(Bronze, 11.5″ × 10″ × 5″, 2019)

"The horse is probably one of the passions that, as a young kid, I can remember. What made me love this is going out to the barn and being around the horses and that grows into the basis for my artwork. I feel the horse definitely shapes why I do this and I would bet you if you were able to talk to many Western artists, it would be the same answer."

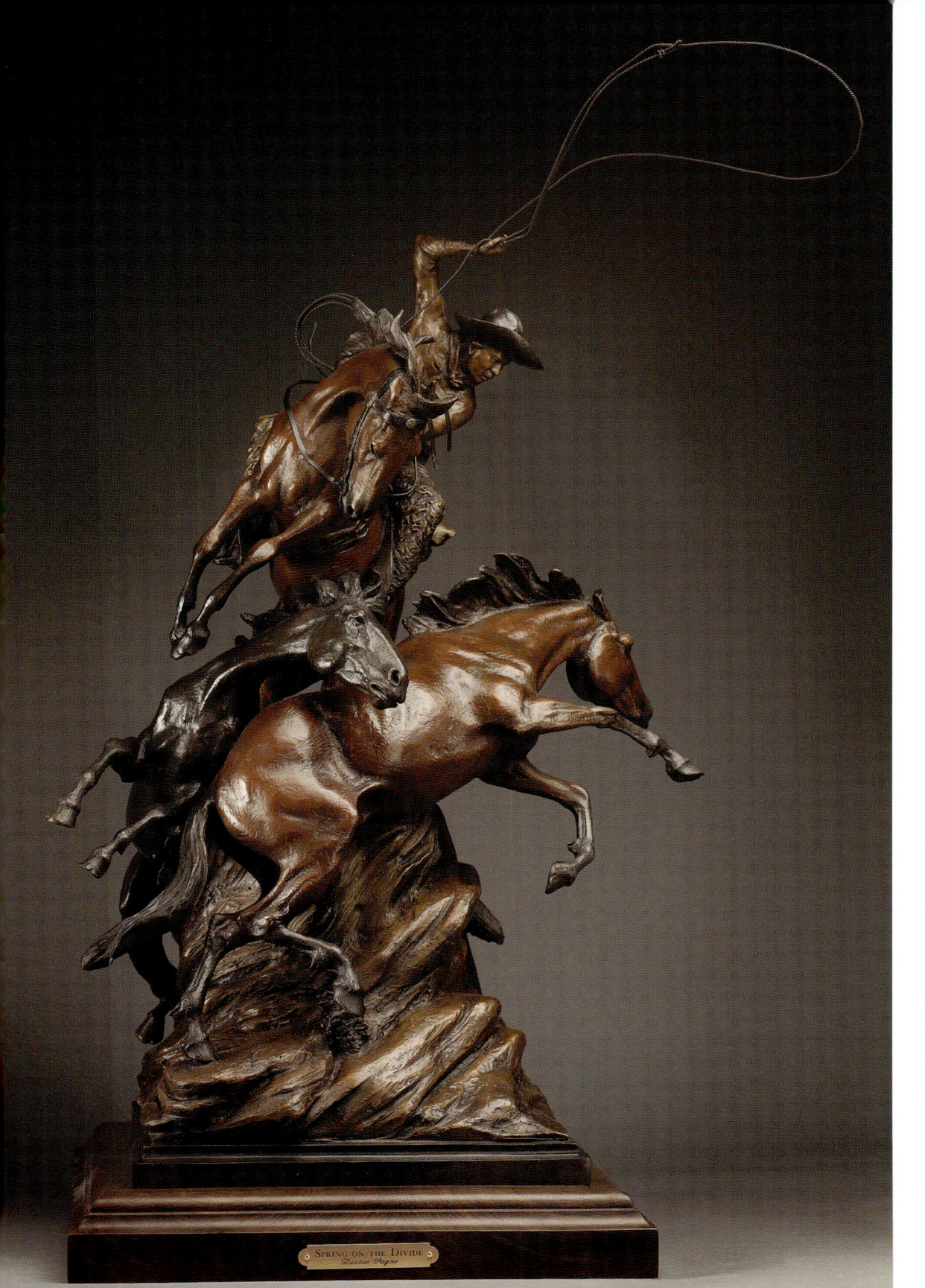

Spring on the Divide

Spring on the Divide

(Bronze, 25" × 15" × 16", 2010)

"Usually I'll have an idea in my head, some kind of concept, something that I'm liking and so then I'll do like these little clay studies or just little, little sketches of clay. You can really get more feeling because you're not thinking about proportions, you're not thinking about the correctness, you're just feeling it. And then from there, if I get something that I'm really feeling and really like and well then I'll take that to the next size and level and then that's where I start going and working with live horses and models and things like that."

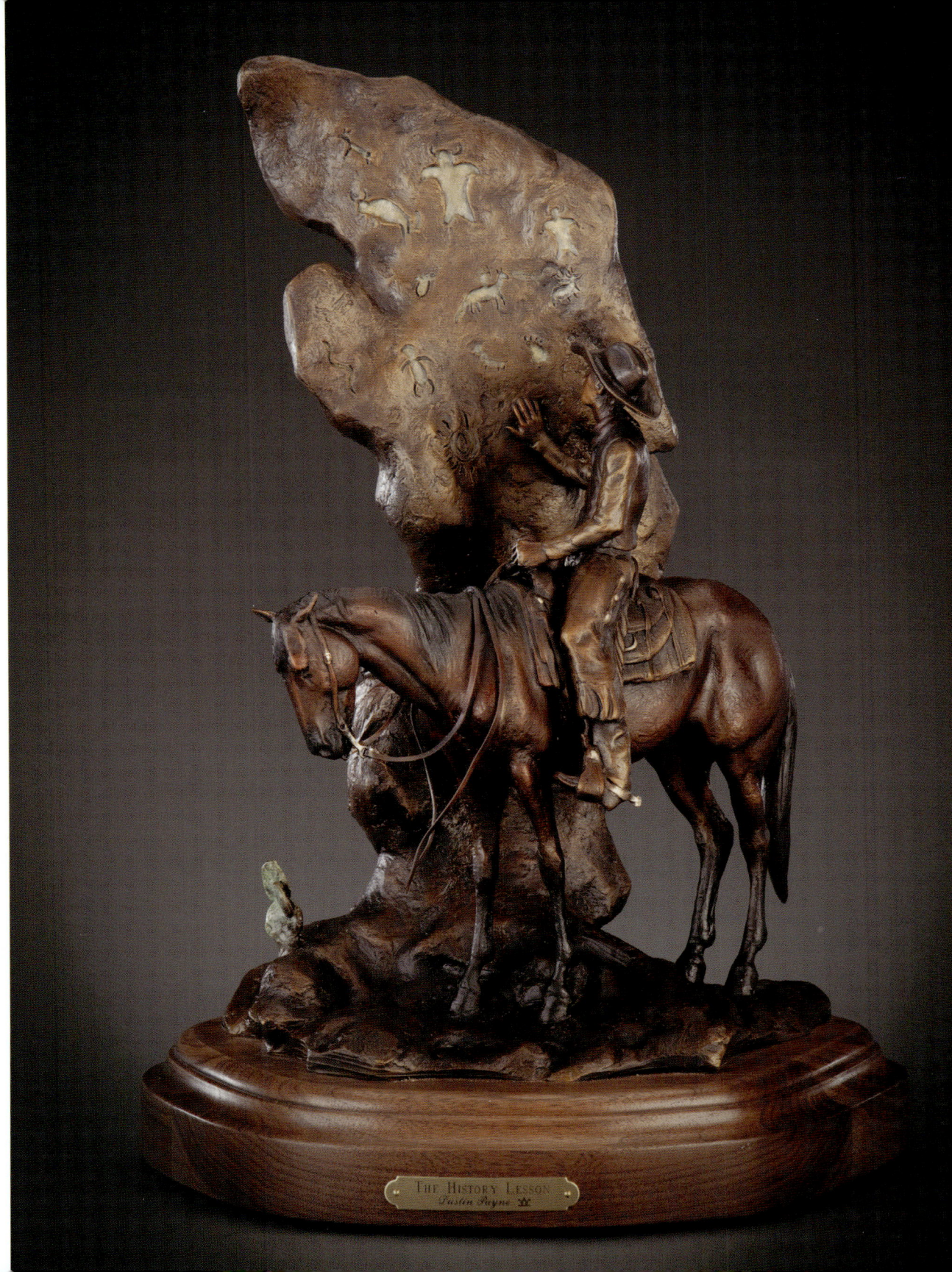

The History Lesson

(Bronze, 15" × 10" × 7", 2010)

"I'd go down to the Buffalo Bill Museum every day for a long time whenever I was starting to try to do this, and there was a saying in the roping world: 'You're only as good as the guys you're up against.' And so I started thinking what I'm going to try to go down there to the museum every day and look at a lot of the sculptures that they had there. And those were some of those early nineteenth-century artists and sculptors, which is whenever I feel sculpture was the best in America."

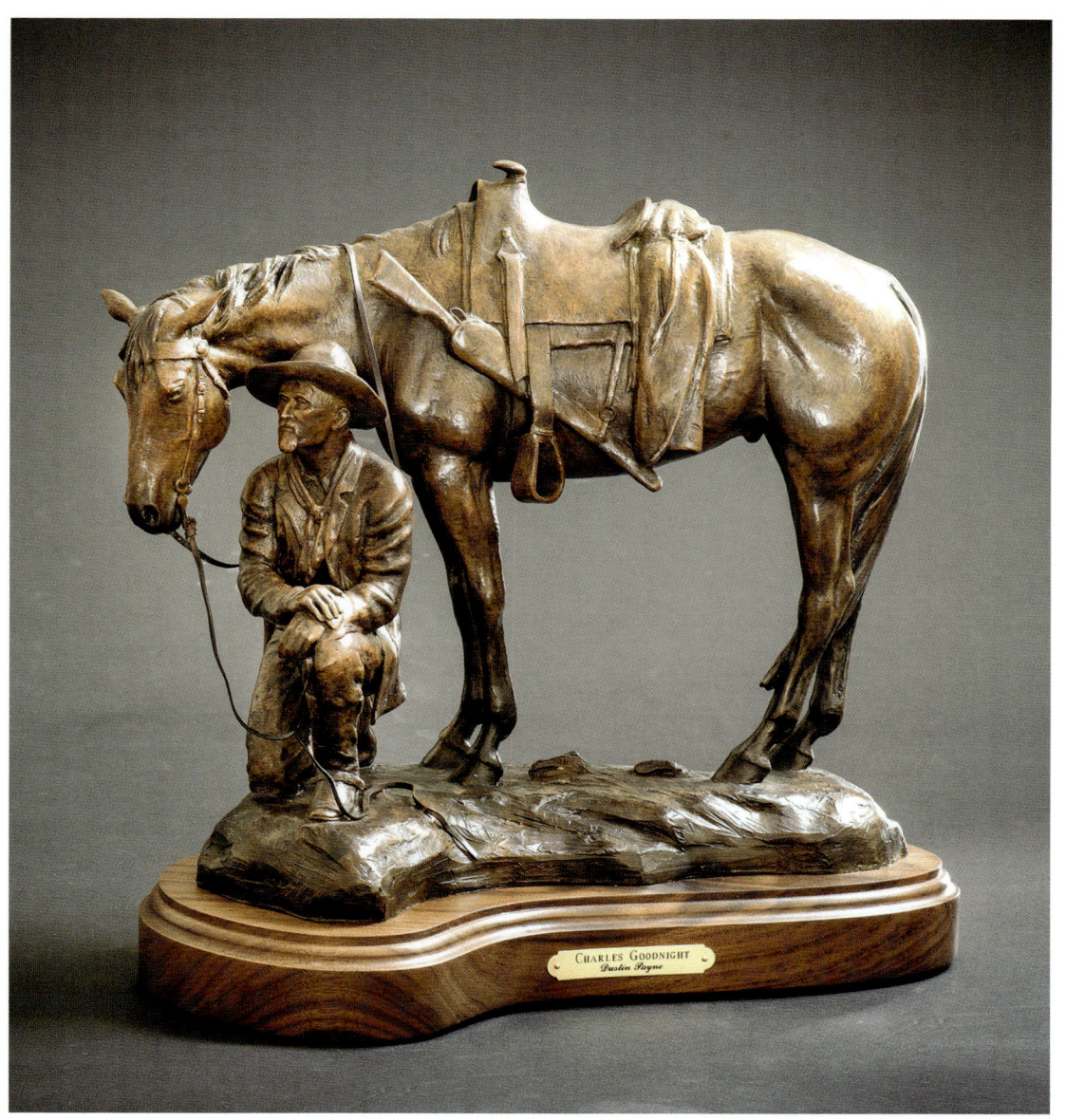

CHARLES GOODNIGHT
Dustin Payne

Charlie Goodnight

(Bronze, 14.5" × 15" × 8", 2018)
(also cast as a life-size monument)

"This one was more personal. My fifth-great uncle, or something, married Goodnight's mom in Illinois and he was the one who brought Charlie to Texas. He ended up marrying Goodnight's older sister after a divorce and they had twelve kids and I descended from that lot. I think it goes back to what I said earlier about our period of the West and how amazing it is what our ancestors went through. In the country that we built with all the Depression and the Dust Bowl— and just the strength of the people. And a lot of that comes down to the land and the people that work the land and the horse."

The Legend, The Lore, The Law

(Bronze, life-size, 2016)

"Before completing the life-size monument *The Legend, The Lore, The Law* in Fredericksburg, Texas, at the Heritage Center, I researched all of the historical gear, clothing, tack, and weapons used by the Texas Rangers throughout the different generations and met with retired Rangers to ensure the preciseness of the piece. I found a neighbor down the road that had an old Mustang that he'd adopted and I use that for the oldest horse."

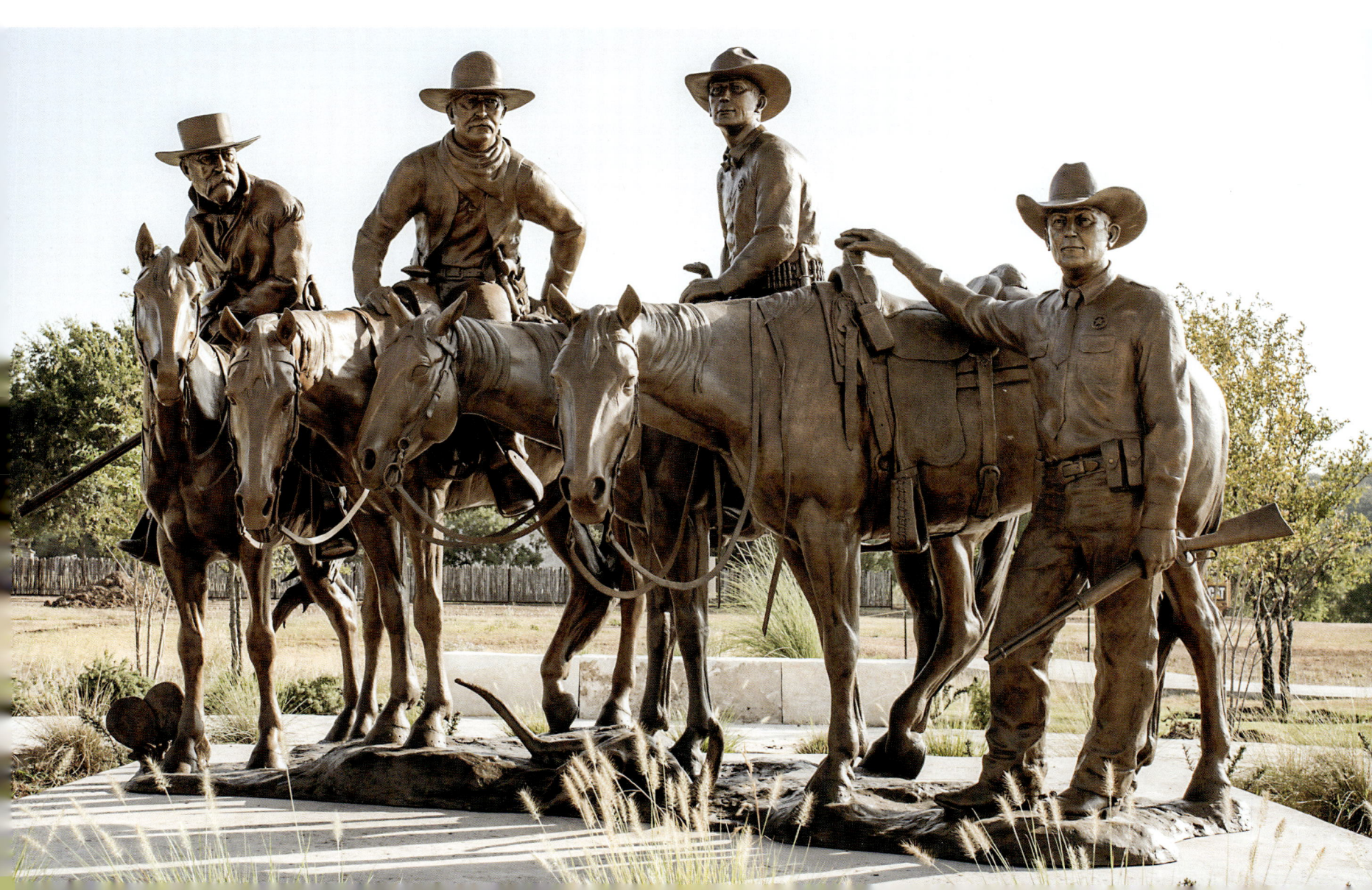

Con Williams

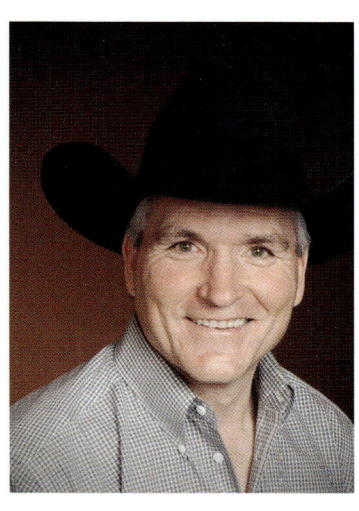

CHAPTER 19

Con Williams

Con Williams comes from a long line of hard-working cowboys. He has led a life intertwining work, rodeo, and sculpture: a combination that has been the perfect blend. Born in Seattle, he was raised on large ranches in Canada and worked in construction with his dad, Roy Williams, in the state of Washington. His father was a horseman, rancher, and journey-man carpenter. While living and working at the Gang Ranch in British Columbia, his father was the steer boss. Eventually, the family moved back to Washington for Roy to do construction work and "get healed up financially."

Dad was a true cowboy. He loved the ranch lifestyle and everything about it but with six kids to clothe and feed, it wasn't the most prosperous career.

Con was in third grade when the family moved back to a large ranch in South Central British Columbia, the Quilchena Cattle Company Ranch. There, Williams learned from an early age about working on a large cattle ranch and came to appreciate the functional beauty of horses, the land, and the cattle. He said, "When we got to Quilchena, I thought we had gone to heaven." During this time, he also began sketching the ranch animals as well as the wildlife in the area.

When we were on the ranch or at cow camp, Dad really pushed Will James books on us. Will James was a major influence on me. I loved his drawings, loved his stories, and I spent countless hours copying Will James's illustrations.

When Williams was in high school, his parents, Roy and Jeanenne, moved the family back to Washington where they bought some acreage to raise cattle and horses. His high school art teacher told him he could make a living out of drawing; however, Williams did not believe him at the time. This idea of the possibility of making a living in art, however, stayed with Williams.

Williams began college and was on the rodeo team at Casper, Wyoming, where he met his wife, Sharon. They transferred to Montana State and decided to settle down in the Bozeman area. Williams was attracted to the Gallatin Valley area from the beginning. His great-great-grandfather, John William Williams, is in the *Prominent Men of Montana* book and made his homestead at the mouth of the Gallatin Canyon, near Bozeman.

Williams's father purchased an old commercial ambulance at a construction site for Con to use to travel to the rodeos. The old ambulance provided both transportation and a place to sleep. "It even had a working siren," according to Con. Many of the rodeo cowboys today still remember Con and his unique means of travelling from rodeo to rodeo. While rodeoing, he was able to return home and sculpt. He also worked in a foundry where he learned the bronze casting process.

When I went to school at Montana State, I ran into some other bronc riders that were doing sculpture and bronzes, and so I kind of fell in with them. They had a foundry and I kind of started from there.

Williams soon began to sculpt more seriously and was able to take his works to the professional rodeos to sell. He shared a commercial booth at the PRCA (Professional Rodeo Cowboys Association) events with his friends and fellow saddle bronc riders, painter Dyrk Godby and sculptor Bob Burkhart. Williams, Godby, and Burkhart would compete in their events and share time in the booth selling their works of art. Williams said, "It was a good way to go down the road, selling artwork and trying to win

some." Despite graduating with a teaching degree in agricultural education from Montana State, Williams never taught school, as his life was filled with rodeo and sculpting. Gradually, the artwork "kind of took over."

It is no surprise that the focus of Williams's sculpture is his main event in rodeo, saddle bronc riding. Each performance or slack of the rodeo provided endless inspiration for his works. Getting the emotions and movements of the horse and rider correct sprang from his experience in rough stock competition.

It just comes more naturally when you have done it . . . a horse is just full of tension and energy. Just being around horses brings back that feeling of getting on. It helps a lot to have that experience. We get it . . . because you've felt their power.

His saddle bronc sculptures are dynamic works and catch the emotion and rawness of the event in bronze. Being a competitor himself for so many years, Williams can capture the horse in motion in a very authentic way. He says, "The explosive ones. . . . I have found they are the most fun to get on and the most fun to sculpt." Williams feels that in his art, the horse is everything. He continued to rodeo professionally but eventually began to sculpt full-time. His rodeo and ranching experiences continue to provide inspiration for new artworks.

In his sculpture, Williams often embellishes in order to get the movement and tension that he wants. He admires the sculptures of CAA Emeritus Western artist T. D. Kelsey because of his skill at exaggerating elements and stretching parts of the horse out to get the motion in his works that he was seeking. William says:

I found over the years, to get the motion that you really want, you must exaggerate things . . . but that takes trial and error. So, you do a sculpture, and it just doesn't have as much energy or doesn't portray what you really want it to, so you have to start stretching things.

Williams was helped along the way by many artists, an occurrence that he feels is common in the Western art community. He compared this to the help that contestants give to each other and to each other's kids in rodeo.

For the fine details, he goes back and uses his own saddle and equipment, which he keeps in the studio. Williams says, "I've got many saddles and gear in my studio that I use for reference. With every new sculpture, I pull the gear that I need out, to help keep my work authentic." To get the proportions of his sculptures correct, he measures his sculptures with calipers. In his work, everything is based on the head of the horse. Using that element as a scale, Williams can adjust it for any size and action.

For the muscles and movement, Williams says that you just use the knowledge of how the muscles and bones work, although it helps to watch horses in action. The most important thing, he says, is to "put my hands on them and that's always the best way." According to Williams, the bucking horses today are far different from the ones in the past. Williams notes, "They take these bloodlines of these big, beautiful horses and they've created unbelievable broncs, and most of them have some size. I think it's a really good time to be a bronc rider."

Williams's art career was interrupted when he was injured working a part-time job in construction. He fell and broke his neck and his wrist, sidelining him for over a year. He now enjoys sculpting again and has become involved in the foundry process. He prepares his own works for casting.

Williams lives and works in a studio outside of Banner, Wyoming, with his wife Sharon. They have three grown children and five grandchildren and enjoy the outdoors together. Williams has been invited to show his sculptures in many juried art shows, and his works are in many private collections. He has been chosen to sculpt for the Calgary Stampede, where over a period of twenty years he has cast eighty trophy bronzes for this rodeo. In these works and his other sculptures, he is strongly motivated to authentically capture the West. Williams sums it up by noting, "I appreciate the opportunity just to be able to talk about this. Because as artists, I don't think about these things. I think we need to foster and keep this Western heritage alive."

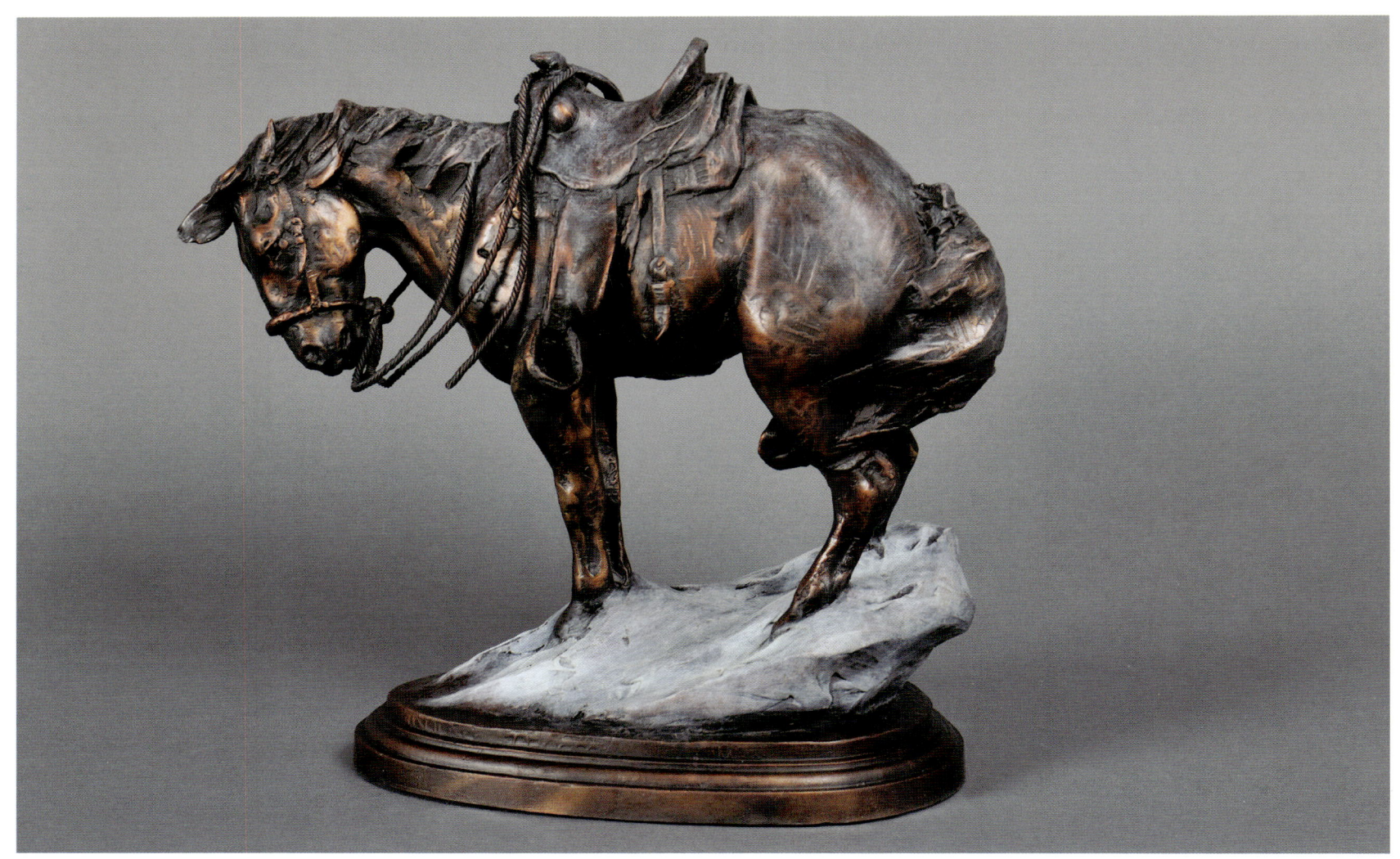

Wind Chill

(Bronze, 11" × 12" × 6", 2020)

"I had an artist friend that was coming over to sculpt, so we started from the skeletal form, which is made from wire into the armature. I created this horse in the process, or just the rough image of this horse in that day. By changing the angle and changing a few things, I can make this horse feel like it's cold. Most of the people that come into the studio where I sculpt don't know anything about horses or cows, so I spend a lot of time explaining why a horse is doing something. But this one, you don't really have to do a lot of explaining. It's just right there. I like that. Sometimes the title on the sculpture helps too. And that's not my forte. Great titles help tell the story. That's what I'm trying to do here, is tell a story. It's nice when one comes together."

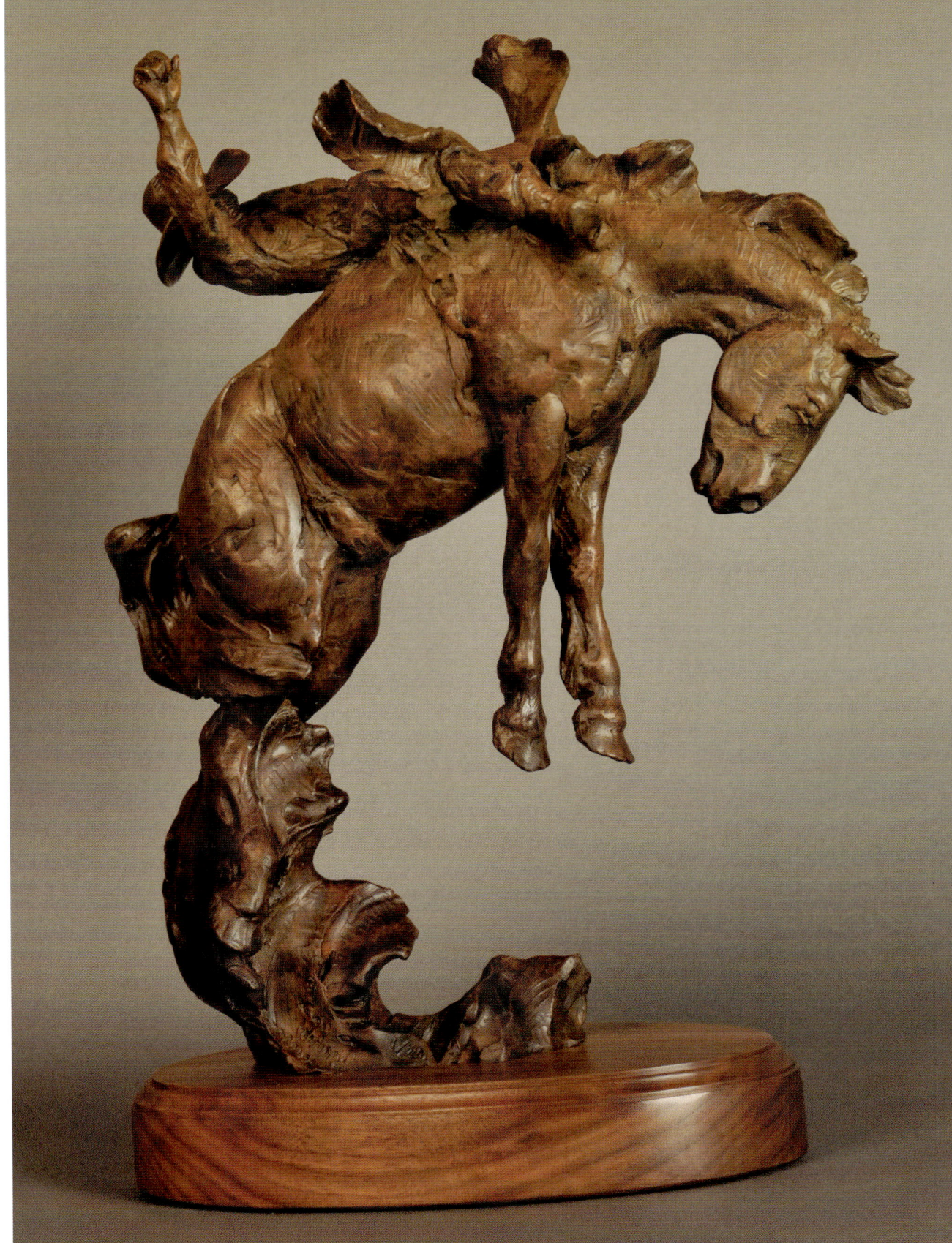

Glory Seeker

(Bronze, 14" × 17" × 7", 2020)

"This bronze was done for the Calgary Stampede as a trophy for the Novice Bareback Riding event. The Calgary trophies are awarded for five consecutive years, and seven sculptures are ordered for each trophy. Every five years, Calgary Stampede holds a competition for the new trophies for the next five years."

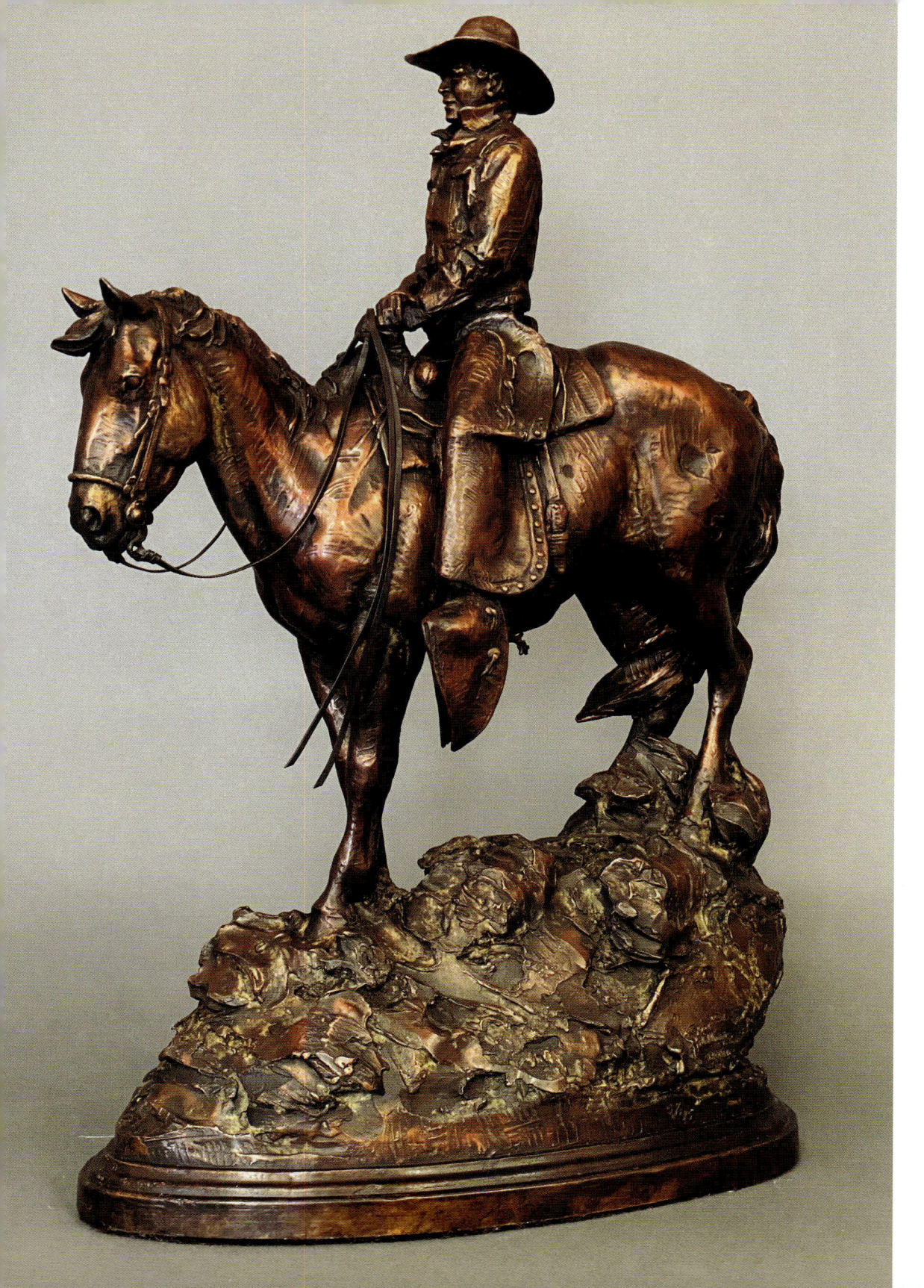

God's Country

(Bronze, 21" × 15" × 7", 2021)

"It seems like every time I get on a good horse, ride into good country, I can't help but think of The Creator . . . This is God's Country. This piece reminds me of that feeling."

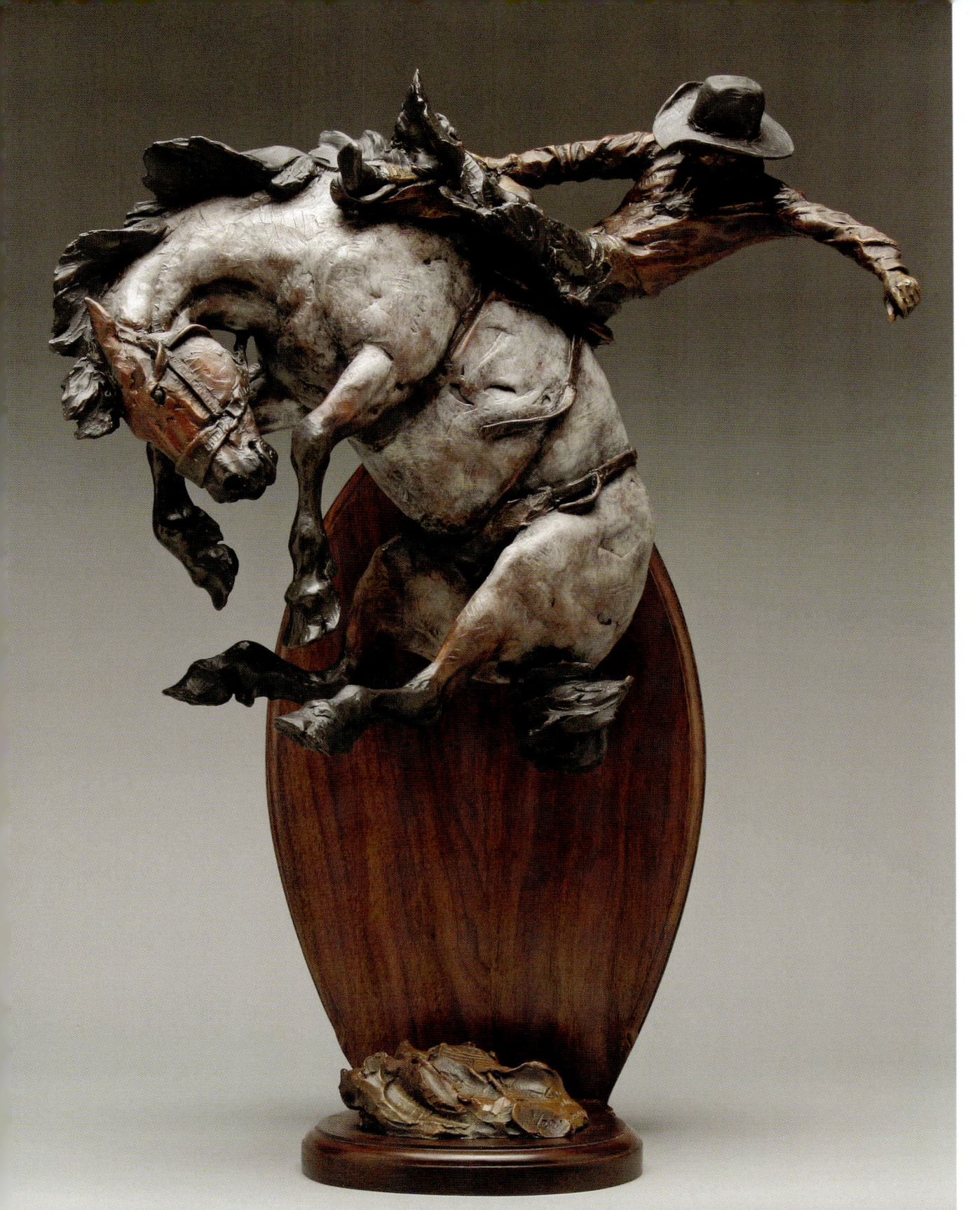

First Jump

(Bronze, 22" × 16" × 8",
2007)

"This is a another Calgary
Stampede trophy for the
saddle bronc riding. This
bronze was designed to
hang on the wall, making it
unique. Not many bronzes
are displayed by hanging
on a wall. I don't do a lot
of color on my pieces but
some pieces I think kind of
demand it."

To the Fire

(Bronze, 17" × 35" × 9", n.d.)

"The thing I liked about this piece is that I believe a lot of our horsemanship and Western heritage go back to these vaqueros. That is where the horsemanship came up through Mexico and from there, went throughout the West. So, this, to me, was giving the homage back to the early horseman."

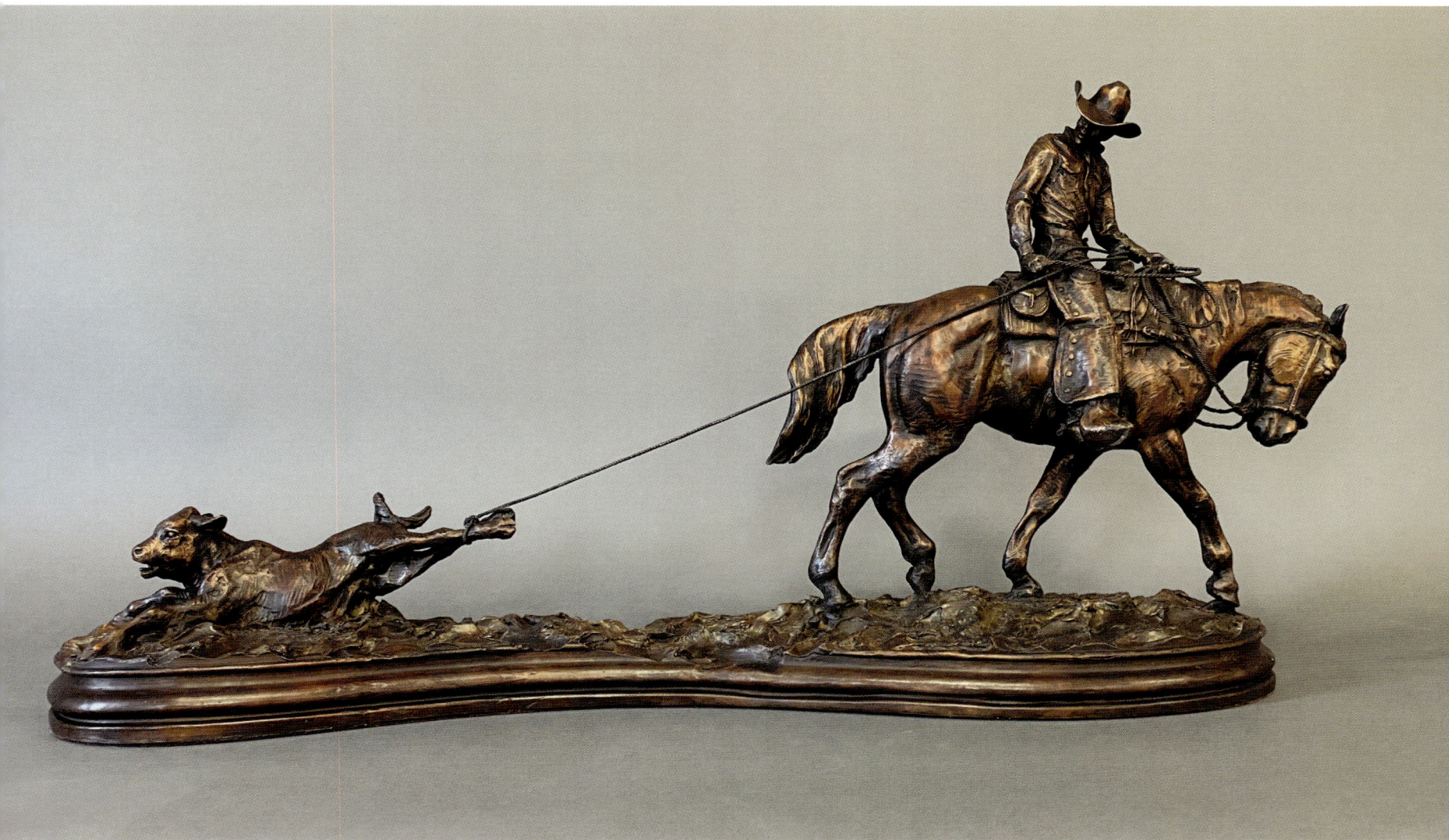

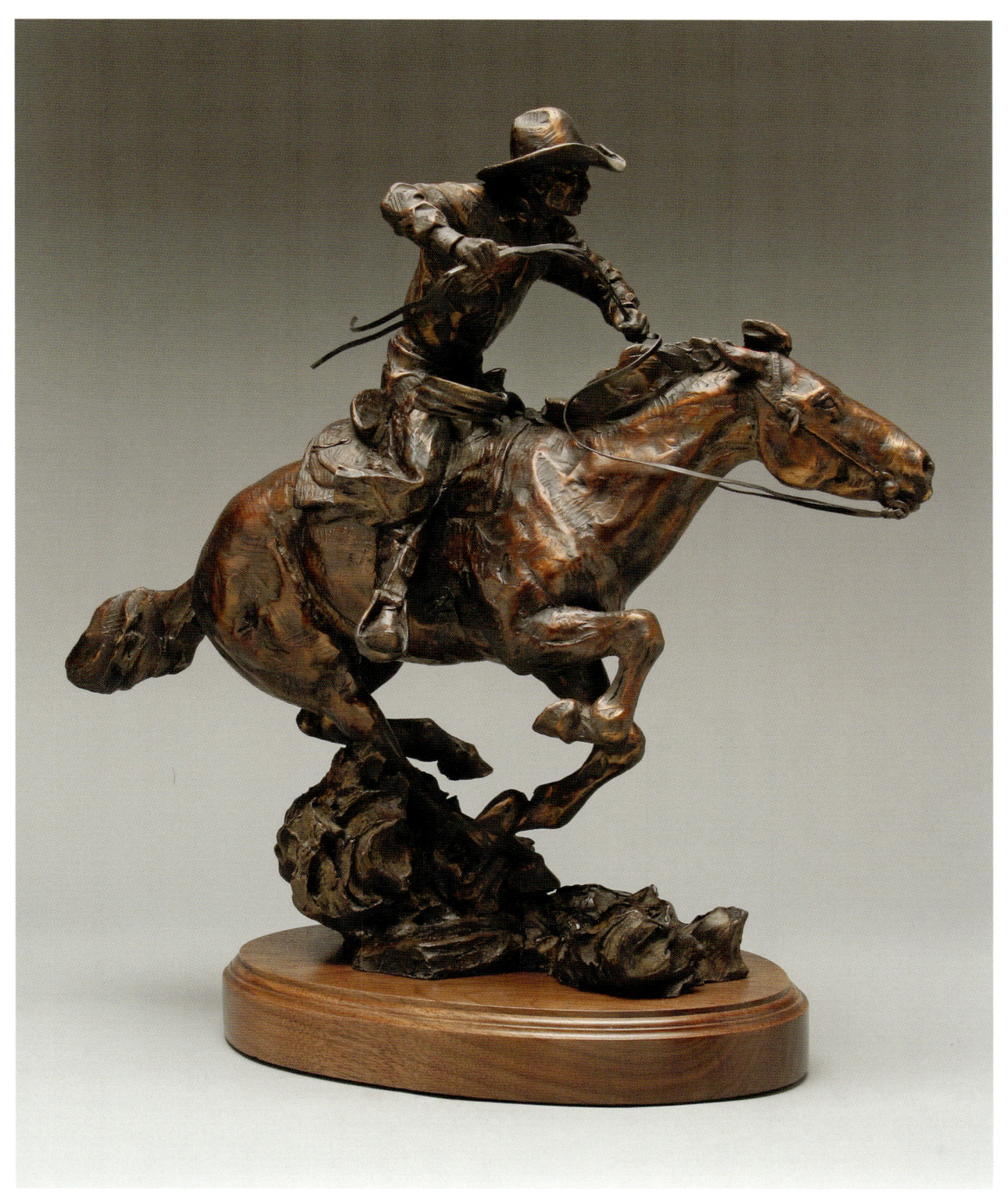

Whip N Spur

(Bronze, 18" × 20" × 10", 2007)

"This piece was created in a noticeably short amount of time. I was on a deadline to turn in new pieces, in two days, for the Calgary Stampede competition and honestly believe I had help from the Lord. *Whip N Spur* was chosen to be the Safety Award for the Chuckwagon Races."

Jason Scull

Jason Scull

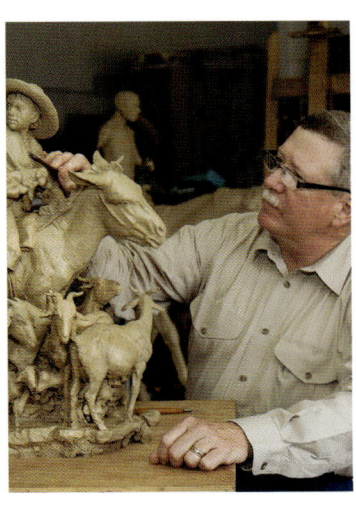

Jason Scull's pioneering family came to Texas in the 1820s and remained in the ranching business until 2010. For this reason, he and his work are deeply rooted in preserving the early history of Texas and Western art. On his father's side, the family moved from North Carolina to Southeast Texas in 1830 and later to the southeast of San Antonio engaging in a large cattle operation, running up to 3,000 head of cattle and 700 horses. When Scull was five weeks old, the family moved to the San Marcos area, which was "beautiful, a kid's paradise." He remembers first getting on a horse around three or four years of age, riding a little Quarter Horse mare named Ladybug, who taught all the kids in the family to ride. Scull had an early interest in art that was fostered by his mother, who fed this interest with books and art materials at Christmas and birthdays. He remembers that he would draw "little cowboys on horses" at church services as a four-year-old child.

Scull attended Texas A&M University from 1976 to 1978 to study animal sciences but returned to work with the family ranch. In 1980, he enrolled in Southwest Texas State University to study business and art. It was while taking a drawing course there that Scull first thought a career in Western art was a possibility. In 1987, he attended the first of many Western art workshops including a Cowboy Artists of America (CAA) workshop taught by Jack Swanson. Swanson and fellow CAA artist Mehl Lawson have been mentors and friends of Scull since 1987. Scull says, "Jack Swanson and Mehl Lawson really formed the basis of what

I do today." Within a year, he was able to start selling some pieces. Scull recounts, "I think the first commission I ever got was doing a portrait of a Methodist minister for a friend of mine's dad." His first successful piece was a cowboy standing by a saddle. His career was greatly helped by early collectors who bought number one of the sculptures he did for more than twenty-five years.

Scull continued to work in the family ranching business until 2010 while also pursuing a career in sculpture. He and his wife Dianne moved to Colorado to be closer to the foundry he was using in 2011 but they returned to Texas in 2013. He continued to sculpt and focus his sculptures on the horse, which he says can be a difficult subject to capture. Scull considers the most difficult aspects of correctly portraying the horse to be achieving accuracy of proportions and anatomy and capturing the emotion of the horse. He says, "Horses are extremely complex creatures both physically and psychologically."

Many of Scull's works focus on the ranching culture of South Texas. Scull is very interested in the accurate historical representation of the horse and cow culture of South Texas. He takes great care to accurately portray the gear of the South Texas cowboy and the tack of the horse. He prefers the look of cowboys from the 1950s through the 1970s as opposed to the contemporary cowboys. In any event, he makes sure that the look of the horse fits the era he is portraying. In the sculpture of horses, none of Scull's works is actually based on specific horses. He will study real horses and spend time looking at angles and muscles; however, he does not reproduce a single, individual horse in his art.

They're kind of my ideal in a way. Are they ideal animals or people? No, but they're just working horses and working people.

Scull has received commissions to create historical works of sculpture for towns in Texas. He created a life-sized sculpture of early Texas Ranger John C. "Jack" Hays that was installed in front of the Hays County Courthouse in San Marcos, Texas. Scull also has studied the history of the early vaqueros entering South Texas and has created several sculptures depicting what the horse and vaquero of this time looked like. Scull's life-sized sculpture of a vaquero from the Spanish Colonial era was installed at the Convention Center in McAllen, Texas.

The horse of that era would have been a Spanish Creole kind of horse. The story is that they would leave a young bull calf and five or six heifers at each river crossing as well as a young stud horse and some young fillies that would end up populating the area. So [when] the Spanish would go through those areas, there would be cattle and horses, their descendants being the early Mustang.

Scull refers to himself as an "accidental sculptor." He says, "I wanted to be a painter. And I kind of wish I had kept on that path at the same time. But I had more proficiency as a sculptor . . . than I did as a draftsman." He now realizes that his drawing has improved as a result of his three-dimensional work in sculpture. He feels much of his work in sculpture is based on muscle memory. His inspirations in art are not limited to Western artists. He has a book of equine artists that have inspired him, including British painters Sir Alfred Munnings and Lionel Edwards.

Scull likes designs in his sculptures that incorporate opposite forces, often creating a tension for the viewer. For example, in *Cowtastrophe*, the horse is moving one way, but chaos is not far off as the cow and calf are moving in the other direction, entangled in the rope. Scull says, "[The cow's] mouth is opening and the calf's mouth is open and he's bellerin'. And it's just a South Texas kind of thing that I enjoy portraying." Scull feels that keen observation of the subject is essential.

Bill Moyers said, "The difference between greatness and mediocrity is observation." And that's, in essence, becoming familiar with your subject, knowing and picking up the little nuances and bumps and dips, and everything about whatever work you're trying to portray.

Scull also teaches workshops at the Museum of Western Art in Kerrville, Texas, the Scottsdale Artist School in Arizona, and others across the Southwest. He held sculpture workshops at the National Ranching Heritage Center in Lubbock, Texas, in 2019 and 2022. He believes it is his duty to give back to others, as he once had the fortune of receiving mentorship. He teaches the importance of learning when to end a sculpture. Scull feels that knowing when to end a piece one is working on can be challenging to painters and sculptors. He is fond of this quote from Antoine de Saint-Exupéry: "Perfection is achieved not when there's nothing more to add, but when there is nothing left to take away."

Today, Scull lives outside of Kerrville, Texas, with his wife, Dianne. His studio, built for visiting artists, is within the grounds of the Museum of Western Art. Visitors to the museum can observe Scull sculpt and visit with the artist. Scull was a member of the Cowboy Artists of America from 2011 until 2022. His awards include 1st place sculpture in The Classic (Albuquerque), 1st place sculpture in the Phippen Western Art Show, 2013 Western Artist of the Year of the Academy of Western Artists in Fort Worth, Texas, the Ray Swanson Memorial Award at the 2017 Cowboy Artists of America Show and Sale in Oklahoma City, and the James Bowie Award for Sculpture at the 2023 Night of Artists, Briscoe Western Art Museum, San Antonio, Texas.

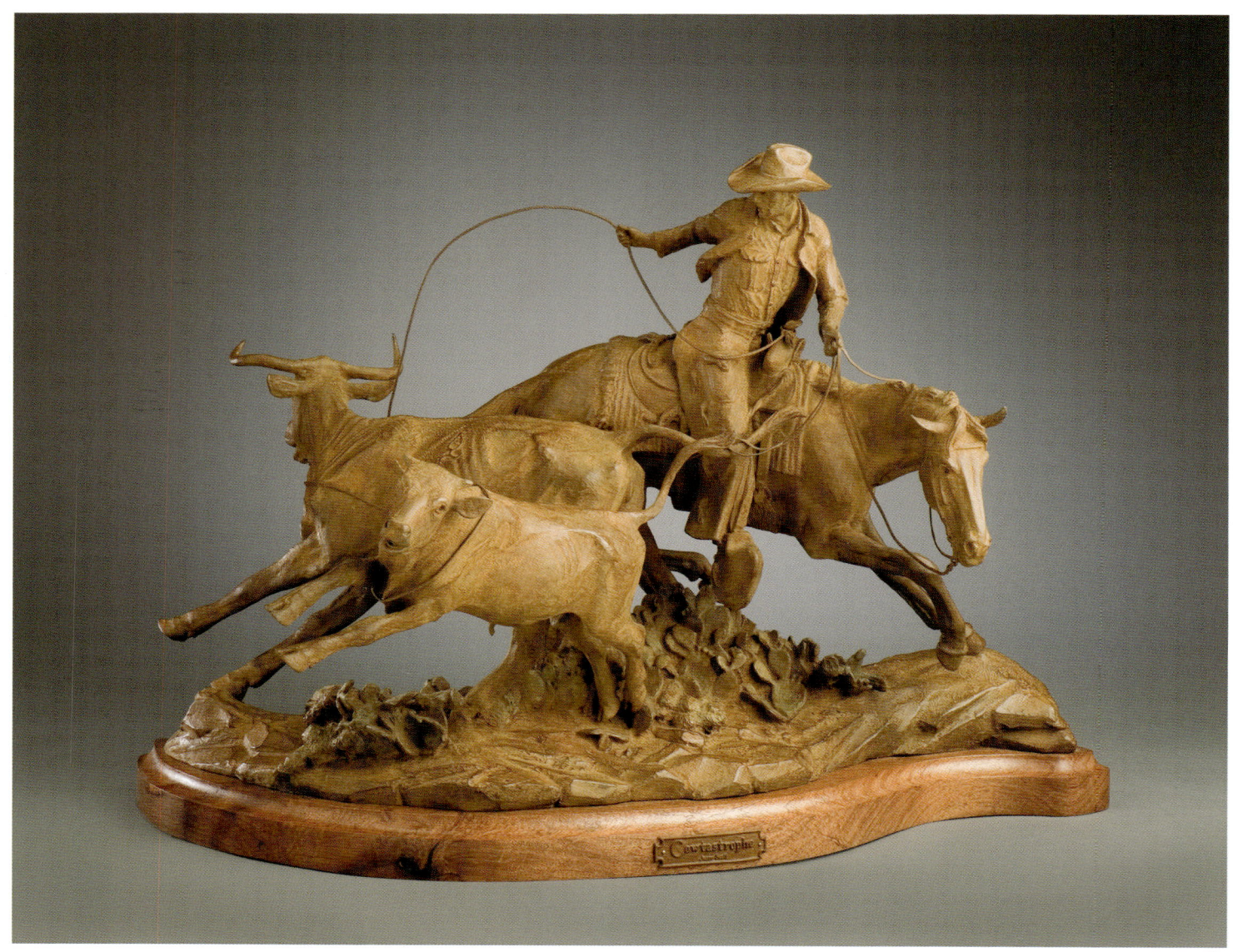

Cowtastrophe

(Bronze, 19" × 28" × 16", 2006)

"This is one of my favorite pieces. I don't know why. This fellow roped a good big bull calf and it's got a rope around the neck where you don't really [want it]—that wasn't a really good move. And the cow runs between the calf and the horse and that rope is tied off hard and fast on the saddle. Once that cow hits the end of that rope, it's gonna be a wreck in the making."

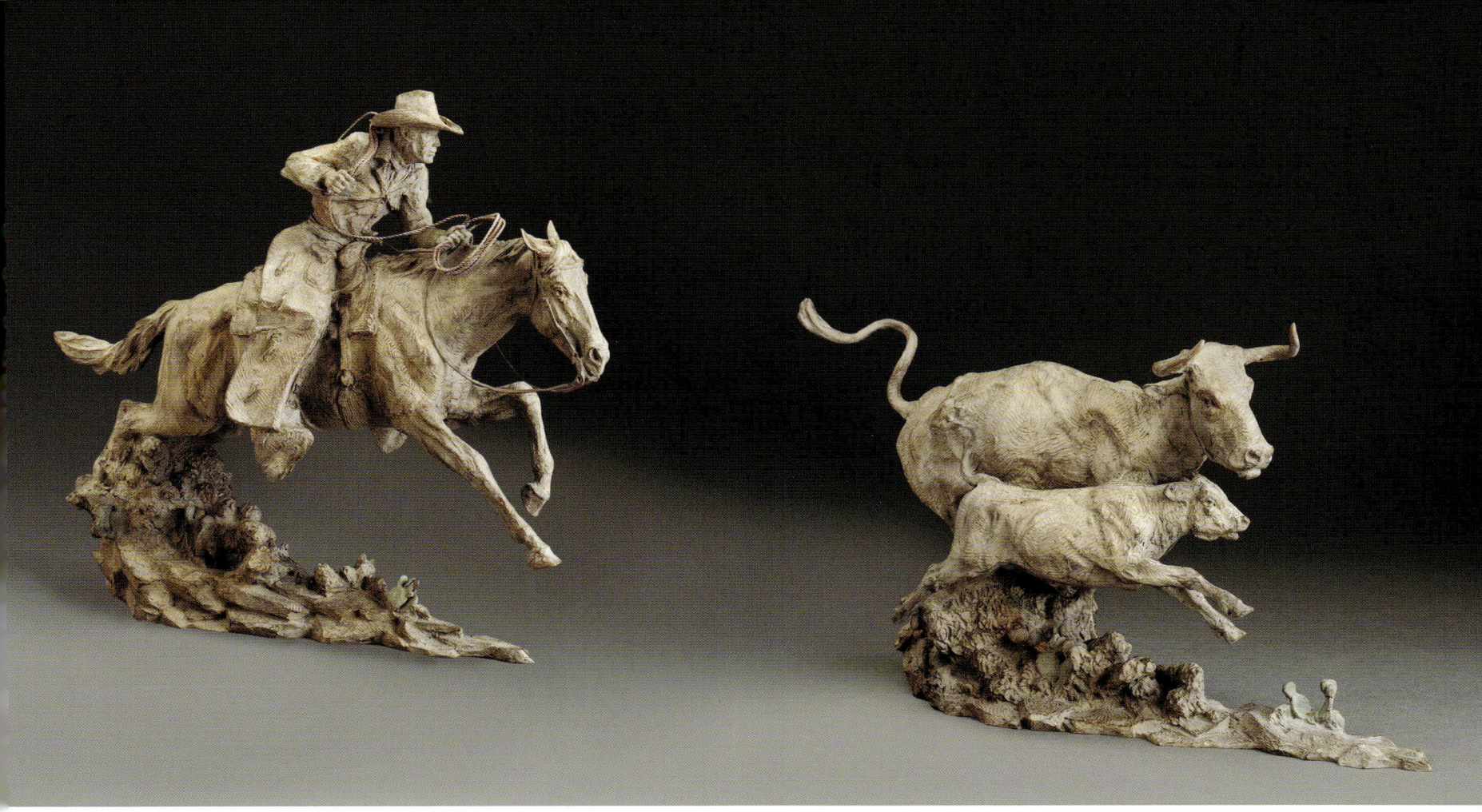

Wild Cows and Wilder Men

(Bronze, 16.5" × 22" × 6" (horseman) / 10.5" × 22" × 6" (cow and calf), 2023)

"I designed *Wild Cows and Wilder Men* to be flexible in its placement in an individual's home or office, whether on a mantle, library table, or credenza to be arranged at their discretion. This piece shows the horse and cowboy's love of the chase and the cow and calf's determination to evade their pursuit."

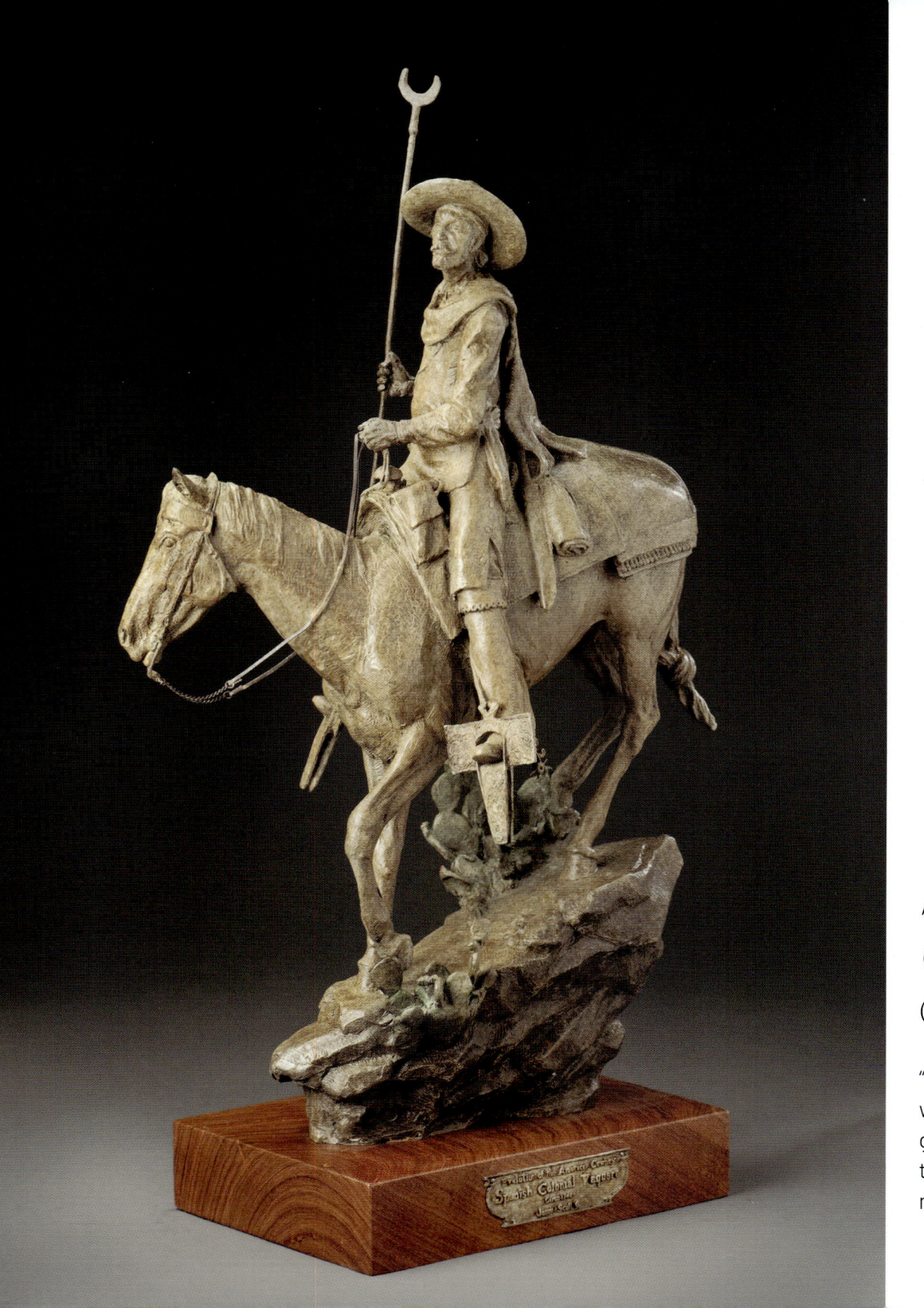

Spanish Colonial Vaquero Circa 1740

(Bronze, 26" × 15" × 8", 2013)

"This to me is one of the first vaqueros as they would have come into Texas. These men were generally soldiers and so much of the gear that they would have was related to their time in the military in Mexico and for the Spanish crown."

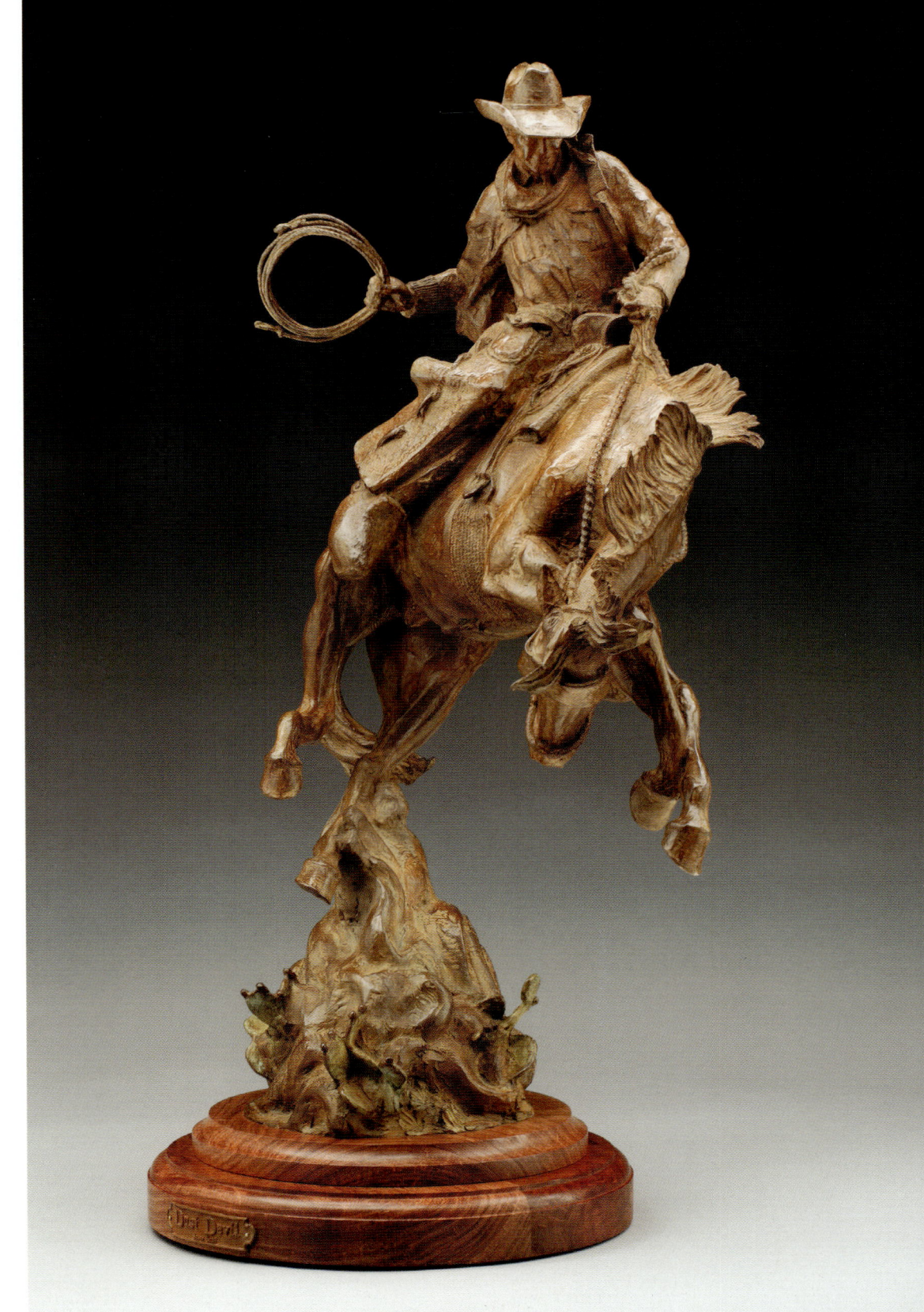

Dust Devil

(Bronze, 26″ × 19″ × 12″, 2010)

"For whatever reason, this horse has decided to break in two on this cowboy. But in this stance the man is in complete control and a match for the actions of this horse. You know, kicking up the dust . . . and thusly I titled it *Dust Devil* . . . because of just the cyclonic effects of what we think of as dust devils."

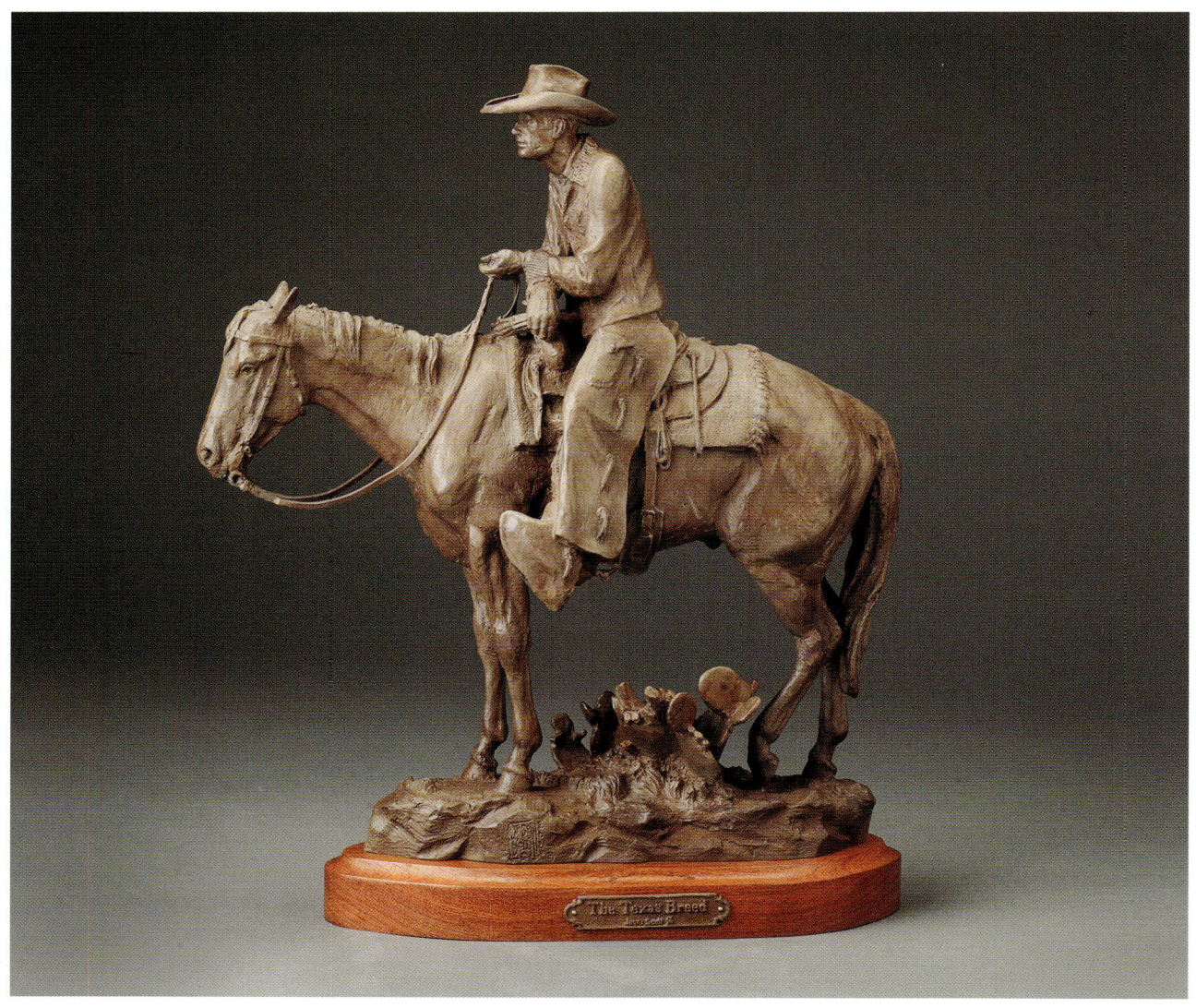

The Texas Breed

(Bronze, 15″ × 13″ × 6″, 2020)

"A very dear friend, Don Hedgpeth, who was a writer—did a lot of books on Western artists . . . had been a friend of thirty, almost thirty-five years. I'd carry things over to him to show because I knew he was interested in what I was doing. One of the early books Don wrote was an anthology of cowboy books that he always thought were indicative of what he thought of as The Texas Breed. And that's where that title comes from. This piece is a tip of the hat to Don."

Out Where the Wild Ones Run

(Bronze, 24" × 27" × 16", 2022)

"This sculpture conjures up images in my mind of wild cow hunters in the rough country of the greater Southwest but, more specifically, the brush country of South Texas. The spiraling force of descent, the brush-wise horse, the crouching figure intent on his quarry are all elements that contribute to what I hope is the excitement of this sculpture."

Conclusion

Compiling this book of contemporary American Western artists has been a rewarding endeavor. We were given the opportunity to not only meet and become friends with the artists in this book, but we also got a chance to see each artwork from a different perspective than what we would find from simply viewing the art in a gallery or publication. The dedication and skill of each of these artists, who have developed their own uniquely recognizable styles and methods of storytelling through imagery, showed why they have become renowned for their craft. The view of Western life shown to the rest of us through each artist's eye makes each painting, drawing, photograph, or sculpture a bit magical. The mystery of each image is discovered in the color, detail, texture, or light used by each artist. It is our hope that this book will help the reader find a deeper appreciation of these artists, their work, and a deeper understanding of the American West.

Index

Note: *Page numbers in italics refer to images.*

About the Authors

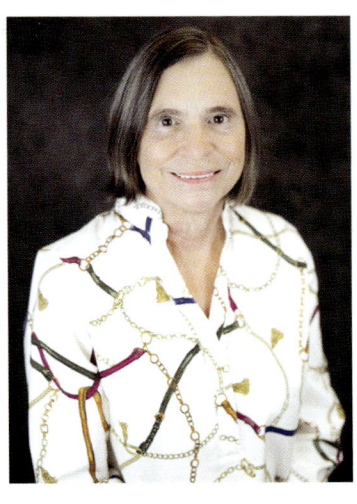

Dr. Heidi Brady is a professor in the Department of Animal and Food Sciences at Texas Tech University, having taught equine-related classes for thirty-one years. She is co-author of two books, including *Horses in the American West: Portrayals by Twenty-Four Artists*, which is used in her unique class, The Horse in World Art. She is also co-author of *The Comprehensive Guide to Equine-Assisted Activities and Therapies*. Dr. Brady is a member of the Texas Tech University Teaching Academy and earned the Texas Tech Excellence in Engaged Teaching and Research Award in 2025. She has a strong faith in God and enjoys spending time with her husband Wade and their family, riding horses, and traveling.

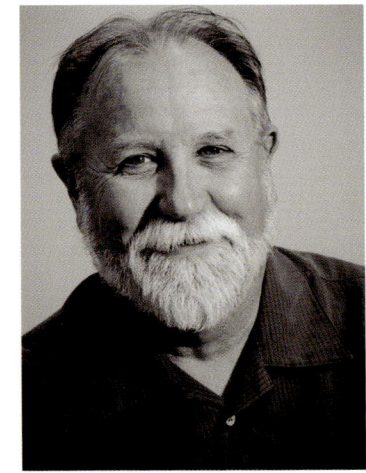

Dr. Scott White grew up in the West Texas town of Odessa amid pumpjacks, sagebrush, horses, and cowboys. He attended Odessa High School then started on an accounting degree at Odessa College until deciding the world was too big to look at through a set of books. His parents introduced him to art when they owned a frame shop and art supply business. He was surrounded by the art of the West there. He pursued interests in music, art, and history while working as a construction contractor. After acquiring an AA, a BA, an MA, and a PhD, he combined all his interests in pursuing museum work. Now retired, he lives in Lubbock, Texas.